THE
INFLUENCE
MACHINE

THE
INFLUENCE
MACHINE

THE U.S. CHAMBER OF COMMERCE
AND THE CORPORATE CAPTURE
OF AMERICAN LIFE

Alyssa Katz

SPIEGEL & GRAU

NEW YORK

Published in the United States by Spiegel & Grau, an imprint of Random House,
a division of Penguin Random House LLC, New York.

SPIEGEL & GRAU and the HOUSE colophon are registered trademarks
of Penguin Random House LLC.

Library of Congress Cataloging-in-Publication Data
Katz, Alyssa.
The Influence Machine : The U.S. Chamber of Commerce and the
Corporate Capture of American Life / Alyssa Katz.
        pages   cm
Includes index.
ISBN 978-0-8129-9328-8
eBook ISBN 978-0-679-64506-1
1. Chamber of Commerce of the United States of America—History.
2. United States. Congress—History.   3. Business and politics—United States—
History.   4. Power (Social sciences)—United States—History.   I. Title.
HF295.K37 2015
381.06'073—dc23   2014038034

Printed in the United States of America on acid-free paper

www.spiegelandgrau.com

2 4 6 8 9 7 5 3 1

First Edition

Book design by Victoria Wong

To Bryan and Thalia

"Full of the know-how that made America great; efficient, straightforward, honest, the chief executives, it is often said, ought really to be allowed to run the government, for if only such men were in charge there would be no waste, no corruption, no infiltration. Dirty politics, in short, would become clean business."

—C. Wright Mills, *The Power Elite*

Contents

Preface

This is a book about the single most influential organization in American politics, outside the Republican and Democratic Parties apparatuses. But more than the story of a solitary institution—no matter how powerful—it is the story of how democracy works today and why, for most of us, it doesn't.

I write it in gratitude for living in a country where it is possible for an operation like the U.S. Chamber of Commerce to thrive. In the United States, individuals and groups are free to express themselves politically; to organize among themselves; and to fight for what they believe in—or at the very least, for what is in their material self-interest—with the expectation that government will pay attention. This is a good thing.

If you, like me, want workers, environmentalists, consumers, and other groups to have such power, it means accepting that private companies big and small do too. This makes sense—it's fair and reasonable, at least in the abstract. But in reality, the power exerted by business in the United States has, over the last generation, overwhelmed the voices of other stakeholders, with enormous consequences for our health and safety as consumers, our rights as workers, and even the power of our votes. One institution in particular has concentrated the energies embedded in our democracy as potently as any the nation has ever seen, and it has used that power to undermine that same democracy, all while maintaining a cloak of secrecy around the funders who call its shots. This is not how it's supposed to work.

The U.S. Chamber of Commerce declined to make staff members available for interview. It invited me to send them questions by e-mail instead; they refused to answer my inquiries. In response to factual questions about their activities, I received only a scolding response, informing me that I had an unacceptable agenda:

> The nature and tone of these questions reveal an obvious slant— one that seeks to paint the Chamber in a solely negative way. Based on these questions, it seems that you have already reached your conclusion about the Chamber, so we see no reason to respond.

In the absence of any cooperation from the Chamber, I've made every effort to be fair, thorough, and accurate in my account—and I am grateful to Chamber alumni and associates who did take the time to lend their insights. I hardly think my account is "solely negative," as I hope you'll see as you read on, but I also want to be clear up front about my own ideological point of view: I believe that government regulation of business is, more often than not, helpful to economies, and that government ought to wield such power in ways that promote the greater good of the nation and its citizens. The U.S. Chamber ostensibly operates on a different premise: that less regulation leads to better outcomes, for society as well as for executives and shareholders. As I discovered while researching this book, the Chamber has been more than willing to invite government regulation and participation in the economy when it suits its clients.

Driven by that combination of ideology and self-interest, the U.S. Chamber of Commerce has been in the vanguard of a business movement to redirect our national priorities through political warfare. Fueled by contributions from member corporations, it has in recent years invested more than a billion dollars in lobbying and campaign spending to win results that, by definition, are not those the public would have otherwise demanded. The U.S. Chamber is not just a lobbying group, and not just a massive political spending apparatus, and not just a policy shop, and not just a prolific combatant in the courts. It is, rather, all those things wrapped into one—a well-funded influence machine seeking to build an economy where government becomes a tool of big business.

It has built its recent success in large part by advancing the interests of industries whose prosperity is threatened not only by intense global competition but by emerging trends in human history—by the evolution of our values, technology, scientific knowledge, and notions of environmental stewardship. Its constituents—and the political metaphor is apt—are mature industries that provide vital goods and services but at mounting costs to society: coal, oil, defense, and other polluters running away from a reckoning; insurers seeking to protect their place at the heart of health care, preserving a convoluted and numbingly expensive payment system; tobacco peddlers who insist they should not bear the costs of caring for those their products injure and kill, and who even deny, still, that their products are addictive; sweatshop-patronizing retailers, off-books debt-peddlers, and even miners and marketers of salt. What unites all these industries, and the household names that lead them, is that achieving business success depends on inflicting collateral damage on public well-being. That is their competitive advantage, the secret sauce in their shareholder returns.

These companies' undisclosed financial contributions to the U.S. Chamber of Commerce provide something of great value: protection against a government that might otherwise seek to curb environmental harm, threats to worker safety, price manipulation, and other noxious by-products of businesses' quest to elevate stock prices—with near-absolute brand protection for the companies involved, which launder their antisocial advocacy through the Chamber. It's a role that the organization has openly embraced. CEO Tom Donohue describes its work as "reinsurance"—the business term for an insurance policy on an insurance policy, offloading risk in order to increase companies' ability to swallow more.

What he means is that when a company or industry association needs to get something done, and the political heat is unmanageable, the Chamber can step in and take the blows on its behalf. By doing their political and lobbying spending through the Chamber, beloved brand names are never sullied with the causes they finance, whether it's defeating climate change action, involving themselves in dark, negative electoral campaigning, or diluting financial reform. In an impressive feat of alchemy, the Chamber frames the objectives of these specific companies and industries as those of "business" generally. The causes of some of the most retrograde and rent-seeking industries in America become, in the hands of the Chamber's propaganda machine, the causes of "free enterprise."

Of course, in the political realm, businesses habitually join together as trade associations to press their interests and obtain benefits of substantial value. In fact, the U.S. Chamber of Commerce was the very first such association to get official sanction from the U.S. government, a century ago, and in the most literal sense it's just one of hundreds of groups that lobby on behalf of corporate members.

But the game is entirely different when a lobbying group also injects tens of millions of dollars into campaign-season attack ads in order to remove members of Congress who fail to fall in line—and advertises its intentions before those members have even voted on the bills in question. It's also different when the courts and regulators that will enforce those laws are influenced by well-funded teams of lawyers paid by the same organization, and when loyal senators block judicial nominees that the organization perceives as hostile. This is vertically integrated influence, and it's how we end up with Frankensteins like the Affordable Care Act: a universal health care initiative perversely crafted in deference to the insurance industry. Keeping that industry at the heart of the health care system made the act unnecessarily complex, deeply compromised by the Supreme

Court, and relentlessly attacked on the political stage. None of this was an accident.

The Chamber of Commerce holds members of Congress in vulnerable seats hostage and terrorizes them with threats of removal. The problem with terror politics is that it distorts the political marketplace. Ironically, in the name of free enterprise, the Chamber has been perpetuating the opposite of market discipline in the political realm. The result is action in Washington that is shaped not by what's best for the nation or for the planet but by what's best for business. It's a literal manifestation of the old credo "What's good for General Motors is good for the country."

As it happens, before it went bust, GM was a major contributor to the U.S. Chamber, which on behalf of the company and other auto giants dutifully fought efforts by Congress to improve automobile safety. And it worked. A 2000 bill sponsored by Senator John McCain (R-AZ) that would have imposed stiff penalties—including criminal punishment in extreme cases—on vehicle and tire manufacturers that failed to disclose safety problems died under lobbyist assault. In its place rose a second measure, championed by Chamber lobbyists, that McCain bemoaned "creates an environment where meaningful enforcement is impossible."

The measure did little to improve the company's plummeting market share or to protect passengers. In other words, it achieved nothing to improve American business or protect American consumers. What it did do was bolster the Chamber's reputation for controlling legislation. Multiply that example by hundreds, and you get a sense of how the Chamber has altered the balance in Washington.

It's no longer alone in the accomplishment. Other configurations have rushed into the vast space the Chamber has created for business to exercise outsize influence in politics. Freedom Partners Chamber of Commerce, closely linked to the billionaire brothers Charles and David Koch, has cloned the U.S. Chamber's skeleton: legally, it's a trade association, set up to promote the commercial interests of its members. For 2012, the Kochs' chamber pulled in an astonishing

$255 million in anonymous contributions and spat them back out at a constellation of groups—including the U.S. Chamber—which in turn used the funds to buy ads attacking President Obama, Democratic candidates for Congress, and the Affordable Care Act.

That's a lot of money. But unlike the U.S. Chamber, Freedom Partners and most of its beneficiaries don't lobby in between elections to keep members of Congress in line. Organizations like Americans for Prosperity, also funded by the Koch brothers, and Karl Rove's Crossroads empire have made their might felt with massive infusions of campaign spending, but they do not mess around with the sweaty work of crafting bill language, blocking judicial nominations, waging court battles, writing obscure regulations, or otherwise scripting the code of power. Membership groups like the Business Roundtable and the National Federation of Independent Business may lobby Congress fiercely on behalf of business, but they remain marginal players in the campaign fray.

Only the U.S. Chamber of Commerce has centralized the political might of corporate America within one organization, playing every instrument of power, at all levels of federal government, on behalf of anonymous industry sponsors. It has persuaded judges to rewrite the laws that govern campaign spending, overwhelmed Congress and regulators with lobbyists, swayed elections, and dangerously warped the government response on the most urgent issues of our age—climate change, the financial crisis, access to health care, and more.

Even a casual observer can see that our political system puts the needs of business before the needs of citizens—and those priorities are reflected in every aspect of our lives, from how we work to the food we eat to our options at the ballot box. But how did we get here? The Chamber is a singular institution, and its history tells the story of how American democracy fell into the hands of big business.

Here is that story.

PART I

The Making of the Machine

CHAPTER 1

One Hour

On a clear Monday morning in August 2010, Susan Slattery was driving along the Ohio Turnpike in her Ford Focus, heading home to Maryland from an annual family reunion in Rocky River, outside Cleveland, with one of her two adolescent sons in the backseat and the other at her side. Susan's husband, Ed, had stayed behind because he was recovering from shoulder surgery.

Traffic ahead of her slowed as she approached a work zone, and Slattery slowed with it. But behind her, an enormous truck—an eighteen-wheeler traveling at fifty-five miles per hour—didn't slow at all. It approached the Ford's bumper and violently slammed into the car. The truck's driver, Douglas Bouch of the Virginia company Estes Express, never braked.

The force of the collision rocketed the Slatterys' car into the back door of the trailer in front of them. Susan was crushed to death in the driver's seat. Her twelve-year-old son, Matthew, was in the front passenger seat, bleeding profusely from deep gashes in his head. Behind him was his older brother, Peter, the bones in his pelvis now broken and the socket under his left eye crushed.

Bouch's truck hit five other cars before coming to a stop at a concrete barrier. Uninjured, Bouch fled the cab just before it burst into flames that consumed its engine and roof—along with the logs containing the details of the trucker's journey. Behind the burning cab were linked three trailers, each emblazoned with the bright yellow "E" of his employer set against a field of red.

As they waited for emergency vehicles, Bouch told another truck driver at the scene that he had fallen asleep at the wheel. When a state trooper arrived, Bouch told him the same thing. He could not remember what time exactly he had set out in the predawn hours that morning, only that it was sometime before three a.m., which meant he had been driving for at least nine hours, and possibly more, without a break when he fell asleep.

Thousands of people die every year on the nation's highways in collisions between trucks and cars—more than 3,500 in 2012 alone—a death toll that would be unimaginable if we were talking about the collateral damage from air travel or collapsing buildings. Hundreds of thousands more are injured in truck crashes. This is a price of commerce—of circulating furniture and electronics and food and aircraft components and all the other stuff we consume from the ports and factories where the goods arrive or are manufactured to distributors and stores and, eventually, to us, the consumers. Trucking is the circulatory system of the American economy, hauling some $8.3 trillion in merchandise a year. But do we have to pay such a high cost in death and injury?

In 1993, when President Bill Clinton was in the White House, Congress asked federal regulators to take action to deal with truck driver fatigue, one of the primary causes of lethal highway accidents. A mounting death toll heightened the urgency of action. From 1992 to 1999, the annual number of truck crash fatalities, which had been stable for years, leaped 21 percent, from 4,462 to 5,380. While the rate of crashes-per-mile had remained steady, a surge of trucks on the road, driving more miles, had increased the bloodshed. So in 2000 the federal Department of Transportation proposed the first changes to the nation's truck safety rules since 1937.

By the Clinton administration's calculations, the proposed rules would prevent 2,600 crashes, saving 115 lives, and many more serious injuries, every year. It wouldn't take a great feat of engineering to reach these results. The key was to give drivers more rest.

Data on truck crashes show that drivers careening into their eleventh hour are nearly twice as likely as those who quit at hour ten to end up in a crash, and they are even more likely to have that crash caused by fatigue. Clinton administration regulators estimated that fatigue was a leading factor in at least 15 percent of crashes. And government studies found fatigue to be a likely factor in more than 30 percent of crashes that were fatal to the driver.

The proposed rules would mandate that drivers stay behind the wheel no more than twelve hours in every twenty-four-hour cycle, instead of the sixteen allowed under the law at the time, and no more than ten hours at a stretch, affirming a limit that had been in place since the 1930s. "Even with this change, drivers could be behind the wheel 50 percent longer than the average citizen's normal work day," noted an administration official.

Drivers frequently hit the road exhausted—a study in *The New England Journal of Medicine* found that they were getting about five hours of sleep in every twenty-four—so the Department of Transportation also proposed granting drivers the right to refuse to start their engines if they were too tired to drive safely. And with the new rules in place, drivers would no longer be able to lie in their paper logbooks about their hours, as many did, since miles and hours would now be tracked electronically.

White House officials seemed to have little reason to fear they wouldn't prevail. Making sure companies operated safely was simply what government regulators had done, under Republican and Democratic presidents alike, since the 1970s for many industries, and in some cases for much longer. Even Ronald Reagan, who came into the White House in 1980 with promises to unshackle business from "paternalistic" government rules, backed off such efforts as his bid for reelection in 1984 approached. Cutting back on public safety and health was just far too unpopular to campaign on.

But things were different now. The Clinton administration found itself facing a hostile audience. Congress had turned from longtime Democratic control to Republican in 1994, and the trucking industry, under the new rules, would be forced to put more vehicles on the road and hire more workers to maintain their pace of deliveries. It opposed the new rules determinedly. Coordinating the attacks was the U.S. Chamber of Commerce.

Tom Donohue had been a leader in the trucking industry for many years, as the head of the American Trucking Associations. Now at the helm of the U.S. Chamber, he was determined not to let the driving-hours limits move ahead. The Chamber's board of directors had unanimously voted to oppose the Clinton administration's proposed safety rules restricting drivers' time on the road, and the organization had successfully lobbied for a clause in the federal budget—passed by a newly sympathetic Republican Congress—that blocked any funding even to research the question of how to craft an improved safety rule for truckers.

Donohue, in congressional testimony, went to elaborate lengths to discredit the proposed limits on driving hours. A one-hour reduction in truckers' allowable time on the road each day, he testified, would add to pollution, the cost of food and products, and morning commute traffic, and would even force "altered school schedules." The number of trucks on the road, the Chamber warned, could rise as much as 50 percent. The new rules would put a flood of inexperienced drivers behind the wheel. Limiting truck drivers' hours in the cause of reducing accidents would actually have the opposite effect: it would lead to a bloodbath on the roadways. "Our members, as well as the entire American business community, are unwilling to accept the deaths, injuries and damage which the proposed regulation will cause," Donohue declared.

The rules, at long last finalized in the waning days of the Clinton administration, never made it into legal effect, thanks to a few hanging chads in Florida and the U.S. Supreme Court. Once President George W. Bush arrived in Washington, his election backed by the

Chamber, the White House push to improve truck safety—itself the result of a congressional mandate—vanished.

The trucking rules are just one obscure chunk of the millions of lines of code that run the federal government. But this story powerfully illustrates the way the Chamber has burrowed into the political process, with serious consequences in everyday life. Its vision of business enterprise unfettered by government has upended decades of painstaking work to turn the public sector into an effective steward of the public interest.

If the effects of the Chamber's actions don't reach you on the highway, perhaps they will in the emergency room, when you get a bill for treatment and have no coverage because your state's governor opted out of expanding Medicaid. Or at the state courthouse, where filing a class action suit against the manufacturer of a harmful product is now an uphill battle. The soot in the air you breathe, the chemicals in the water you drink, the fees on the financial products you buy, working conditions that ravage your body—all these and more are at the center of a battle over businesses' freedom to gamble with your well-being. And in each of these arenas, the Chamber has played a pivotal role in shifting the balance of power to business.

It wasn't always so. During the 1970s and 1980s and into the 1990s, the power of consumer, labor, and environmental advocates was considered unshakable. An overwhelmingly pro-regulation Congress, and voting public, stood in the way of greater influence for business lobbyists. And the Chamber was nowhere close to changing that balance. In that not-so-distant era, it was business, and the Chamber itself, that were divided and feeble in Washington.

The trucking industry, which touches nearly every corner of the economy, neatly symbolized its weakness. Up until the 1970s, many trucking companies secured scarce government licenses to carry freight, doled out during the Great Depression; they had come to find this to be a surprisingly comfortable, and profitable, arrangement. Not so happy were manufacturers and other businesses, which had to pay the truckers to ship goods and which shouldered the high costs that resulted from the trucking monopolies. With the business community divided between comfortable truckers and dissatisfied manufacturers and retailers, the Chamber was paralyzed. The 1970s push to deregulate the trucking industry didn't stem from the Chamber or from conservative ideologues in Congress, who were a rare breed back then, but from leading Washington liberals, including Senator Edward Kennedy (D-MA). In the face of a political consensus that supported regulation and distrusted business, the Chamber was divided and powerless.

But dramatic change would come to the Chamber with new leadership, drawn from the trucking industry itself. Even before he officially started at the Chamber in 1997, Tom Donohue showed his true colors when he talked to a *New York Times* reporter. "Sweeney," Donohue said of the head of the AFL-CIO, the nation's biggest labor group, "somebody's got to go hit him in the mouth."

Joan Claybrook, a Nader colleague who headed the National Highway Traffic Safety Administration under President Jimmy Carter and went on to run Public Citizen for twenty-seven years, remembers first confronting that pugilist in the ring in 1991. That's when she and Donohue, then head of the American Trucking Associations, sat next to each other on a panel testifying on a proposal in Congress to halt the rollout of triple-trailer trucks to the nation's highways. That's the kind of monster rig that careened into the Slatterys' car.

The two were set for a collision course. Claybrook had just helped found Citizens for Reliable and Safe Highways (CRASH)—a national group of public safety advocates and survivors pressing for truck safety—largely to counter the trucking lobby's might under Donohue. CRASH's advocacy had helped energize the sponsors of a bill that would put the brakes on triple-trailers. The measure, which Senators Frank Lautenberg (D-NJ) and Lincoln Chafee (R-RI) sought to insert into a federal highway funding bill, would keep three-trailer trucks out of the thirty-one states that had not already legalized the behemoths on their stretches of interstate. Claybrook's group wanted them banned from interstates entirely.

Donohue's strategy on the witness panel was to destroy the credibility of CRASH. Because some of its funding came from a railway boxcar company that would stand to gain business at the expense of truckers, he accused CRASH of being a "front group" for the railroad industry. Never mind that its diverse, volunteer board included the head of trauma services at Stanford University Hospital, the president of the trade association for property insurance companies, and the Republican former governor of Massachusetts John Volpe, whom President Richard Nixon had appointed secretary of transportation. Donohue insisted they were all doing the bidding of an unseen hand. "The railroads are trying to do through public policy and government intervention what they have not been able to do in the marketplace: compete effectively for market share," he told the House environment subcommittee.

Meanwhile Donohue expected the representatives to take at face value the safety claims of the American Trucking Associations— whose budget was orders of magnitude greater than that of CRASH and which was funded by the trucking industry.

Claybrook brought with her a brochure warning of the dangers of triple-trailers. Like a rig pulling cars behind it, the brochure unfolded, panel after panel, into a wide panorama many feet long. As she unfurled it, Donohue grew visibly flushed. "Don't ever put me at the same table as that lady," he fumed to a congressional aide after the panel concluded.

The bout didn't end there. The American Trucking Associations filed a complaint with the IRS asserting that CRASH had not filed proper paperwork. For good measure, it sent threatening letters to the board members of an insurance group that supported CRASH to pressure it out of the coalition. The moratorium on triple-trailers ultimately went ahead, dealing a defeat to the trucking industry. Still, Donohue had the last word: crushed by debt, the boxcar company soon went out of business.

In 1992 Donohue wasn't deterred by the arrival of a Democrat in the White House. The Clinton administration's man in charge of trucking regulation, George Reagle, was a career federal highway safety regulator who had started in Washington during the Johnson administration. He made for a wide-open target.

The trucking lobbyists set the tone from the beginning. In 1995 Donohue secured an invitation from the Federal Highway Administration to be its keynote speaker at a national truck and bus safety summit—but not before he threatened to pull out, objecting to the press release sent out by Transportation Secretary Federico Peña highlighting a recent increase in fatalities. At the meeting, safety experts and trucking leaders identified driver fatigue as the number-one safety problem faced by their industry.

Amid the carnage, public safety groups pleaded for reductions in the number of hours truckers could stay on the road. Reagle commissioned a study—unusually for a government research project, partly paid for by Donohue's organization and other trucking industry trade groups. "The most dangerous thing in the world is to let these people out at night doing their own study, writing press releases about what they think they found," said Donohue in 1995 of public interest activists like Claybrook. "Quite frankly, I want to beat them to the punch. I don't want them to define the agenda."

Instead, the industry took the reins. In a scathing 1999 report looking back at this period, the Department of Transportation's inspector general described an agency that had largely abandoned its mission of ensuring public safety and instead saw itself as an enabler of the trucking industry. Under official policy, enforcement actions for violations of safety regulations, such as fines and other sanctions, were to kick in only as a last resort and only "if unsuccessful in changing the safety performance of a particular motor carrier when there was clear reason to"—that is, after the accidents had already happened. Not surprisingly, the number of citations declined, and what fines were imposed amounted to just a fraction of what the law allowed. Trucks from companies with poor safety records, the inspector general found, continued to roll without sanction.

As enforcement steeply declined, truck crash fatalities increased by 21 percent, reversing a decade of progress. "This number of fatalities is unacceptable," concluded the inspector general, who equated the 5,355 deaths from large-truck crashes in 1997 "to a major airline crash with 200 fatalities every 2 weeks."

Just as damning was a second report, which found that Reagle and other safety officials had lobbied the lobbyists, asking trucking companies and trade groups to complain to Congress about a proposed transfer of enforcement responsibilities from their Office of Motor Carriers to the National Highway Traffic Safety Administration.

Tom Donohue had by then left the trucking associations for the U.S. Chamber of Commerce, and he brought the Clinton administration's man in charge of truck safety along with him. Reagle, after resigning from the federal government, went to work as a consultant, with the U.S. Chamber as his first big client. Donohue paid Reagle less than $10,000, enhanced with a fancy title: "key counsel" on transportation.

Under the leadership of Donohue, who took over in 1997, the Chamber utterly transformed its game. Instead of standing on the sidelines, it took the front lines—and instead of resigning itself to futile struggles with a liberal Congress, it took aggressive measures to change Congress's composition. In campaigns and in the courts, in regulators' offices and in the media, it dove into single-issue, single-industry political combat to mold the Washington environment decisively in businesses' favor.

With Donohue in power, the Chamber was prepared to deal more decisively with issues like the regulation of the trucking industry. Those rules limiting truckers to ten hours on the road, which had been around since the 1930s? The ones that Congress had asked the White House to make safer by reducing driver fatigue? Under Donohue, the Chamber demanded that drivers spend *more* time on the road, not less. The Bush administration, encouraged by the Chamber and other business groups, responded with a rule that allowed truck drivers to work more hours every day and every week. It amped up the limit on consecutive driving hours to eleven. In a single week, truck drivers could be on duty more than twice as long as the typical American worker: up to eighty-four hours. The Bush administration had acted on Congress's call to improve road safety by reducing drivers' fatigue, by increasing the number of hours they spent on the road. It completely ignored the part where Congress said it had to do something to improve drivers' health.

"HAD THE RULE BEEN ten hours, my wife would very likely have been alive and with us today," Ed Slattery says from his home in Maryland, where he now must provide constant care to Matthew, with the help of a special therapeutic school. Until the 2010 accident, Slattery was an economist for the U.S. Department of Agriculture, with a firsthand appreciation for the balance between the hand of government and the freedom of business to prosper. "I understand markets. I've studied them most of my life. I know what markets are good at doing and what they're not good at doing. Markets aren't good at allocating resources to safety. They aren't."

Matthew lost 80 percent of his blood in the collision, and doctors did not expect him to survive. For months he lay in the hospital almost entirely paralyzed. Moving a finger to try to pet a dog was a major accomplishment. Now Matthew can walk only with assistance, so he usually uses a wheelchair. He has severe aphasia, which means he frequently cannot find the words he seeks to express. As a result, he is mostly mute. His recovery is painful and will never be close to complete.

When the White House changed occupants in 2009, the Obama administration, like Clinton's, sought to improve road safety and drivers' health by curbing the length of time drivers could stay on the road. Its transportation department pressed to reduce driving time from eleven straight hours to ten, with longer periods of rest every day and week.

The Chamber of Commerce calculated the cost of the proposed

regulations—the rules that could have saved Susan Slattery's life—at $700 million. A driver working at a standard rate of 30 cents a mile earns about $22.50 for that eleventh hour. That extra pay is not the cost the Chamber is talking about, or why it has lobbied aggressively and gone to court to fight for longer hours for truck drivers.

Of the nearly $12 trillion in goods that companies ship across the country every year, more than $8 trillion go by truck, and that extra hour is one more that a driver can spend getting one load to its destination. Trucks keep Walmarts and Targets stocked, they keep consumers spending, and they keep the nation's economy churning. It's no accident that the Chamber's vice-chair at the time was the third-generation head of an Iowa trucking megacompany, Ruan Transportation.

In the face of intractable unemployment, coupled with soaring oil prices, global warming, and other existential threats to companies and the larger economy, one might have expected the leading organization for American business to seek to seed a domestic manufacturing revival. That way, instead of trucking goods from coastal ports to the heartland, the heartland would sprout jobs once again that produced goods consumed within the region, which would reduce the need for truckers to spend so much time on the road delivering goods. But the logic of the businesses that drive the U.S. Chamber doesn't work that way. Manufacturing is still cheaper overseas, and pushing drivers and diesel until both are spent is better for their bottom line.

The Obama administration ultimately opted to stick with eleven hours on duty, as the trucking industry sought, but with a tougher seventy-hour weekly max for a driver's time behind the wheel. The measure, which went into effect in July 2013, didn't prevent the deadly crash a year later that badly injured comedian Tracy Morgan on the New Jersey Turnpike, and killed his fellow performer Jimmy Mack, when a Walmart truck barreled into the rear of their tour van. Prosecutors alleged the driver had been awake for at least twenty-four hours prior.

. . .

SINCE 2010, WHEN ED Slattery got the horrific calls from Akron Children's Hospital and the Portage County coroner, he has guided his sons' recovery and has also become active in CRASH, the public safety advocacy group co-chaired by Joan Claybrook.

Besides truck safety and automobile airbags, which you can thank her for, Claybrook's other career-defining fight was against what business groups call "tort reform": the ongoing campaign by businesses and their insurers to limit legal damages available to consumers who have been harmed by companies' products and conduct. Try to use that term with Claybrook, and she'll throw back a chilly pause. "Don't call it 'tort reform,' please," she instructs. "We view it as a 'deform.'"

Public Citizen has an annual budget of about $3 million; its nonprofit research foundation, with much stricter legal limits on its political advocacy, has $9 million more to work with. And the U.S. Chamber? In 2012 it spent $207 million. Less than a third of that went to staff salaries, including CEO Donohue's $5.4 million in compensation.

In the 2010 and 2012 election years, the greatest share of the Chamber's spending went to lobbying federal officials and influencing congressional elections. And that doesn't count the Chamber's spawn organizations. The National Chamber Litigation Center, its in-house law firm that fights regulations opposed by the Chamber, on its own has a budget triple the size of Public Citizen's. And the Institute for Legal Reform, the Chamber's force behind a national campaign to tip the courts in businesses' favor, spent $42 million in 2010 alone.

That year all those divisions combined channeled $157 million into federal lobbying—money that translated into an extraordinary outpouring of lobbyists who filled the halls of the Capitol and the House and Senate offices—one lobbyist for every two members of the House. The Chamber's roster of lobbyists includes two former members of Congress, Lauch Faircloth (R-NC) and David McIntosh (R-

IN), and dozens of former congressional staffers. Between 1998 and 2012 the Chamber invested just over $1 billion in lobbying—more than three times as much as the next-biggest business lobbying force in Washington, General Electric.

When it comes to the work of the federal government, lawmaking is only the part of the iceberg that floats above water. The details that really matter are in the arcane realm of rulemaking—the specific regulations and guidelines that determine what paperwork needs to be filed when, how many parts per million of a pollutant can hit the air before sanctions slam down, or the precise manner in which a trucker has to document his lunch breaks. Each of these millions of lines of code comes with costs and consequences for businesses. Members of Congress can be lured with the honey of campaign contributions, but regulators at federal agencies require more aggressive means of persuasion.

Usually that persuasion comes at the hands of the federal judges on the D.C. District Court, where critical cases concerning government regulation are heard. In 2010 alone, the U.S. Chamber stepped in to press a dozen appeals fighting regulations in the D.C. court, including actions to stop the Securities and Exchange Commission (SEC) from opening corporate board elections to insurgent candidates and to block California from creating its own fuel efficiency standards.

Another suit sought to block a move by the Environmental Protection Agency (EPA) to regulate greenhouse gases as a pollutant, even though the U.S. Supreme Court had already made clear that greenhouse gases were covered under the Clean Air Act. The Chamber has used the D.C. court to successfully prevent the Teamsters union from organizing FedEx drivers, and it has beat back an effort to speed union elections. In a rare moment of convergence with progressive interests, it sued the state of Arizona to block a law compelling employers to check the immigration status of every worker against a national database.

The Chamber also generates hundreds of "friend of the court" briefs that it files in federal appeals courts and in the Supreme Court. The arguments in these briefs often find their way into judges' decisions.

In some of these fights, the Chamber faces well-motivated and relatively well-resourced adversaries—most reliably, trial lawyers, labor unions, and the government itself. Some of its most aggressive assaults in the courts have hit federal agencies under the Obama and Clinton administrations, including the National Labor Relations Board, the EPA, and the SEC.

But in other cases, where there's no identifiable group with a ready source of funding available to fight the Chamber, it falls to relatively puny public interest advocacy organizations to push back. And on that front Public Citizen has been the Chamber's most stalwart nemesis, especially when it comes to so-called tort reform.

When regulations fail or don't exist in the first place, the courts are the recourse for those who have been harmed. In a small bit of consolation for Ed Slattery and his family, Estes Express Lines had $150 million worth of insurance. Things could have been much worse: the same federal law that had deregulated the trucking industry and put swarms of new rigs on the road required them to carry only $750,000 in coverage.

The question was where Slattery and his sons could make a claim. Maryland, the Slatterys' home state, was out of the question. Just a month after the crash, the state's supreme court, urged on by a brief from the U.S. Chamber and from individual state chambers of commerce with trucking, insurance, and chemical industry groups, had upheld a half-million-dollar cap on noneconomic damages (a category that includes pain and suffering and loss of companionship) in lawsuits.

The Slatterys seriously considered suing in Ohio, where the accident had taken place, even though it would have been a fraught proposition. In 2005, following heavy lobbying by the Ohio Chamber of Commerce, an affiliate of the national organization, the state put strict financial caps on noneconomic damages. "Ohio Chamber members are urged to contact their state representatives and ask them to make passage of SB 80 their number one priority when they return to Columbus in January," the Ohio Chamber's political team urged businesses across the state. After the measure passed, the group published a list of all the legislators who supported the measure and asked members to thank them.

The U.S. Chamber thanked the bill's sponsor, Steve Stivers, in the best way it could: by helping him get elected to Congress in 2010, with more than $260,000 in campaign ads attacking the Democratic incumbent, Mary Jo Kilroy. He was one of dozens of Republicans who were swept into office that fall aloft the Chamber's $33 million in election advertising, spending that helped hand the GOP control of the House of Representatives. In Ohio alone five Republican challengers supported by the Chamber ousted incumbent Democrats.

In office, Stivers received a 100 percent rating from the Ohio Chamber. He dutifully echoed the local and national Chamber's main talking point: that beating back "frivolous" lawsuits would boost the economy and create jobs. His Ohio crackdown on lawsuit payouts poses as a carefully crafted surgery attacking excessive payouts in questionable cases, since the cap on payouts doesn't apply in cases where plaintiffs, like Matthew Slattery, are no longer able to care for themselves.

But the rest of the law tells a different story. Juries are not allowed to consider the defendant's wrongdoing in calculating the size of the award. In catastrophic injury cases, judges have to follow restrictive guidelines for setting awards. And when all is said and done, the defendant can go back after the fact and challenge an award as excessive or appeal to a higher court.

Ohio is not a place to take any chances in the courts. In 2004 in Ohio and fifteen other states, the U.S. Chamber and affiliated local chambers had contributed to and in many cases coordinated political campaigns on behalf of their favored candidates for seats on state high courts. The Ohio Chamber created a group called Citizens for a Strong Ohio to "distribute information about Ohio's economic climate and the importance of job creation," as it advised the IRS. But what it in fact did during election years—flouting IRS rules limiting nonprofits' political activity—was sponsor a war chest to elect judges sympathetic to the Chamber's interests.

In 2004 that pot of money totaled more than $3 million, $1 million of which came from the Institute for Legal Reform—that sister group of the U.S. Chamber's devoted to limiting payouts in lawsuits, whose board of directors (and, though undisclosed, funding) has heavy representation from the insurance industry. The Chamber's project fueled a record-setting $7 million-plus advertising arms race that saturated TV stations with an astonishing fourteen thousand–plus ads for and against judges seeking seats on the bench. And in Ohio it had the intended result: all three of its candidates won, including one newcomer to an open seat, widening the Republican majority on the state supreme court to a six-to-one margin.

The Ohio Chamber was already assured of loyalty from Governor Bob Taft, whose political dynasty had for a century helped business build its platform of political influence. His grandfather, Senate majority leader Robert Taft, had sponsored the 1940s law that to this day limits workers' ability to go on strike and that has allowed twenty-three "right to work" states to forbid obligations to join a union as a condition of employment. And the national Chamber owes its existence to his great-grandfather, President William Howard Taft, who early in the twentieth century first called on warring factions of business to join forces around their common interests and create the U.S. Chamber of Commerce.

Ed Slattery never had to put the Ohio courts to the test. "We are very lucky in our private little hell," he remarks. Before the Slatterys launched a suit, the driver admitted he had fallen asleep at the wheel—an act of criminal negligence that put him in jail for two years—and Estes Express entered into a $40.8 million settlement with the Slatterys, certified by a Missouri court. Slattery used some of the proceeds to set up a fund at Akron Children's Hospital for the care of kids whose families can't afford to pay their bills. The rest is now covering the mounting medical costs for Matthew, and for Ed's retirement so that he can become a full-time caretaker for his sons.

THE U.S. CHAMBER OF Commerce is notorious for waging big, dramatic fights in the public eye, like the tens of millions of dollars in campaign spending that helped swing the House to Republican control in 2010; for its aggressive campaign against the Affordable Care Act that expanded health insurance—a law that but for the vote of one justice would have gone down to defeat in the Supreme Court; and for its successful lobbying to kill cap-and-trade regulation on carbon dioxide emissions.

But much of the influence of the Chamber happens in battles that most Americans never hear about yet that have profound effects on our lives. The victories that the Chamber has won in trench warfare affect safety on the road and our ability to sue for damages when an injury is done. They shape our prospects of getting affordable insurance, or a mortgage that won't devour our household budgets. The Chamber is why companies that have repeatedly violated federal laws can still get government contracts. And it has played a pivotal role in widening the economic divide between the very wealthiest in the United States and everyone else.

The dwindling of labor union membership to just one in every fourteen private-sector workers. A seven-year delay in advancing standards under the Clean Air Act to reduce smog-inducing ozone emissions and the release of the tiny particles that plague asthma sufferers. The ability of companies to contribute infinite amounts of cash to political campaigns without having to disclose their involvement. The obliteration of a new SEC rule that gave shareholders the power to nominate their own members to corporate boards. These are just some of the sharp legacies of the U.S. Chamber's singular power.

The Chamber is something unique in the annals of American politics: a single institution that shapes the balance of power in the courts, at the ballot box, in the halls of state legislatures, and in the U.S. Congress. It is protected by the IRS as a trade organization, which means it does not have to pay taxes or disclose its sources of funds. That isn't new: it lobbied Congress a century ago to secure such special status for industry and for "social welfare" groups—a privilege that today has opened a pipeline of corporate cash into our elections, much of it arriving courtesy of the Chamber itself.

In the nation that the Chamber seeks, carbon dioxide would not be regulated as a pollutant, even though science has proven its devastating impact on the environment beyond any doubt. The United States would remain the only developed nation without universal health care, and agents of U.S. companies would be free to bribe officials overseas. Homeowners would not have easy-to-read disclosure forms to explain their mortgages' true costs or enforcers to respond when they're bilked, courtesy of the Consumer Financial Protection Bureau. Risky financial derivatives would trade with high leverage, and without outside scrutiny, but with potentially catastrophic consequences for the larger economy. The federal health agency would not even be able to inform the public that reducing salt consumption lowers blood pressure for most people.

That all of the above objectives have largely been thwarted, at least at the time of this writing, is testament to an easy-to-overlook reality: the Chamber's rise as the most fully realized political influence machine the nation has ever seen was a direct reaction to the stunning success of consumer, environmental, and labor groups in driving Washington's actions over the previous decades to regulate businesses. And it's the continued combat of those counterforces that has kept those rules of the road in place and, here and there, in response to grave crises, even expanded them.

The Chamber machine is also a reaction to the firmly entrenched power of labor unions in Democratic politics, which even in their diminished and divided state continue to organize and mobilize voters in high-stakes congressional races. Taken together, unions spend more than $600 million a year on lobbying and politics. The leader among them, the Service Employees International Union, spent an average of $54 million a year between 2005 and 2011, and on the state and local level its affiliates spent millions more.

By law, unions have to disclose the totality of their political spending. Companies don't, and entities and individual business leaders spend far more than labor ever could. The Chamber has openly advertised itself to them as a vehicle for influence, which in exchange for contributions will carry out intensive lobbying and political campaigns designed to neuter government activism.

One important channel for its influence doesn't have to be paid for: provocative and sometimes downright offensive public statements that serve as deliberate bids for free media attention. Though the Chamber has backpedaled from it, a call from its environmental chief, William Kovacs, for a "Scopes Monkey Trial" to air arguments for and against global warming continues to draw public mockery— but also guarantees that the Chamber remains perpetually visible as a player in climate change politics.

In a 2004 speech to the Commonwealth Club of California, Tom Donohue told tech workers who had lost their jobs to offshoring to "stop whining" because ultimately exporting jobs creates more economic opportunity than it destroys.

Six years later Donohue's words still resonated through the Capitol, as liberal Senator Bernie Sanders (I-VT) delivered his grand filibuster against the Obama tax cut. "'U.S. Chamber of Commerce President and CEO Thomas Donohue urged American companies to send jobs overseas,'" Sanders quoted a headline in hour five or so. "What more do we need to understand why we have lost millions of good-paying manufacturing jobs, why wages are going down? What more do we need when the president of the Chamber of Commerce tells us he thinks it is good public policy to send jobs to China?"

THE CHAMBER IS BUT one business trade organization out of hundreds that make their influence felt in Washington, seeking favors and advantage. It jockeys alongside three other industry supergroups—

the National Federation of Independent Business, the Business Roundtable, and the National Association of Manufacturers—for members and influence.

If the name Chamber of Commerce triggers any associations for most nonmembers, it's of a small-town organization that helps keep Main Street clean, perhaps lined with brightly painted fiberglass cows, and that provides a civic platform for local businesses usually preoccupied with the rigors of keeping cash coming in and the lights turned on. About 2,800 local associations remain dues-paying members of the national organization, and across the country business owners proudly display the trade group's red, white, and blue schematic eagle emblem in shop windows and on office doors.

But the Chamber's recent incarnation as an ideological machine with a fundamentalist vision of how capitalism ought to work, and whose political spending has overwhelmingly benefited Republican candidates for public office, has riven the landscape of American business. The local Chamber of Commerce in Rocky River, the Ohio town where Susan Slattery spent her last day, runs a bright red disclaimer at the very top of its Web homepage: "The Rocky River Chamber of Commerce is NOT affiliated with the U.S. Chamber of Commerce in any way. Every Chamber of Commerce is an independent membership organization." Other local chambers have published similar disclaimers:

> The Santa Cruz Area Chamber of Commerce is not affiliated with the U.S. Chamber and has not been a U.S. Chamber member for many years.

> The Greater Nashua Chamber of Commerce is a completely independent organization from the U.S. Chamber of Commerce.

On and on across the country, local chambers face Web rants and angry phone calls from area residents who are convinced that they are doing the national group's bidding.

Hundreds of local chambers remain members of the national group, paying modest dues of $300 and up. But by 2014, just 213 out of seven thousand local chambers remained officially accredited members of the national organization, having passed a rigorous questionnaire about their management and membership practices—and their political organizing.

The U.S. Chamber's prior leaders invested heavily in cultivating the local groups as the building blocks of the national cause. But while it continues to provide helpful services for the member chambers and their members, the supercharged U.S. Chamber that arrived with Donohue in 1997 has unapologetically devoted itself to deciding elections, laws, regulations, court cases—pressing every available lever of power—to advance a highly specific view of businesses' interests. In the process Donohue has styled himself as bizarro Nader—a cantankerous, confrontational, media-hungry advocate every bit as uncompromising and committed to transforming the national landscape as Ralph Nader himself.

Large companies with political problems to solve turn to the Chamber of Commerce when they need to alter the political climate enough to ease through the outcome they seek—but want their own company's fingerprints to stay off an unpopular cause. It's one thing to lobby on an issue; it's quite another to lobby on that same issue while spending millions of dollars, as everyone on the Hill knows, to decide who gets to keep their seats in the House, based on votes and even mere public statements on that very subject. And it's still another to put teams of lobbyists on the task of whittling down regulations, holding a big club behind their back: the prospect of lawsuits blocking the rules entirely.

Dow Chemical gave the U.S. Chamber $2.9 million in 2012, even as it spent another $11.5 million on its own lobbying—more than double its contribution to the American Chemistry Council and far outstripping its $84,000 to the Business Roundtable.

In 2011–12 Chevron gave the Chamber $1.5 million, in addition to spending more than $19 million on its own lobbying.

In 2009 one single contributor, its identity undisclosed on the Chamber's IRS filing for that year, gave $86.2 million. *Bloomberg News* figured out that it was America's Health Insurance Plans (AHIP), a coalition that included WellPoint, Cigna, Aetna, Humana, and UnitedHealth and that had itself reported contributing a similar amount for "grassroots outreach, education and mobilization, print, online, and broadcast advertising and coalition building efforts." At 40 percent of the Chamber's entire spending for that year, the contribution came dangerously close to violating the IRS directive that nonprofit civic groups like the Chamber must do more than serve the interests of individual members. The following year, as the fight over health care reform came to a head, AHIP gave another $16.2 million to the Chamber for its campaign against the health care bill.

As the obscure fight over truckers' work hours shows, the Chamber doesn't always get exactly what it wants. Some of its most fiercely fought campaigns—like its salvos against the Affordable Care Act and the EPA's move to regulate greenhouse gases as a pollutant—have ended in stinging losses.

But these losses are never complete. Even the Supreme Court's decision to uphold the Obama administration's health care plan—an immediate defeat—contains within it the seeds for history-changing litigation to challenge federal mandates to states. The Chamber is relentless in its cause, and its cause is nothing less than dominance of the American political system.

CHAPTER 2

The Bastard Child

From its beginning a century ago, the U.S. Chamber of Commerce has been snared in a tangle of paradoxes. It stands for the principle that businesses should be free to compete, yet pulls them together for common purpose; it demands independence from government, yet sets as its primary purpose the capture of the government's attention for its own demands. Against all odds, this strange hybrid beast amassed influence—but only after decades of impotence.

Local chambers of commerce and similar industry groups have long existed in this country. New York State's chamber dates back to before the Revolutionary War. The National Association of Manufacturers emerged from the depths of a late 1800s recession. Almost always these groups represented a narrow slice of business life—an industry, a city—and looked after its welfare. Sometimes that mission took local chambers in decidedly progressive directions; for instance, advocating for laws improving housing, food safety, and other basics of healthy communities. But more often self-serving objectives beckoned.

In 1890 Congress passed the Sherman Antitrust Act in response to the rising power of monopolies like Standard Oil. The act gave the government the authority and tools to break up monopolies and prevent businesses from dominating the nation through sheer bulk and brawn—most famously used in 1911 when a Supreme Court decision led to Standard Oil's dissolution. With the antitrust act, the federal government became involved in American commerce to an unprecedented degree—and trade associations and business groups responded by coming to Washington, in delegations of a hundred and more, to make their demands heard and to press for advantages. The voices of these various associations were often raised against one another, however, divided between rural and urban interests, southern and northern, big and small, those who benefited from government regulation and those who were hurt by it.

President Theodore Roosevelt planted the seeds to unify clamorous commercial interests into a single force with the 1907 formation of the U.S. Department of Commerce, whose secretary, the New York City business leader Oscar Straus, invited a group of other business leaders to his office to serve as a kind of advisory group. But company executives, it turned out, didn't want to be the kept consorts of the government; nor did pro-tariff businesses appreciate the Roosevelt administration's agenda to lower trade barriers.

Still, business chieftains were not about to let go of the invitation to influence. They saw threats on the horizon—like Europe, where in a protectionist fit nations were raising taxes on imported U.S. goods, making it harder for American businesses to compete. European companies, the Americans noticed, possessed another advantage: they had a habit of teaming up into national associations and often worked closely with their governments to expand foreign markets. Germany was a particular object of obsession, viewed by some business leaders as a powerful machine that scrappy American companies and their government needed to emulate.

Leaders of local and regional chambers asked the administration of Roosevelt's successor, William Howard Taft, to work with them to form a national group, sanctioned by the government as an official voice of business. In his 1912 State of the Union address, Taft took up the call for a national organization that would advance the cause of trade, and in March of that year he called for a summit to found a U.S. Chamber of Commerce. His intention was that the organization would work with the White House and Congress as they developed laws and policies that affected business.

The details of the new group would be up to its private-sector leaders, but the president stressed two "essential principles" that he believed needed to govern the organization. One, it had to be "broadly representative of the commercial interests of the whole country." And two, those in charge needed to allow democracy to flourish within that broadly representative organization, so that the will of the majority of members decided its actions.

In April 1912 more than seven hundred merchants, bankers, tradesmen, and manufacturers, doing commerce in hides, cotton, dollars, wood, groceries, metals, and more, converged at Washington's new Willard Hotel to establish a national Chamber of Commerce. Local business associations in forty states and territories, even the Philippines, delivered delegates; many, figuring they already had a man in D.C., simply sent their local members of Congress.

The president gave the members of the new Chamber of Commerce a very good reason to be there: a loud say in the shaping of government regulation. Taft had something to gain too. Instead of having to navigate the thorny politics of competing business interests on red-hot issues like tariffs or corporate taxes, and field lobbying from dozens of regions and industries, he could let the national Chamber decide on one majority position, and then he would take it from there.

"We want your association to work in conjunction with the government," President Taft addressed the gathered men. "We need your assistance and we ask it." Specifically, he sought their direct input on policy actions taken by the feds. "Regulating measures which have been adopted in the past may have suffered from lack of advice from those who should be best qualified by experience and training to give it. . . . The disinterested advice of those who are to live by the measures is of first importance."

The following January the newly formed Chamber of Commerce held its first convention in Washington, and delegates and their wives attended tea at the White House with President and First Lady Taft. The Chamber also advocated and secured a privilege that has shielded its resources and activities ever since: a clause in a tariff law that exempted it and other business trade groups from paying taxes.

In its first decades, the Chamber was a careful and not especially vocal presence in Washington. The group operated with painstaking formality, in deference to the kaleidoscope of different business interests under its tent and the founding mandate to do business by rule of majority. Merchants who loathed tariffs had to get along with manufacturers who demanded them. Businesses that chafed at the Sherman Antitrust Act had to get along with companies that stood to be crushed by mergers and monopolies. Referendum votes of the entire membership, supported by pamphlets detailing arguments for both sides of each issue, were the sole means of decision making. While business leaders in the Chamber met and deliberated and approved referenda sedulously, their adversaries in the American Federation of Labor were organizing millions of workers, whose voices and votes—and lobbyists—rang loudly in Congress.

IN 1924 THE CHAMBER settled into a grand Grecian fortress designed by the architect Cass Gilbert on H Street, across from the White House. Now that it occupied a building that loomed larger than its impact on government, it decided to up its game. Flush with the prosperity of the mid-1920s and eager to counter the influence of the fast-mobilizing labor movement, its leaders began to offer a more forceful vision for what the organization should be. "American business must become militant," Chamber president Lewis E. Pierson exhorted his members at a meeting in Indiana. It had to stop looking to government, he demanded, for favors and endorsements.

But the great stone edifice could not withstand the forces building up outside its bronze doors, demanding a new, never-before-seen activism from government—and controls on the bankers and business enterprises that had reached beyond sustainable limits. The ravages of the Great Depression would not only propel government into superpowered, muscular action to stimulate and steer the economy, with wide popular support; they would also cast out business into a new wilderness, from a cozy partner with Washington into a realm on the defensive, in need of caging and control like a wild animal trapped after a rampage.

It would take decades before business as a political force could pull out from under the Great Depression's mighty shadow. Meanwhile, in a confounding post-war prosperity—an era in which workers and capitalist kingpins both shared in America's wealth, thanks to progressive taxation, unionization, militarization, and the newly strong hand of government regulation—the Chamber of Commerce retreated into the comfort and power of Cold War paranoia, fueling the national panic that the forces of socialism had infected the unions, workplaces, and movie lots of America, fatally if not stopped.

At first the stock market crash, the bank failures, and the commercial paralysis of 1929 did nothing to change the means or message. A year and a half after the crash, the next Chamber president wrote a letter to Congress saying the best thing representatives could do was leave business alone; it would recover just fine without help. He wrote of "the inherent strength of our economic position."

The reality of the Great Depression, however, soon obliterated hope that the sick marketplace would recover on its own. Virtually every American business saw its sales plummet and its markets dry up. In many industries, in particular the garment trade, firms began to turn on one another in a brutal fight to undercut prices, wages, anything that would give them an edge and make a sale. Capitalism had turned to cannibalism.

The Chamber began to make the case for businesses to organize as a bloc to coordinate economic activity: "We have left the period of extreme individualism and are living in a period in which national economy must be recognized as a controlling factor." It sought to allow businesses to band together to set controls on industrial production, so companies didn't dump unneeded goods in the marketplace. And it pushed for job sharing by workers as a way to reduce unemployment. But these ideas, which required the kind of collusion that ran afoul of antitrust laws, never progressed. Instead, businesses clung to the hope offered by President Herbert Hoover, the former secretary of commerce: his Reconstruction Finance Corporation offered them desperately needed loans to maintain operations during the early days of the Great Depression.

With the arrival of Franklin Delano Roosevelt's New Deal, the Chamber was faced with a new threat. Price controls, the right to organize labor unions (and an end to the company unions favored by the Chamber), new taxes for Social Security and unemployment insurance—President Roosevelt and his New Deal engineers would bring on a succession of repulsive obligations for American businesses, most of which they would have to live with indefinitely.

The U.S. Chamber nonetheless embraced the White House in the hope of having some influence. Chamber president Henry Harriman, a former textile manufacturer, spent much of the spring of 1933 across Lafayette Square from the Chamber of Commerce headquarters, collaborating with Roosevelt's brain trust to develop the National Recovery Act (NRA). The NRA suspended much-loathed antitrust laws that made it difficult for industries to coordinate, in order to make way for codes of fair competition within industries. Those codes could include agreements on wages, hours, and conditions for workers. If trade associations could not agree on their own codes, then the White House had the power to impose its own.

As Chamber members complained loudly and bitterly about most of the New Deal, Harriman sought to dampen the furor. He traveled the nation to make the case to local business groups that the NRA stimulus program, and by implication President Roosevelt, was not their enemy. When the administration sought to renew the act in 1935, the Chamber's membership voted overwhelmingly in favor of renewal and called for codes to include minimum wages, maximum hours, and collective bargaining for workers.

A month later the Supreme Court ruled that the NRA, whose industry codes the Chamber so cherished, was unconstitutional. This decision left the Chamber's constituent businesses with the new obligations imposed by the New Deal, without new opportunities. Social Security would force businesses to pay a new tax on every employee. Unemployment insurance pushed another big tax onto businesses. Price controls were anathema to business. The National Labor Relations Act gave workers vast power to organize into unions and shut down businesses with strikes. And the Chamber loathed the big public works projects that received mountains of government cash and that directly competed with private business and drove up wages.

The Chamber's warnings of government overreach weren't entirely unfounded. Protected by Senator Robert Wagner's Labor Relations Act, unions organized and grew. Sit-down strikes forced General Motors and other companies into deals they didn't want. Between 1936 and 1937 the number of strikes more than doubled, to more than 4,700.

By 1946 more than 4.6 million workers were involved in strikes, some of them vicious. In the minds of the Chamber's leadership and backers, the rise of unions, abetted by government, was driven by a deeper and more insidious threat to American business: socialism. Fully empowering American business would mean destroying socialism on American soil.

The battle against socialism, which defined the Chamber for much of the twentieth century, had begun while the country was still in the depths of the Great Depression. In 1934, the Washington investigative journalist I. F. Stone discovered, the Chamber's committee on communism and socialism had recommended that the Department of Justice set up an agency "to investigate, record, control, and prosecute all subversive agitators." Specifically, the Chamber urged changing the law to make advocating the violent overthrow of the U.S. government, even in a pamphlet, a criminal act of sedition; to ban "subversive doctrines" from using the U.S. Postal Service; and to deny naturalization to members of the Communist Party or other groups deemed subversive. The Chamber approved that proposal at its 1935 annual meeting.

The Chamber went on to compile an aggressive and exhaustive series of reports and to distribute some three-quarters of a million copies of them, detailing Communist infiltration into American society, government, and workplaces. The reports called for Congress to create a loyalty check for current and prospective federal employees and to purge anyone found to have engaged in "pro-Communist activities." Shortly afterward President Harry Truman ordered just such a sweep at the FBI. The bureau, in a move endorsed by the Chamber, also gained new powers to investigate the scourge.

The Chamber had estimated that some four hundred individuals within the federal government, some in influential positions within the State and Budget Departments, were members or sympathizers of the Communist Party, and that forty thousand more were members of the "Communist-dominated" Congress of Industrial Organizations or other supposed agents of Moscow working in U.S. operations overseas. "Secret communist cells are continuously at work in the nation's capital," the Chamber's report stated, and the workers within these cells were using patronage to hire fellow travelers into key positions in numerous government agencies: "Communists and their followers have achieved positions in our government where they can do immense harm to national welfare and security."

The Chamber claimed, in its pamphlet on Communist infiltration into America, that it had produced the first comprehensive look at the Communist conspiracy's influence in media, Hollywood, government, and labor. American businesses had a "duty to show both in theory and practice the superior merits of our present way of life." The information campaign and testimony to Congress legitimized what had been a fringe movement and set the table for the paranoia and purges soon to follow.

The Chamber pioneered McCarthyism while Senator Joe McCarthy (R-WI) was still in law school. It would go on to push the Justice Department to "investigate, record, control, and prosecute all subversive agitators," and later it distributed handbooks detailing how local anti-Communist committees could ferret out and blacklist Communists hiding in consumer, women's, civil liberties, school, and church groups.

Going after the Communists wouldn't be enough. The Chamber's membership had to fill the nation with its own ranks of believers in the capitalist system. In the face of supposed (and highly debatable) union power in politics, members decided in the late 1950s to make the voice of business heard loudly in Congress. With members General Electric, Gulf Oil, and the American Can Company in the vanguard, the Chamber's leaders urged members to sway elections, through political organizing and pro-business education at the local level.

A Gulf vice-president explained the stakes in a letter to employees and shareholders in 1958, calling them to mobilize in a grassroots political offensive to make sure capitalism—not Adlai Stevenson or his liberal ilk—won the 1960 election. "If our free, competitive institutions are to be preserved from destruction by the unholy combination of predatory gangsterism and crackpot socialism that is thriving and expanding under labor's Congressional benevolence," wrote Archie Gray, "then business has no choice. It must do likewise, or throw in the towel."

The Chamber joined the fray with its Political Participation Program (slogan: "Unleashing the Creative Energies of People") and in 1959 distributed some forty thousand sets of an audiovisual education series called Action Course in Practical Politics. Some 150,000 business executives and employees signed up for the training. With painstaking precision, the course detailed every step a local chamber of commerce or company would need to take to influence an election, from the best seating arrangements at rallies to the art of a door-to-door canvass and the usual ticket prices for fund-raising dinners ($100 max). Participants received detailed instruction on how to form a political club and how to set up and run an effective campaign for political office.

Monsanto used the program to train its employees and found that the number of them who donated to political candidates, distributed literature, and joined local political clubs tripled. Ford and Caterpillar trained their employees to similar effect.

The project never had much influence on local or national politics. As Harvard Business School professor Theodore Levitt observed at the time, employees had little incentive to get involved in the rambunctious, working-class world of local politics, with its laborious door-knocking on all sides of the tracks. "The usual plums for politicking are patronage jobs," he noted, "and these have neither prestige nor financial appeal for aspiring executives." Golfing with Ike this wasn't.

The means were all wrong and showed a clumsiness in politics that in hindsight is downright charming. But the dream lived on. Business had to find a way to assert itself as a political force.

IN THE 1950S THE government had passed barely more than two dozen laws dictating the rules American businesses had to work by. In the 1960s into 1970, the decade of Great Society programs like Medicaid, nearly fifty new laws thunked onto the books. The Occupational Safety and Health Act, Clean Air Act, National Environmental Policy Act, Civil Rights Act, and a slew of more obscure measures created a new mandate on American businesses—to work not just in their own economic interest but for the good of the nation.

But the 1970s brought an even more activist government, determined to rein in American business. Consumer groups, labor unions, and crusading investigative journalists made common cause with ambitious members of Congress to form a juggernaut that tapped into many Americans' growing sense that the land of the free had lost its way, polluting its own water and soil, exploiting those who did low-paid and dangerous work like crop harvesting and coal mining, endangering drivers and passengers in death-machine automobiles. The Great Society had fueled hope that progress was possible. The Watergate crisis only deepened a nagging sense that Washington had to reinvent itself and prove its worth to a discouraged nation.

During that decade, the federal government spawned twenty-one new regulatory agencies, the fruits of movements for environmental, consumer, and worker safety. Along the way Congress went somewhat regulation-crazy. Inspired by exhortations of consumer and labor groups who spoke to the very real needs and concerns of voters, some 120 regulatory measures emerged from Congress in the 1970s. The Foreign Corrupt Practices Act (1977) forbade American businesses from bribing officials outside the United States. The Toxic Substances Control Act (1976) subjected all new chemical compounds to review by the EPA. The Community Reinvestment Act (1977) required banks to do business and open branches in areas where they had previously refused to tread. The list went on.

The popular imagination puts consumer advocate Ralph Nader at the vortex of the regulation revolution, largely because of his success in driving the landmark 1966 Highway Safety Act. But the new regulatory state was created by politicians fighting for popular support, and responding on their own to the smell of revolution in the air. For example, the Occupational Safety and Health Administration (OSHA) first took shape as a few lines from a speechwriter that were uttered by President Lyndon Johnson; the speechwriter's brother happened to work in a tiny unit within the federal welfare agency assigned to keep an eye on worker safety and saw an opportunity to step up government's authority in the area. When Congress took up the idea, the Chamber and other business groups opposed it, while the AFL-CIO rallied in favor—all what you'd expect.

But in 1968, one month into the newly elected Nixon administration, a coal mine explosion claimed seventy-eight lives and drew the nation's attention to the miners' dangerous and unregulated working conditions, pushing the Nixon administration to craft what would become OSHA. The Chamber supported Nixon's carefully calibrated vision of OSHA, but that's not the creature that ultimately stomped out of Congress, which was instead a bipartisan Frankenstein of Chamber members' nightmares. This new agency's powerful inspectors could show up at a workplace and levy hefty fines for any of-fenses they found, without opportunity for the business owner to appeal.

And in some instances, the Republican president himself became the source of businesses' troubles. Nixon created the EPA in 1970 by asking Congress to combine the functions of a scattering of different federal departments into one superagency. "Our national government today," Nixon wrote in his memo, "is not structured to make a coor-dinated attack on the pollutants which debase the air we breathe, the water we drink, and the land that grows our food."

The president was acting on a promise he had already made in that year's State of the Union address, and it's worth hearing him out here to understand just how strong a stand he took.

> We can no longer afford to consider air and water common property, free to be abused by anyone without regard to the consequences. Instead, we should begin now to treat them as scarce resources, which we are no freer to contaminate than we are free to throw garbage into our neighbor's yard.
>
> This requires comprehensive new regulations. It also re-quires that, to the extent possible, the price of goods should be made to include the costs of producing and disposing of them without damage to the environment.

Nixon went on to debunk conventional wisdom that a better envi-ronment and quality of life must come at the expense of economic growth. In fact, he insisted, America could reap great economic op-portunity by channeling its "inventive genius" into solving environ-mental ills.

Now, Nixon was as sensitive as any politician to the prevailing political winds. He knew his expected 1972 election rival, Edmund Muskie, had stirred up environmentalist fervor and tapped into the nascent green movement. What Nixon wasn't getting was serious pressure from the other side—from the businesses that would have to pay the price for all of these new regulations.

What was the U.S. Chamber of Commerce doing as this great threat to business brewed in the White House? Not much. Despite earlier efforts at getting business involved in politics, in light of this new political mood, the Chamber's influence against the sheer force of the Great Society remained tepid.

On the sidelines of Washington power, the Chamber held forums and hurled recommendations over the gates of the White House—to cut funding for antipoverty programs, to move administration from one federal agency to another, to switch to block grants that states could spend as they wished. When an 8 percent hike in Social Security payments was on the table, the Chamber sent a letter to all 435 members of the House of Representatives suggesting they consider a more modest increase.

None of these polite requests had much of an effect on politicians, now entranced by popular momentum to push for an expanded, activist government. By the mid-1970s Washington was a hellish place for a believer in unfettered private enterprise. The name Ralph Nader, far from being a Washington epithet, referred to a man whose voice resounded in the Capitol and set into motion new national laws on consumer and worker safety. "Nader's Raiders," and idealists inspired by them, went to work for federal agencies, drafting regulations to keep corporate behavior in line.

An episode of *Mad Men* would later deftly reflect Nader's capture of the national conversation about corporate responsibility to the public. Roger Sterling is on the phone with a client. "Oldsmobile. He wants to know if there's any way around Nader," Sterling tells Pete Campbell, his hand on the mouthpiece. Responds Campbell, without hesitating: "There isn't."

A generation earlier, middle-class young people might have embraced the identity of the Organization Man and aspired to don a hat, accede to authority, and work for a brand-name corporation. But instead they now chose to protest and subvert the companies that dared to profit on the labor of workers, exploit natural resources, and produce the machinery and chemicals deployed in the Vietnam War.

Even a best-selling children's book by the revered Dr. Seuss mocked corporate activity and growth as a despoiler of the earth. "Business is business and business must grow!" incanted the greedy Once-ler of *The Lorax,* whose production of useless Thneeds claims every last tree in the forest and the creatures that depend on them. If the current generation was skeptical of the value of profit and production, the next one would surely grow up convinced of their evils.

BUT EVEN IF THE Chamber leadership was asleep, one person saw the threat inherent in this antibusiness political and cultural consensus. Lewis Powell was then a lawyer for the Richmond Corporation and would soon be, thanks to President Nixon, a justice of the U.S. Supreme Court.

American free enterprise, Powell warned the Chamber's brass in a 1971 letter leaked to Jack Anderson of *The Washington Post,* was coming under sustained attack. Most alarmingly, the New Left had taken root in many of the nation's college campuses, and its members were feeding the mother's milk of anticapitalism to the next generation's leaders. "One of the bewildering paradoxes of our time," Powell wrote, "is the extent to which the enterprise system tolerates, if not participates in, its own destruction." He advised the Chamber that it was at war and that it would have to arm itself to counter the ideological programming of the anticapitalist movements. "The first essential—a prerequisite to any effective action—is for businessmen to confront this problem as a primary responsibility of corporate management." He viewed the Chamber as the best-equipped group in the country to lead the way.

His proposed course of action went much further than college campuses. Powell saw a need for an infrastructure to support pro-business, conservative thought and action. "This is a vast area of opportunity for the Chamber, if it is willing to undertake the role of spokesman for American business and if, in turn, business is willing to provide the funds." He concluded with a dark warning: "Business and the enterprise system are in deep trouble, and the hour is late."

The missive served its intended function both as a wake-up call and as a call to action. Twenty-five years later the Chamber would credit the Powell letter as the instigation that enabled it to help "create a business environment in which the debate in Congress and between Congress and the White House is no longer on how much more to tax, spend, and regulate but on how much less to tax, spend, and regulate."

The memo inspired Colorado brewer Joseph Coors to pour his money into creating a new Washington think tank, the Heritage Foundation, in 1973, during conservatism's darkest hours in Washington. Unlike the existing American Enterprise Institute, Heritage set out to change not just the intellectual cast of Washington but the outcomes on specific pieces of legislation with a bearing on business, taxes, and regulation. It would work closely with the U.S. Chamber of Commerce along the way.

The Powell letter wasn't the only spur to the coming conservative wave, but it created a rough blueprint for a new chapter in the Chamber's history. The sleeping beast had awakened.

CHAPTER 3

The Astroturf Assault

Just months before Powell wrote his memo, Tom Donohue arrived in Washington, settling with his wife, Elizabeth, into a house on Greyswood Road, just outside the Beltway in Bethesda. The man who would eventually lead the Chamber's most militant phase in defense of "free enterprise" hadn't made his way in the world as an entrepreneur or an innovator or a risk-taking steward of American industry. His income had almost always derived from institutions operating by the grace of the American taxpayer.

Donohue came from a humble household that started out in a four-story brick apartment building in Prospect Heights, Brooklyn; the $50 monthly rent was paid on father Thomas's $1,800 annual salary as a timekeeper at a can factory. As the Great Depression ebbed, Thomas Sr., unlike many of his neighbors, was employed full-time, and he transmitted his work ethic to his son.

Donohue Jr.'s exposure to the private, for-profit sector came when he worked his way through St. John's University in Queens as a truck driver; he graduated in 1963. Otherwise, in the first years of his career he worked as a fund-raiser for nonprofits like the Human Resources Foundation, where he tapped into government funds newly unleashed by Great Society programs.

Donohue continued to trade in federal funds as head of development for the College of New Rochelle and then, starting in 1967, directing fund-raising and public relations for another Catholic college, Fairfield University. While he was there, more than $1 million in government funds sponsored the construction of a new library and science center—and had the ancillary benefit of giving young Tom Donohue his first exposure to high-stakes combat in the courts.

Fairfield University was the target of a 1968 lawsuit from the ACLU and the American Jewish Congress that sought to bar the college and hundreds of other religious schools across the country from receiving federal funds for their facilities.

As *Tilton v. Richardson* made its way to the U.S. Supreme Court, Donohue served as a trustee for the Catholic school's legal defense fund. Fund-raising involved elaborate deal making between colleges and dioceses, to determine their fair share of the sponsorship, and a call to all religiously affiliated colleges in the country to chip in to defend the case. In 1971 a five-to-four Supreme Court majority decided in the Catholic school's favor.

Donohue saw his future. The *Tilton* fight demonstrated the raw power of a coordinated fund-raising campaign among financially interested players to decide a legal case with far more future money at stake than they would have to pay out up front.

Donohue started his rise to power in Washington with a position in the Nixon administration working for Ted Klassen, the former president of American Can—coincidentally or not, the company that employed Donohue Sr. as a manager. Klassen had been tapped by the Nixon administration to run what was then called the Post Office Department. It was a time of turmoil for the agency. Postal carriers hadn't had a raise in years; many earned so little they qualified for food stamps. In 1970 postal workers went on an unauthorized strike that shut down mail delivery around the country. Nixon called in the army to transport and sort letters—and then he called in Klassen to fix the problem. In the subsequent settlement, workers received a raise and the right to bargain for wages and benefits, but it was a right they couldn't exercise: they were forbidden to strike and were required to go into arbitration in the event of a dispute.

Donohue was hired as part of a cadre charged under President Nixon with privatizing the postal service and imposing tough new work rules on a labor force that was, at the time, the second largest in the country, with 750,000 workers. As a regional deputy in the San Francisco office and then district manager for New York, Donohue was responsible for snuffing out such conflicts.

Donohue wasn't the only American Can Company connection on the postal service payroll. At least nine other Klassen associates secured high-paid positions or no-bid contracts. Klassen gave hundreds of thousands of dollars in contracts for promotional media, without a contract, to the former American Can film crew.

In San Francisco, Donohue tried to implement new cost-cutting work rules—such as putting all coffee breaks off the clock—that sought to squeeze every possible minute out of employees' time. "You will be surprised how much time you can capture," he wrote in a memo to postal supervisors. "Remember, if you have 48 routes and can save an average of 45 minutes per route, you can reduce your total by three. This is a savings of 24 hours per day."

The restive union didn't respond well to Donohue's push for new rules. "Labor-management in San Francisco has deteriorated to an all-time low," the local union president declared. "In our office today there is absolutely no labor-management communication."

Donohue received a transfer home to New York, where he became a district manager.

In a portent of deregulatory disasters to come, the privatization plan did not work out as promised. The new U.S. Postal Service was supposed to be financially self-supporting. Instead, by the time Klassen resigned in 1975, it had a deficit of almost half a billion dollars, even with $1.7 billion in financial support from Congress. Postage rate increases became routine, while mail delivery slowed.

More than two decades later, as Donohue took the helm of the U.S. Chamber of Commerce, Steven Pearlstein of *The Washington Post* asked him to name his mentor. Donohue said "Ted Klassen." Klassen's patronage had given young Tom Donohue a chance to earn more than $40,000 a year, the equivalent of $182,000 today. But Donohue secured more than a sweet salary; he got a crash course in Washington influence.

In Donohue's colorful later retelling of his first days in Washington, all it took to cut deals in the good-old-boy days was a drink in a stairwell with the Wyoming senator who headed the postal committee. Whatever the substance of the transaction, Donohue had had his first taste of power as a Washington lobbyist.

IN 1975, AS DONOHUE carried on without his postmaster, a new president, Dr. Richard Lesher, arrived at the U.S. Chamber of Commerce. He was greeted by declining membership rolls and a lingering sense of uncertainty about how exactly the Chamber could reverse the ill fortune of business in the political sphere.

Dr. Lesher (he insisted on the "Dr.," earned for a dissertation on the industrial application of aerospace research) was, like Donohue, not a businessman. He had worked for NASA, helping run the space program as it put men on the moon. His most recent job had been running a trade group for the budding business of recycling industrial waste. Now Dr. Lesher had an equally daunting mandate: to make Congress friendly to business, when all it seemed to be doing was piling on more taxes and regulations every session.

Once he took the Chamber's helm in 1975, Dr. Lesher built a team that was well stocked with Ph.D.'s like himself. Dr. Jack Carlson served as chief economist. Dr. Carl Grant, a former TV anchorman in Philadelphia, ran communications. At the height of the feminist movement, the entire executive leadership was male. Dr. Lesher's wife, Agnes, served as his executive assistant.

When Lesher started out, the Chamber had fewer than fifty thousand members and had been marginalized in the midst of a regulatory revolution. Particularly crippling was an internal policy that kept it on the sidelines on any issues that concerned specific industries instead of business in general. So in 1975, when the federal EPA sought sweeping power to test and regulate chemicals used in consumer products and manufacturing via the Toxic Substances Control Act—an issue that struck at the heart of businesses' freedom to operate in the marketplace—the Chamber, pre-Lesher, officially took no position whatsoever. "This communication should not be deemed to indicate either our approval or disapproval of the proposal in whole or in part," its lawyers disclaimed in testimony to Congress just weeks before Lesher took over, as they quibbled with an amendment to the bill.

But under Lesher, the Chamber changed tactics: no more would it stay on the sidelines of major fights. It would fight fire with fire. If the grassroots action waged by Nader and his allies was a source of its misery, the Chamber could use the same tactics to achieve power itself. It was grossly outnumbered by the ranks of the consumer groups, but it had an edge in resources and technology. The least it could do was try.

When the Chamber did finally mobilize its army of members against the tide of government regulation, it did so against a bill whose supposed harm to business was a paranoid fantasy of the conservative imagination. The Chamber chose to stir ideological passions among the membership that didn't align with reality, didn't help American business, and caused unnecessary harm to the average citizen and the country's larger needs. But it worked.

The bill, sponsored by Representative Mo Udall (D-AZ), would have given $50 million in urban planning grants to cities and states to help them slow suburban sprawl. The OPEC oil embargo of 1973 had made it all too clear that something had to be done about U.S. dependence on foreign sources of petroleum. Udall and other supporters thought the urban planning grants would be a way to help local governments find solutions that worked for them, without imposing edicts from Washington. State and local governments had planned their streets and highways and infrastructure for years; the federal funds would help them do that in a way that consumed less oil. As its language made amply clear, the bill would leave cities and states to decide how to spend the funds, without interference from Washington.

The Chamber, however, saw the bill through a funhouse mirror. The land use planning grants would be "merely the first step on the road toward more public control over the use of private property," as Chamber natural resources point man James Graham griped to Udall. As a result of the antisprawl grants, he warned without supporting evidence, states would likely take private property from its owners without any compensation. Never mind that such action would have been plainly unconstitutional, and that cities for years had been condemning urban real estate on behalf of urban renewal projects under their legal power of eminent domain, paying owners in return, and doing it all with federal funding arrangements that did, unlike Udall's bill, tell cities exactly what they had to do with the money.

The facts of the law didn't matter: Lesher's new Chamber had found an issue on which it could call its constituents to arms, and that was enough. The Chamber sent out a letter to every member in districts where its lobbyists felt congressmen could be persuaded to oppose Representative Udall's grants. (In 1975 this feat called on the Chamber's new $1.3 million computer dedicated to member mailings.) The letter urged them and their employees to write letters to their congressman in defense of private property in America and against federal control of local zoning.

Decades before ubiquitous e-mail blasts diluted the impact of letter-writing campaigns, the mailed letters served as a potent source of persuasion. Representative Roy Taylor (D-NC), a key vote on the committee considering the bill, received thousands of letters—more than he had ever received on any issue. He professed ignorance of the organized campaign to defeat the bill. "I never heard from the Chamber of Commerce," Taylor was later said to have remarked. "I responded to the 15,000 letters I got from my district." And as the Chamber had intended, Udall's urban planning grants bill did not make it out of committee.

. . .

"LOBBYING THAT COUNTS IS done through the grassroots process," Lesher had been known to attest. He had perhaps a half-dozen registered lobbyists at work in the Capitol at any given time. But lobbying, he realized, was more effective when backed by numbers. His success against the Udall bill proved that putting his member companies' employees, retirees, and shareholders to work as a grassroots lobbying force could tip the scales in favor of big business in a way that simple lobbying never could. But to generate the numbers needed, the Chamber would have to go beyond its members and their employees. Unfortunately for them, IRS rules restricted it from mobilizing anyone other than its own members.

In order for the Chamber of Commerce to grow its grassroots campaigns, Citizen's Choice was born in 1976 as the vehicle the Chamber would use to counter the Nader-inspired crusades and "fight the unnecessary growth of the federal government." Organized as its own nonprofit advocacy group but launched with a loan from the Chamber, Citizen's Choice was designed to take the heat off the Chamber and give the appearance of grassroots support for its positions on a wide range of issues. It could also call a pro-business grassroots to arms without running afoul of the laws that restricted the Chamber's own organizing. Members would pay fifteen dollars a month and in exchange would receive a newsletter and access to a special toll-free phone-in hotline updating them on the latest action in Washington. The idea was to create grassroots campaigns to show members of Congress that lowering taxes and reducing regulation were causes cherished by large numbers of voters whose voices—and votes—would have to be heard.

Chaired by Jay Van Andel, the chief executive of Amway, Citizen's Choice was housed in the Chamber's headquarters at 1615 H Street in Washington, but the letters and calls its members made to Congress had no discernible connection to the Chamber. And those letters would come flooding in, opposing a minimum wage hike, universal voter registration, a consumer protection agency, and other manifestations of big government. In 1976 the U.S. Chamber of Commerce hired Tom Donohue to serve as executive vice-president of Citizen's Choice.

Tapping Donohue's experience in management at the postal service and Van Andel's in multilevel marketing, Citizen's Choice sought to recruit members through a massive direct mail campaign, which Van Andel promised would reach ten million Americans. "Our members are housewives, teachers, professionals, stockholders, small businessmen and retired citizens," Donohue testified to Congress in 1977, in support of a bill that would force government spending programs to automatically expire after six years.

But this alleged voice of the outraged, overburdened citizen was not going to be a genuine grassroots organization. With Citizen's Choice, the Chamber pioneered "Astroturf" lobbying—deploying purported citizens' groups to advocate for laws and regulations favored by the businesses that were paying the bills. Eight hundred Chamber member companies endorsed Citizen's Choice and encouraged employees and shareholders to join. Some simply signed up their employees to join whether they wanted to or not. And Amway itself was a crucial recruiting hub: the multilevel marketing company encouraged its 300,000 distributors to enroll. Moreover, its board was hardly representative of the typical taxpayer. Fifteen of the sixteen members, the exception being a Dallas attorney, were chief executives of corporations and trade groups, including Marriott, PepsiCo, the National Association of Realtors, and the Manufacturing Chemists Association.

Today mobilizing Astroturf is standard operating procedure in corporate lobbying. But back then creating a false popular front was an innovation in political warfare. In the aftermath of the Carter election, the ranks of Citizen's Choice grew quickly. In 1978 it claimed 20,000 members; by 1980 it had 50,000. At its peak in 1982, it claimed to have 75,000 members, and to be able to mobilize some 12,000 phone calls to Congress from a committed core of volunteers in just twenty-four hours.

But the causes that Citizen's Choice took on were hardly the sort of reforms regular Americans would dream up over a backyard barbecue. When the Carter administration moved to fight the oil embargo by setting thermostats to sixty-five degrees, Citizen's Choice rallied hundreds of letters to Congress opposing this "arbitrary regulation" that "could be injurious to health" and "will certainly lead to a reduction in the nation's productivity." The proposed regulation disappeared.

Citizen's Choice went on to launch campaigns opposing public financing of congressional elections (1977) and demanding lower and less complex taxes. Chamber officials admitted they had no way of measuring the impact of Citizen's Choice; one described the grassroots venture as "a blind man searching for a black cat in a coal bin at midnight." But they also boasted of the success of the business mobilization against the proposed Nader-inspired consumer protection agency, which went down to defeat after members of Congress received a blitz of phone calls, letters, telegrams, and visits.

Still, for all its resources, Citizen's Choice barely slowed the regulatory machinery of OSHA, the EPA, and other new federal agencies that put new demands and boundaries on business operations. The choice of actual citizens was still for a larger, more aggressive government. New public interest populism had helped bring Jimmy Carter to the White House, and his administration gave Washington regulators unprecedented power.

But even if it couldn't yet reverse the tide of history, Citizen's Choice joined the newly formed American Enterprise Institute as a boldly assertive conservative lobbying force in Washington, one that granted political legitimacy to the movement for shrinking government. These developments built directly on Lewis Powell's call for the Chamber to counter the assaults on business, and they established conservative action and communications in Washington that attempted, in practical ways, to shift the Capitol's cultural climate.

For example, members participated in cleverly framed "opinion polls," like one that asked members to rank the federal agencies "whose budgets most need to be cut." (The winner: the Department of Health, Education and Welfare, with OSHA in the number-two spot.) The poll questions, distributed by postage-paid mail, invariably primed respondents to deliver the desired answer. Citizen's Choice then delivered the results to members of Congress.

One member who heard the message was Senator H. John Heinz III (R-PA), who met with Marvin Kosters of the American Enterprise Institute on Halloween 1978 to brainstorm ideas on how to shrink the federal budget. "According to a Citizen's Choice poll: 93% of those surveyed felt govt. is the major cause of inflation," Heinz's notes duly transcribed.

If members believed that government spending had caused inflation, it was because they had heard it from their leadership over and over again. "Citizen's Choice believes that EXCESSIVE GOVERNMENT SPENDING is the major cause of INFLATION and has called for significant spending cuts in the fiscal 1980 budget," read a booklet circulated to members of Congress. And they heard it from the board chair who succeeded Van Andel when the Amway executive took the helm of the U.S. Chamber in 1979. "Only Congress has the power to reduce the rate of federal spending and thus stem inflation," J. Willard Marriott Jr., CEO of Marriott Corporation, wrote in one communiqué. "The American people in general, and Citizen's Choice in particular, will be watching to see what the Congress decides to do."

In his own statements as chief of Citizen's Choice, delivered in his deep Long Island accent, Tom Donohue took the opportunity to blame government regulation for the scourge of inflation—carefully crediting this information to his members. "Citizen's Choice members feel strongly that government regulation is a major cause of inflation and is reducing the spending power of individual citizens," he told a congressional committee that was considering public financing of elections coupled with sharp restrictions on political campaign spending. "Americans want less regulation in their lives, not more. They do not want more bureaucracy."

But neither regulation nor spending had much of anything to do with the inflation that plagued the U.S. economy in the 1970s. With the exception of a few industries then under heavy regulation—like airlines, where government rules kept prices high and competitors from entering the industry—economic research at the time suggested the larger problem was the exact opposite. Inflation rapidly raised costs for companies, which then faced pressure from consumer groups to keep their prices low. In industries like power generation, where government agencies had some control over the prices consumers paid, this led to serious headaches, as utilities still had to contend with higher costs from their suppliers—but inflation tended to be the precipitating cause of regulation, not the effect.

Nor has government spending been a spur to inflation—with the notable exception of wartime defense spending, something the Chamber and its many military contractor members had never opposed. Much later, economists Casey Mulligan of the University of Chicago and Song Han of the Federal Reserve Board staff looked at past levels of government spending in the United States and Great Britain and could find no relationship between the volume of nonmilitary government spending and inflation.

But the anti-inflation crusade of Citizen's Choice didn't need any actual facts. It was a campaign built on volume and repetition, which eventually put the specious notion of government-induced inflation into the national conversation. In sync with the Heritage Foundation, through Citizen's Choice, the Chamber helped launch a new era in Washington lobbying, in which conservative ideology and messaging—and above all, a determination to downsize government—described their own reality. Without more than the sentiment of its members to justify their positions, Citizen's Choice freely made dramatic claims in its campaigns to weaken government.

This form of crude propaganda—relentless and strident repetition of a fiction till it gains respectability and becomes part of the political lexicon—has by now become a fixture of right-wing messaging. (Just think of how familiar we all are with terms like *Whitewater, swiftboat,* and *Benghazi.*) But in the 1970s this kind of brazen campaign was just being tested out. And it worked.

After the anti-inflation campaign succeeded, Citizen's Choice turned to taxes. At the time, pre–Reagan presidency, the now-commonplace sentiment that American households and companies suffer the ravages of overtaxation resided in Washington's conservative think tanks, not its political mainstream.

Via Citizen's Choice, the Chamber of Commerce injected the think-tankers' notion into the political arena. On Halloween 1979, based on "complaints and frustrations expressed by thousands of citizens and small businesses throughout the country," it launched a campaign for a massive federal tax cut, in sync with a proposal being pushed in Congress by Senator Bill Roth (R-DE) and Representative Jack Kemp (R-NY). Chamber chair Jay Van Andel and Citizen's Choice chair J. Willard Marriott Jr. sent their colleagues on the Hill a dire message telling them they had to take action because if they didn't, American taxpayers would revolt en masse and simply stop paying taxes.

"The American taxpayer has established a superb record of voluntary tax payments to the nation's treasury," Van Andel warned, in a memo outlining the Citizen's Choice project, but "tax law inconsistencies, IRS harassment, an inflated tax rate and any number of other factors could break down the willingness of the American people to comply with IRS regulations." The threat of a tax strike was chilling and clear—yet it was based on nothing more than willful speculation; the Citizen's Choice National Commission on Taxes and the IRS hadn't even met.

In 1981, the Chamber and other business groups—and the new Reagan administration, which had been swept into office on a pledge to reform the tax code—pressured Congress to push for a historic inversion of the federal tax system—and the ruse of having grassroots support gave it cover. (The Chamber's election spending, which overwhelmingly went in support of Republicans and a trickling of centrist Democrats, eased it along.) At the time, the top tax rate for wealthy households was 70 percent, and capital gains on investments were taxed heavily. By the time Congress finished its overhaul, it had slashed federal taxes across the board, most sharply for the highest-income households and for capital gains and investments. Within a few years, the top rate would plummet to just 33 percent.

The tax cuts that greeted Reagan's entry into the White House left middle-class households shouldering far more of the burden than ever before. They marked a historic shift of the U.S. tax code, from a progressive vehicle for public investment to a tool that enabled the monopolization of wealth by a tiny portion of the population. The nation's investor class, its high earners, and its biggest businesses had received the largest tax cut in history, which immediately swelled the federal deficit—but more than that, the new legislation gave businesses the ability to make money off the tax code at the expense of the federal Treasury.

This triumph was in part the handiwork of the Carlton Group, a regular meeting of lobbyists from the Chamber and other business associations named for the Washington hotel where they had met every other Tuesday since 1975. The ringleader who brought the group together, Charls Walker, had successfully advocated for a massive cut on capital gains taxes during the Carter administration, via his think tank the American Council for Capital Formation. The Carlton Group, the Chamber, and the incoming Reagan administration worked closely together on crafting the new tax package, in part by exchanging staff members.

One member of the Carlton Group, Richard Rahn, went to work for the U.S. Chamber as its chief economist. The Chamber embedded a staffer on the incoming administration's transition team: Citizen's Choice vice-president David Chew worked with Washington lawyer Stanton Anderson to coordinate the hiring of Reagan's economic staff. Anderson would go on to be a major player at the Chamber, serving as Donohue's own counsel. Walker, meanwhile, headed Reagan's transition team on taxes and worked with Treasury officials to come up with Reagan's tax cut and depreciation plan.

With other members of the group, Rahn and Walker had devised the depreciation scheme that would gain business hundreds of billions of dollars in public subsidies in the name of reviving a tepid economy. Rahn was a fervent supporter of so-called supply-side economics, which held that reductions in taxes and other burdens on business would stimulate economic growth.

Rahn promised Congress an economic Eden. "Such a tax package would increase both the demand and supply of labor, greatly increase needed savings and productive investment, and cause a boom in venture capital that is desperately needed to revitalize America," he inveigled as Reagan took the White House. "These tax changes would substantially lower the rate of unemployment and increase the rate of productivity growth, thereby increasing real per capita income to all Americans."

With the encouragement of Lear planeloads of lobbyists who rushed to defend the proposed depreciation deal, Rahn and the Chamber won the massive tax cut they sought. This single provision—an arcane change to depreciation schedules for business equipment—would cost the U.S. Treasury *half a trillion* dollars in less than a decade.

While business groups had a strong consensus in support of the depreciation changes, some had big problems with the sheer scale of the proposed 30 percent cut to personal income taxes—among them, the Business Roundtable, a tighter group of large corporations. The loss of revenue to government would be staggering and scary. But the Chamber expressed no such reservations, and it and Citizen's Choice loyally advocated for the tax cuts.

They had achieved a seemingly perfect alliance with a White House whose economic advisers included the father of supply-side economics, Arthur Laffer. But while the Chamber would take ample credit for pushing through the Kemp-Roth tax cut, which Reagan eagerly signed, the recession that descended in 1981 changed the game very quickly.

As unemployment surged, the Reagan administration had to do

something to stimulate the economy, and budget director David Stockman was among those forced to challenge supply-side orthodoxy to do it.

By early 1982, staring down a stalling economy and growing budget deficit, the White House advanced the unthinkable: a tax *increase*. And not just any tax hike, but specifically one that would fall on business, while preserving the personal income tax cut set the previous year.

The proposed hike put the U.S. Chamber on an embarrassing and highly public collision course with the White House, which Lesher had visited weekly in the first year of the Reagan administration. The Chamber held out for months against the Reagan tax hike, only to be outflanked by other industry groups that decided to work with the White House.

The Chamber's tax committee, representing a constellation of interests among its growing membership, just couldn't come to agreement on a tax increase they could live with. Its board chair, the powerful defense contractor Paul Thayer, had personally promised President Reagan that the Chamber would back him up on the tax hike, only to find that the group's rules forbade him from acting against the prior vote of the board opposing tax increases.

Thayer pressed his case to the Chamber's sixty-one-member board and got thirty-one to sign on to a commitment to support the tax hike—a tally he passed on to Lesher. But it would take a two-thirds vote of the massive board to make a change in this or any other policy position of the Chamber.

In the meantime the Chamber, now out of step with its former friends in the Reagan White House and even with half of its own board, pushed for cuts to welfare programs as an alternative to the tax hike. Relations between the White House and the Chamber got so tattered that Reagan aide James Baker dismissed Chamber economist Rahn as a "supply side kook."

Richard Lesher was forced to appeal to Congress for support, writing:

If H.R. 4961 is passed in these troublesome economic times, we have no doubt that it will curb the economic recovery everyone wants. It will mean a lower cash flow as more businesses pay more taxes, with a depressing effect on stock prices. It will reduce incentives for the increased savings and investment so badly needed to improve productivity and create more jobs. It will mean higher prices for many products and services. It will increase government costs in caring for those who, because the economy is held down, cannot find employment.

At the time, one of the most vocal advocates on Capitol Hill for Lesher's hard-line take on tax hikes was Bruce Bartlett, an economic adviser to congressional Republicans—so much so that Citizen's Choice published a lengthy interview with Bartlett to bolster its cause. But as Bartlett noted years later, following the 1982 tax increases, the economy grew at a rapid clip by every measure: gross domestic product swelled, unemployment declined, and the stock market raged.

Reagan later teased Lesher about the episode, in a speech at the U.S. Chamber's headquarters: the president called him "the man who is to federal tax rates what Conan the Barbarian was to anyone who got in his way."

The Chamber's sword of choice remained fear-mongering. At Citizen's Choice, Donohue continued to peddle the apocalyptic idea that fed-up taxpayers were on the verge of a national revolt. "Unless something is done immediately to improve the relationship between the taxpayer and the IRS and to massively simplify the present tax system," he told the House Ways and Means Committee in 1982, "our system of voluntary tax compliance will collapse."

But the damage was done, and the insults from the Reagan administration kept coming. At the end of 1982, labor was demanding that airline pilots who had been furloughed as a result of airline mergers in the wake of deregulation receive up to 60 percent of their salaries for five years. The administration caved—a costly concession that the Chamber vigorously opposed.

. . .

IN 1976 THE CHAMBER had 49,350 firms as members. By 1982, after aggressive mobilization of grassroots campaigns and membership recruitment, it had 234,000. Habitually, the Chamber claimed far more troops in its army—in the 1970s, its magazine masthead described it as "the national federation of organizations representing more than 5 million business and professional people and companies"—presumably members of their local chambers.

Bigger was not necessarily better or stronger in the world of Washington influence. New members brought in dues payments, but they also brought a cacophony of needs and demands and points of view on the proper role of government in the life of American business. For some, the tax showdown and other internecine feuds provided excuses to exit. And local chambers around the country were already discovering that on those occasions when they needed a voice in Washington, they could simply hire their own lobbyists. After peaking in Reagan's first year in the White House, by the mid-1980s Chamber membership had declined by some thirty thousand, as rival business groups poached members.

In what should have been its moment of triumph, with the rise of a free enterprise champion in the White House, the Chamber reeled from setbacks. It was burdened not only by a gargantuan, often paralyzed board but also by a far-flung membership that, in the pre-Internet age, had to wait to get its alerts and information by mail.

Donohue left Citizen's Choice in 1984 to run the American Trucking Associations. Citizen's Choice soon afterward disappeared as suddenly as it had emerged, unable to attract enough funding, Richard Lesher says. It was a "grassroots" political movement that lived and died by its leader, Tom Donohue.

The Chamber still had its own version of grassroots recruitment: in small towns and big cities around the nation, squads of hundreds of suited salesmen went door to door in a hunt for new members, starting at $125 a year for the smallest enterprises. But ironically, the perception that business had a close friend in the White House hurt its recruitment. "For the last six and a half years, you've had a President in the White House who said he'd veto anything antibusiness. So why should business people bother to join?" asked Lawrence Kraus, a senior official with the Chamber.

To reap the members and dues payments it could, the Chamber had to take extreme care not to alienate any of them—even if that meant remaining on the sidelines on issues of intense concern to many businesses. So despite Lesher's commitment to a more aggressive Chamber, it once again found itself returning to timidity. "If we haven't got a strong consensus, we just don't move," admitted the director of the Chamber's tax policy center.

This strategy had diminishing returns. By 1985—with Reagan in the White House, and Donohue gone to the American Trucking Associations—Chamber membership sank to 180,000 companies. And those members, according to the Chamber, were broadly and closely polled via committees, subcommittees, and task forces on "positions on national issues" before the Chamber would take action. It was still stuck with its original design, which forced it to be a consensus-centered organization. Despite the increasing ideological militancy of some of its leadership and members, the overall organization still moved with caution.

It was also prepared to compromise and seek incremental change in ways that would be unrecognizable at the Chamber today. When manufacturers found themselves facing a flurry of A Civil Action–style toxic-pollution lawsuits, the Chamber put together a task force that offered the extremely uncontroversial suggestion that courts turn to science to evaluate the risks of environmental poisoning and size up the liability for those who caused it. "A basic ethic in American society is to care for those who may be injured through no fault of their own, or who are unable to care for themselves, however hurt," it concluded. "The American business community proudly subscribes to this effort."

With the first Bush administration, the Chamber undertook a "human capital investment initiative" to figure out how to upgrade the skills of U.S. workers for an age in which technology and literacy increasingly mattered.

The enticements to compromise only deepened when President Bill Clinton entered office in 1992 with an economic agenda that offered growth opportunities for business. "This isn't Mr. Dukakis coming in," the Chamber's policy chief, William Archey, said with a tinge of hope. "This is not a Democrat who is knee-jerk adversarial to business." One positive sign was Clinton's support of a proposed North American Free Trade Agreement (NAFTA), which would open up new opportunities to move American goods—and jobs—to Mexico and Canada.

Archey's quest to build a relationship with the Clinton White House outraged many committed conservatives on the Chamber's staff. Its chief economist, Larry Hunter, put up the strongest fight, signing the Chamber to a petition opposing proposed new energy taxes, a move that positioned the Chamber as hostile to the new president. Archey fired him. The sudden dismissal of one of the most prominent right-wing economists in Washington marked an embarrassing moment of discord within the Chamber family. For many board members, ideological warfare was not what they'd hoped to buy with their membership dues.

The courtship with Bill Clinton came at a price. Ultimately, the Chamber's romance with Clinton ended with a spectacular meltdown—after it came out in favor of the Hillary Clinton national health care plan.

IT WASN'T SOME SUDDEN fling with the idea of universal health care. Fifteen years before Clinton arrived in office, the National Chamber Foundation, the nonprofit research group affiliated with the U.S. Chamber, set out to create what it called a national health care strategy to "achieve adequate health care and health insurance protection for all Americans on an equitable, soundly financed basis."

Back then the Chamber had been responding preemptively to a never-fulfilled promise by President Carter to create a national health insurance plan. But even more urgently, it was reacting to very real financial pressures that the Chamber's own members were facing, as the cost of providing health insurance galloped upward at a rate far higher than the rate of inflation—and the raging 1970s inflation rate was higher than the patrons at Studio 54.

By the time Bill and Hillary Clinton advanced their plan in 1993, the burdens on business had only become heavier. Two out of three Chamber members were paying for their workers' health insurance coverage, at higher and higher prices. A Chamber task force recommended requiring employers to pay for 50 percent of premiums, and the organization's board of directors unanimously supported the plan.

"The Chamber supports the need for universal coverage," policy chief Archey told Congress in October 1993, "and recognizes that it can only become a reality and be paid for through the shared responsibility of employers, employees and government." Archey favored an alternative plan, from Representative Tim Cooper (D-TN), which unlike Clinton's would not have required employers to pay for their workers' insurance.

But Clinton's plan—in which employers would pick up 80 percent of the tab, with the help of government subsidies—was the main event. The Chamber, in its communications to members, stressed the indisputable truth: that most businesses stood to gain tremendously from Washington's proposed reforms. It showcased small-business folk like Marilyn Hart, the president of a Fort Worth, Texas, plastics design company, who attended a Clinton event at a hardware store in Washington and estimated she would save nearly $47,000 a year on insurance costs because of the Clinton aid to help small businesses pay premiums.

The Chamber even enlisted the sage opinion of liberal health care reform advocate and Princeton professor Paul Starr, who was advising the Clinton administration on the plan. "If there is one group that will benefit from health-care reform, it is small business," Starr said in the pages of the Chamber's house magazine, *Nation's Business*.

"They are getting a terrific bargain." He called the planned subsidies a "windfall" for small-business owners and their workers—which is exactly what they were.

Big businesses stood to gain much too. Rising health care costs were hurting the auto and other industries, in which American products had to compete against foreign imports made by workers whose governments covered their health care costs. When workers went on strike in the United States, better health benefits were usually a central demand. In one authoritative survey, more than half of Fortune 200 executives surveyed supported employer mandates to provide health insurance, and another 19 percent didn't entirely oppose them.

The idea, the Chamber's health committee had hoped, was to support the Clinton plan and its employer mandate to offer health insurance, then use that as leverage to get some crucial changes it sought—like exclusions for small businesses. The committee secured a couple of meetings with Clinton point person Ira Magaziner and hoped to score time with Hillary herself.

The man behind the Chamber's suddenly friendly, even progressive face was William Archey, the policy chief, who had been a Commerce Department official under Reagan. Archey's experience in international trade had taught him that nations that invested in education and health were strong economic competitors—and that the United States would have to keep up or suffer the consequences.

But global economic realities didn't hold much sway among conservative congressional Republicans, who began to openly attack the Chamber leadership for its support for health care reform and other items on the Clinton administration's legislative agenda. A group of five House Republican leaders that included Newt Gingrich, Dick Armey, and Tom DeLay sent Lesher a letter threatening the organization with losing Republican support. "The Chamber's current posture is disturbing," they wrote, and warned darkly, "Tactical decisions made in today's political environment will reverberate for years; once made, the ramifications could be quite severe. . . . We wanted to warn you again of the stakes involved."

Representative John Boehner (R-OH), chair of the congressional Conservative Opportunity Society, which included forty House members, sent letters on official stationery to Chamber members asking them to cancel their membership. The National Federation of Independent Business took a hard line in opposition to health care reform, then moved to poach Chamber members and dues.

"The far right considers the Chamber to be its bastion, its home away from home, its mouthpiece," Archey complained. And Lesher asked, "Where do they get the right to tell us how to run our affairs?" He said members called the attacks "McCarthyism of the '90s"; others "fascism" that "has no place in American life." He accused the Chamber's former economists of rallying hard-core conservative opposition to the Chamber's efforts to act in its own members' interests.

Archey and Lesher were hardly renegades in the organization: the Chamber's board chairman, Ivan W. Gorr of Cooper Tire, snapped back at the conservative caucus too. He called the Chamber's 215,000 member companies "unified in their interest in creating and preserving the best business climate . . . whether or not our positions are pleasing to any political party or policy group." Gorr also pointed to the irony of the threat: "a small group of legislators, who espouse the principle of limiting government interference in business, is attempting to interfere in the democratic policy-making process of a business organization."

Those forceful words pushed Gorr right out of the chair's seat: in less than a year, he would be succeeded by a newspaper publisher from Fargo, North Dakota—hardly representative of the needs of most U.S. employers.

The pressure from conservatives was relentless. On February 2, 1994, the head of the Chamber's health and employee benefits committee, managed care executive Robert Patricelli, submitted written—multicolored, even—testimony to Congress that stated, "We accept the proposition that all employers should provide and help pay for insurance on a phased-in basis." This wasn't news: the previous October, he had told a Senate committee that the Chamber would support a plan that required employers to pay 50 percent of premiums. There were things about the Clinton proposal the Chamber certainly didn't like—like a new National Health Board that would run the show.

But Patricelli cheered much of what the reform proposals under consideration would begin to accomplish, including the portability of health care plans when workers left employers and an end to exclusions for preexisting conditions. "We think a compromise is possible, and we look forward to working with members of this committee in forging a workable bill," he told the senators.

The next day everything changed. On February 3 Patricelli appeared to testify to the House Ways and Means Committee—and denounced the written proposal that he had submitted the day before. The Chamber, he told the committee, "cannot support any of the mandate proposals that have been advanced in legislation by President Clinton or members of Congress." He claimed that he had not approved his own written testimony, which he said had been "inadvertently sent to the committee" by the Chamber's staff. "It ain't over till the fat lady sings, and I'm the fat lady when it comes to the Chamber policy," he explained.

What happened? Quite simply, the Chamber had been maumaued by the hard right. Backed by a chorus of angry conservative commentators like Evans and Novak and the *Wall Street Journal's* editorial page, Boehner and other Republicans had phoned local chambers and members to spur them to complain to the national group about its supposed betrayal of its core values. Fearful of a mass defection of members, Lesher ordered the last-minute switch of testimony.

Archey soon found himself out of a job, and Lesher soon moved toward retirement. Many forces doomed health care reform in 1994, but the defection of the largest business trade group affected by it was a crucial turning point.

Some might see the Chamber's initial position on health care reform as consistent with its mission to be a forum for the national business community: many businesses *needed* health care reform in order to be competitive. But when meeting the needs of the larger business community was opposed by a handful of powerfully motivated and ideologically driven members, the larger community lost. This would set a pattern for the future: the Chamber would increasingly respond to its squeakiest wheels, particularly when the squeak took the form of threats to its financial support.

Former economist Richard Rahn, one of the conservative voices who helped derail the Chamber's brief moment of moderation, would later describe the Clintoncare episode as a moment of insanity for an organization that had lost its moorings from small-government, low-tax ideology. "A few individuals within the Chamber who suffered from Washingtonosis and thus were more interested in cultivating their own relationships with the Clinton White House and the Democratic Congress," he lamented, "almost managed to destroy a great legacy and institution."

CHAPTER 4

Business Takes Charge of Congress

In 1997 Tom Donohue returned to the Chamber of Commerce with a promise to reverse the fortunes of business in Washington. He got to work on a complete makeover months before he even started the job.

On July 3 he appeared on C-Span's *Washington Journal,* where the host asked him to choose his "wow" story from that day's Washington headlines. Would the just-named next president of the U.S. Chamber of Commerce want to discuss the expansion of NATO to Poland and Hungary? Or perhaps the Republican Party's proposal to suspend the inheritance tax, which was polling very badly among voters? Maybe the Clinton administration's push to improve air quality?

"I was taken by Jimmy Stewart," Donohue announced, in tribute to the Hollywood star who had died the previous day. "The great thing we all remember about Jimmy Stewart is *Mr. Smith Goes to Washington:* one man can make a difference." Then he recited a quote from the Frank Capra movie's script: " 'I would not give two cents for your fancy rules if behind them they didn't have a little bit of plain ordinary kindness and a little bit of looking out for the other fellow.'

"We need more people like him," Donohue continued. "We need people to understand that one man can make a difference. And in this political system here, it is a collection of 'one men' who have traditionally made the difference."

Donohue had made a typically shrewd choice in casting himself as a besieged and ultimately victorious movie hero, the most beloved in the nation's history. He had taken a page from Ronald Reagan, whose genius lay in packaging conservative ideology in a populist Hollywood script whose heroes and villains were easy to tell apart. Donohue's own twist on the Reagan formula, well practiced during his time at the American Trucking Associations, was to reinvent the conservative hero—and the folksy Mr. Smith—as a Brooklyn-by-way-of-Long-Island-accented Irish street fighter.

As the interview continued, he quickly pivoted from Capra to the capital's business. "I get sick of the whole bit, advanced by a small group of people who say, 'Let's be Robin Hood; let's rob from the rich and give to the poor,'" he said. "After a while the rich don't have any money and there's nobody else to rob." He proceeded to call the estate tax, targeted by Republicans for demolition, "disgusting."

His vigorous performance might have been convincing to someone who wasn't paying attention to the real world. But the fact was that the rich were doing quite well in 1997, and they were prospering more with each passing year. Under the Clinton administration, the wealthiest 1 percent of the population had just achieved an unprecedented increase in its share of the rapidly growing national income, from 14 percent to 22 percent of everything earned in the United States. The wealthiest 10 percent were also seeing a surge in their earnings, capturing more than 40 percent of all income in the nation. That didn't even count capital gains.

And the less rich weren't doing so badly either, historically speaking: the moment when Donohue railed against Robin Hood was one of stunning economic growth and of unemployment of less than 5 percent, lower than some economists even thought possible. Free trade agreements, tax code revisions, banking deregulation, and other actions by the Clinton administration and Congress had unbuckled numerous restraints on the nation's economy. The results were plain to see.

A bonus annoyance for Donohue and other advocates of lower taxes was that the Clinton boom had started not with a tax cut but with a hike in 1993 that brought the top rate within a hair of 40 percent.

Prosperity posed a special challenge for Donohue, who had sought the helm of the Chamber promising to turn it into the most powerful lobbying group in Washington. "Three years from now, the White House, no matter who's in it, is going to have the view, 'Don't do that until you check with the Chamber,'" he vowed once he had settled in his sixth-floor office on H Street. That would take heaps of money, for all kinds of reasons: to make a show of strength, to hire the best lobbyists, and not least to pay for the lavish accessories of power. Donohue had long been a keen believer in indulging the perks of his position. While the truck drivers who ultimately paid his salary as the head of the American Trucking Associations slogged cross country on bumpy roads, Donohue flew a leased jet, and the driver of his Lincoln limousine had formerly chauffeured presidents.

To grow the Chamber, he would also have to rally small-town entrepreneurs and Fortune 1000 companies under the same banner, even though their needs wildly diverged. (At the time, just 250 of the Fortune 1000 were Chamber members, many paying a mere pittance in dues.) He acknowledged as much, telling donors he was "developing a set of compelling issues around which companies of all size can rally."

The Clinton administration, however, had gone out of its way to help business succeed, most emblematically by concluding the North American Free Trade Agreement. A surge of political spending by the AFL-CIO couldn't disguise the fact that in sheer market share, labor unions were as weak as they'd been since the Wagner Act of the New Deal, representing barely 15 percent of American workers.

Donohue was faced with the challenge of convincing businesses large and small that the economic paradise they so greatly enjoyed was in fact a gloomy wasteland of missed opportunities, stolen wealth, and oppressive regulation. He took the express track to unity, available to any politician, and immediately sought to rally them around a common enemy, or enemies:

Lawsuit payouts and the trial lawyers who won them.
Trade protections and the unions that pressed them.
Environmental standards, and the regulators and advocacy groups that enabled them.
Taxes.

Hyperbole and doomsday scenarios were the currency with which the newly ascendant U.S. Chamber would buy precious media attention. In October Donohue rolled them all out in his public debut in front of the Washington media corps, at the National Press Club.

Proposed clean air regulations, by which the EPA would curb emissions of tiny particles of soot, constituted, he said, "economic suicide." Or it would, if the United States didn't kill itself first by failing to sign free trade agreements with other nations, since "we cannot shut the door and keep everyone else out and us home because we will shortly starve to death."

The nation's 107 million workers, he insisted, had as much at stake as anyone in the showdown "between those who would make the American economy more rigid and controlled, or those who would make it more free." Without "major reforms that boost productivity," he warned, "we will not be able to protect our nation's prosperity or provide living standards for most Americans."

Again the rhetoric flew at odds with reality. Even as Donohue spoke, the contract between economic productivity and American workers had already been shattered. Nationally, economic productivity had grown more than 30 percent since 1979, yet workers' wages had stalled, with barely a blip of growth. It was clear from the numbers that the impressive productivity gains, fueled by leaps in technology, were overwhelmingly being realized by the wealthiest 1 percent of society.

The spin about worker productivity was just a cover for Dono-hue's real mission: lowering taxes—especially those that targeted capital gains and inheritances.

Just a month before Donohue started at the Chamber, the Clinton administration had made a deal with the Newt Gingrich–led Repub-licans in Congress for one of the business lobby's top priorities: a cut in the top capital gains tax rate from 28 to 20 percent. The same package nearly doubled the chunk of estates that were exempt from taxation upon death, to $1 million. But that wasn't enough for the Chamber.

Of course, putting all those tax dollars back into the pockets of investors pulled the same funds out of government. Donohue had an answer for that too: he announced that Social Security, Medicaid, and Medicare would all need an overhaul (details unspecified) to bring their costs down to size.

But attacking big, politically sacred benefit programs that almost every American depended on at some point in their lives was not Donohue's most effective tactic. His real gift was to take a machete to thickets of regulation that were too obscure and complex for the pub-lic to even notice. At the American Trucking Associations, he had led a successful search-and-destroy mission against state laws that charged trucks fees for entering state roads or carrying toxic cargoes. Another lawsuit had blocked a Clinton administration attempt to set up a survey and database of workplace injury reports—data that could have showed in gory detail the toll that trucking takes on driv-ers, as well as the number of hours they work.

When the U.S. Chamber's board approached Donohue about the prospect of his return, one of the first things he had done was call a friend, Ed Feulner, president of the Heritage Foundation. Feulner had taken charge of Heritage in 1977, as the fledgling conservative think tank struggled to gain influence in Washington. Feulner told him, Donohue would later recall, that "there was a great need for leadership at the Chamber of Commerce; that a Chamber of Commerce with new ideas, new energy, and new focus would really help Heritage accomplish what it was trying to do. We agreed that if I became president of the Chamber of Commerce, we would work together."

The Heritage Foundation needed all the help it could get. As the Chamber discovered, the Clinton administration had seized the opportunity to forge a new-era capitalism, in which fresh opportunities for business and banking profit went hand in hand with government-leashed efforts to make that wealth more accessible to a robust middle class through tax credits and health care and home ownership incentives. With a heavy dose of disdain, Donohue deemed Bill Clinton's political maneuvers "brilliant."

Yet even as Clinton created space for a pro-business liberalism, conservatives sensed that in the bigger picture they were well positioned for an offensive. The end of the Soviet Union opened new political horizons. For decades, communism had offered American workers the possibility, however stunted, of an alternative economic order crafted to meet their needs. As recently as the 1960s, the U.S. Chamber had felt compelled to publish literature to help companies make the case to their workers that free-market capitalism served their interests better than did redistributive socialism; it had warned them that even the smallest interventions could quickly lead down a slippery slope to a collectivist, state-controlled, and utterly unresponsive economy. But with the Soviet Union collapsed and China reinventing itself as a quasi-capitalist state, business no longer had so much to prove to American workers. Workers would simply have to trust that government actions on behalf of business would ultimately accrue to them.

Donohue arrived at H Street, on Labor Day 1997, with some ready targets for obliteration. He promptly canceled a Chamber TV show that had been created and beloved by Lesher, who had built a costly broadcast studio to support the program, and booted the domestic policy team. Soon Donohue would also kill *Nation's Business,* the monthly magazine that the Chamber had published continuously since 1912. The group's means of influence would henceforth lie elsewhere.

He doubled the size of the lobbying staff to ten, hired dozens of new membership recruiters, and increased the size of the board by one-third: now more than one hundred leaders could be leaned on to bring in big money. And he went on a whirlwind tour to energize the base; in his first five months on the job, he hit forty-four cities with his message rallying local business with nightmares about the three horsemen of the Apocalypse: trial lawyers, unions, and "extreme environmentalists."

Donohue made moves in the media to demonstrate that he was serious on all three fronts, even though he as yet lacked the resources to deliver on his aggressive promises. The Chamber was so eager to publicly display its resurgence that at one point it lobbied congressional staffers to vote for it on a *Fortune* magazine survey of top Washington influence groups.

In another play to pump up its visibility, someone leaked word to reporters that the Chamber would spend millions to take on the trial lawyers, and in the spring of 1998 it founded the Institute for Legal Reform. Donohue's public statements spoke of a bold assault on the power and wealth of the trial lawyers, who they claimed cost businesses and consumers $160 billion a year and made American products uncompetitive in the world market.

The political—and fund-raising—power of such an assault was undeniable. In a briefing memo, the election consultant Frank Luntz assured Republican clients who were running for Congress that year, "It's almost impossible to go too far when it comes to demonizing lawyers."

Yet the game plan laid out by longtime Chamber lawyer Larry Kraus, who was in charge of the trial lawyer project, described only tepid steps to get there: making employees pay their legal costs if they lost lawsuits against their bosses, issuing reports and ratings that would reveal the campaign spending of the trial lawyers on the elections of judges, and "encouraging" businesses in unspecified ways to get involved in those races.

The Chamber's early efforts to combat the political influence of labor were similarly shaky-footed. They also had the downside of being illegal, in the opinion of lawyers for the Federal Election Commission (FEC).

While Donohue was suing the Clinton administration at the American Trucking Associations, the U.S. Chamber was on its ill-fated honeymoon with the White House. But in 1995, following the embarrassment of its reversal on health care reform, the Chamber's board cleaned house—including board chair Ivan Gorr, who had bravely told the Chamber's congressional attackers during the health care battle that their actions were "deeply offensive."

Its new chief strategist would be R. Bruce Josten, a proud free marketeer who'd worked his way up the Chamber ranks, starting out as a telemarketer in 1974 and developing under Donohue's tutelage. Scruffy and blunt, the Harvard grad steered the Chamber toward a decisive alliance with the Republican Party. Where his predecessor William Archey had sought to build bridges with Democrats, Josten looked to burn them down.

REPRESENTATIVE JOHN BOEHNER, ALONG with the tobacco industry, handed Josten a match to strike. In 1995, to steer the power of the new Republican majority that Newt Gingrich had led into the House, and to advance their "Contract with America," Boehner began to convene weekly gatherings of lobbyists in the Capitol, which came to be known as the Thursday Group.

The tobacco companies already knew one item in the contract that they wanted: a bill that would cap punitive damages in product liability lawsuits. In November 1994, shortly after the election that cemented a Republican takeover of the House, Philip Morris strategists planning this campaign saw the Chamber as a likely ally to help shepherd a bill through while the tobacco company remained behind the scenes.

"The Chamber has been kind of a weak sister in recent times. However, based on a meeting we had with Chamber staff last week (and reflective of our sharp reduction in dues), the Chamber is eager to regain its former position of policy influence AND regain its stead in our once upon a time good graces," wrote a lobbyist for the tobacco company Philip Morris. "If we go to them with a specific action agenda, I believe they will do their utmost to attempt to see it through."

That it did. On February 21, 1995, Boehner held a kick-off meeting of a tobacco-industry-driven legal reform coalition in the gilded Cannon Caucus Room. Frank Coleman, who chaired the Chamber's media relations committee, crowed that "everybody . . . is committed to spending what it takes to win." The Chamber did its part by putting radio ads on the air in Washington that used the painful medical plight of an elderly woman for a political attack. It jumped on the tort reform meme of the moment: a jury's $2.9 million award to Stella Liebeck of New Mexico after a cup of McDonald's coffee scorched the skin off her thighs. "Is it fair to get a couple of million dollars from a restaurant just because you spilled hot coffee on yourself?" the ad asked viewers. "Of course not. It's ridiculous. But it happened."

The bill the tobacco industry sought passed both houses of Congress, only to be vetoed by President Clinton. But the Chamber had proven itself willing and able to play ball.

In June, the Chamber picked up the ball as a leader of a new group called the Coalition for a Balanced Budget, which sought to widen the circle that met in the Cannon room and expand its influence in Congress. "We are writing to you at the request of House Republican Conference chairman John Boehner," the overture to prospective members began. Boehner and Senator Paul Coverdell (R-GA) "have been designated by their respective leaderships to build a broad-based coalition."

The Coalition for a Balanced Budget sought to drum up support from business for the Gingrich Republicans' push for a cap on federal spending. A seat on the steering committee came at the bargain price of $2,000, an entry ticket bought by groups that included the National Federation of Independent Business, the National Association of Wholesaler-Distributors, and the National Association of Manufacturers.

Such coordination between industry groups and members of Congress was troubling but not improper, as long as the groups registered their activities as lobbyists. (In fact, the law requiring such disclosure did not pass Congress until later that year; the Chamber supported it, fearing alternative bills would have exposed them far more.) But within a year the Chamber was using "the Coalition" as its label for something quite different: an election-year project to protect the seats of dozens of newly elected Republican members of Congress.

The business groups found a common enemy in the AFL-CIO, the union supergroup. In a move that struck fear among business leaders, AFL-CIO president John Sweeney announced in 1996 that his group was going to blitz dozens of newly elected Republicans with $35 million in campaign ads reminding voters of those members' attacks on Medicare and other anchors of middle-class entitlement.

The Chamber took the lead on the Coalition and fired back at Sweeney in partnership with some of its chief rivals for members and funding, including the industry organizations that had already sponsored the Coalition for a Balanced Budget and the National Restaurant Association.

The price of entry to the Coalition started at $20,000 for the smallest groups and rose to $50,000 or $75,000 for larger ones. The Tobacco Institute, an industry trade group, had a $10,000 stake and had Chamber staff make a presentation in its office—though its name was conveniently left off the letterhead listing the Coalition's members. Also on board was the Heritage Foundation, as well as Americans for Tax Reform—founded by Chamber alumnus Grover Norquist, who would later become notorious for his declaration: "I'm not in favor of abolishing the government. I just want to shrink it down to the size where we can drown it in the bathtub."

"Our effort will be purely educational," one fund-raising pitch promised.

The Coalition looked to raise money for favored candidates—but more important, it signaled to labor unions that they were no longer the only interest groups that could form alliances to give campaign contributions to favored candidates. "We've got this puppy and we're going to try to turn it into a dog," Josten said of the Chamber's plans to expand this experiment in political influence.

"What we're trying to do is bring some truth and honesty back to the political process," he told Mary Matalin on her talk show in July 1996. "It's time that Big Labor's one-way conversation with the American public comes to an end."

By Donohuean standards, the amount of money raised was pitiful, about $5 million—far short of the $20 million initially floated. Working with competing industry groups turned out to be troublesome, too, as disagreements about strategy hindered fund-raising.

But the important thing was that the Coalition got its ads on the air and could prove it made all the difference in tight races to protect the newly elected Republicans' seats. The focus-group-tested ads appeared on the nightly news and on *Oprah,* in support of the Gingrich Republicans that labor believed it could oust.

Ever wonder what happened to American government? Why the system got so ugly? Why nothing gets done? George Nethercutt did exactly what he promised. Voting for lower spending, tax credits for working families, and to protect Medicare. But big labor bosses in Washington, D.C., don't like Nethercutt's vote. They want to return to the days of big spending and higher taxes. Without permission from their union members, labor bosses are taking $35 million from mandatory union dues and spending it to try and pass their special interests agenda. They've flooded us with untrue ads, claiming Nethercutt voted to cut Medicare. The truth? Nethercutt voted to increase Medicare spending more than enough to keep ahead of inflation. It's sad that lying is now part of the system.

The accusation of a lie was itself a lie: Republicans had indeed sought to cut Medicare, by $270 billion under its projected rate of growth.

Still, the ad did the trick: Representative Nethercutt of Washington won reelection, a victory his campaign consultant credited largely to the Coalition. Thanks to twelve thousand runs of four Coalition ads, twenty-seven other candidates that the Coalition backed also kept their seats. "In short: mission accomplished!" gloated a memo to contributors.

In terms of the law, Josten's Coalition project stood at the edge of a steep cliff. Even though it worked directly to influence dozens of campaigns for Congress, it elected not to register as a political committee with the FEC. In 1998 the Democratic National Committee filed a complaint; the FEC staff found sufficient reason to believe that the Coalition—and Josten personally—had violated federal law by funneling corporate contributions to the National Republican Congressional Committee and related GOP committees, in violation of the Federal Election Campaign Act.

The coordination between the Coalition and the House Republicans was close and direct. The Coalition sent seven sets of videotapes of the ads it had created to Boehner's assistant, for distribution to the thirty-seven campaigns the Coalition supported, and the Chamber received a copy of an AFL-CIO script in a crucial race from the House Republican Conference's fax number.

The project was also closely entwined with the Republican National Committee (RNC). The Coalition's consultant Chuck Greener had recently been the communications director for the RNC and had also worked on the campaign that put Boehner into office. The pollsters and media consultants he hired were already working for the RNC and the Republican congressional committee on responding to the labor ads. For $500, the RNC even sent the Coalition footage of labor demonstrations that ended up being used in the antiunion ads.

The FEC subpoenaed Boehner, chair of the House GOP Conference. After a lengthy fight to quash the subpoena, Boehner in the end reluctantly delivered a statement in which he denied talking to Coalition members about the ad campaign.

The Coalition also stayed mum on ties to Boehner: it reneged on an agreement with the FEC to disclose communications with his office, and it would acknowledge only that it was "not aware of any such contacts in advance" of its campaign. Subpoenas of the thirty-seven campaigns involved and their political consultants yielded little more.

But through subpoenas of the Chamber's Bruce Josten and other Coalition members and consultants, the FEC found evidence that Boehner's office was deeply involved in the campaign. Officially, the political consultant Larry McCarthy—the Washington shark who gained notoriety as the creator of the Willie Horton ads that helped defeat presidential candidate Michael Dukakis—was working for the Coalition as a consultant on its ad campaigns. But it was Boehner's Republican Conference that likely advised McCarthy on ad placement.

Another leader of the Coalition, from the Wholesaler-Distributors, screened the ads for Boehner and personally delivered them to the RNC. Josten himself pressed "play" on the videotape at a July Thursday Group screening of the ads, at which Boehner, two aides, and an RNC official were in attendance.

But implausibly, Josten and most other organizers either denied or couldn't recall the anti-AFL-CIO ad campaign ever being discussed at the Thursday Group meetings with Boehner. "It is highly probable that the discussion was more substantial" than anyone would admit, the FEC's lawyer concluded.

Josten told the FEC's investigators that the ads were designed not to aid candidates but rather to "set the record straight on issues." So why had he met in May with freshman Republicans who were under attack by the AFL-CIO ads? Why did this "issues" campaign mail two million candidate "report cards" to voters in forty-four congressional districts with vulnerable Republicans—just ten days before Election Day 1996?

"The facts obtained thus far provide circumstantial evidence that the activities of the Coalition were loosely coordinated with the Republican Party leaders, specifically Representative John Boehner and other candidates," the FEC's general counsel concluded.

Josten and the Chamber got lucky. In 2000 a federal judge set a high bar for proving whether campaigns and political parties had coordinated with advocacy groups: in a pivotal case, she concluded that the Christian Coalition had not campaigned improperly on behalf of GOP candidates, even though it distributed millions of voter guides and worked directly with the campaigns. The FEC would henceforth have to prove that a campaign requested or suggested specific expenditures to benefit a particular candidate, with details of the timing or content worked out between the partners.

As a result, the following year the FEC's counsel concluded that the discussions with Boehner couldn't be proved to be "substantial" enough to hold up under the ruling, and four of five election commissioners who took a vote agreed. The lone dissenter, Commissioner Karl Sandstrom, said he just didn't get it. "It is beyond me," he wrote, "how expenditures for these activities could be considered other than in connection with a federal election."

The Coalition sealed Josten's role as a leading strategist for the Chamber of Commerce. Even before arriving at H Street, Donohue elevated him to the number-two post at the Chamber, in charge of legislative and political activities—lobbying Congress and making sure the right people were elected.

Josten hailed from Pennsauken, New Jersey, on the edge of Camden, where 1960s riots and fires had sent him fleeing on a scholarship for the halls of Mercersburg Academy in Pennsylvania, alma mater of Jimmy Stewart (and Timothy Leary). The turmoil followed Josten to Harvard, where unrest repeatedly closed the campus and burned down the ROTC building. His dorm room was upstairs from the president's office, and at times he couldn't get to his room amid the tear gas. In the smoke of leftist revolution was born a conservative radical.

In business circles Bruce Josten was known as a master of subtlety and strategy, a perfect complement to Donohue's combat-ready persona. Josten's new dog was trained to attack. Tom Donohue inspired an outpouring of sobriquets upon his triumphant return to head the ascendant Chamber: "junkyard dog," "George C. Patton," "militant," "uncompromising."

No longer would the Chamber make pitiable references to its 180,000 dues-paying members; now it would claim to represent "3 million businesses that make up the Chamber federation," 96 percent of them employing fewer than one hundred people. That most were members of their local chambers of commerce, not the national group, remained unspoken.

"MY GOAL IS SIMPLE — to build the biggest gorilla in this town—the most aggressive and vigorous business advocate our nation has ever seen," Donohue told a major donor in January 1998. The recipient of that letter was an executive from Philip Morris, the tobacco company that had months earlier dismissed the Chamber as a "weak sister." The cigarette giant had nonetheless been paying $50,000 in annual dues to the Chamber. Now the Chamber was a hot suitor. It was telling the public that its Institute for Legal Reform was not taking money from tobacco companies, yet the Chamber itself actively sought and received funds from them.

The opportunity came that spring as Senator John McCain (R-AZ) introduced a bill that proposed to increase taxes on each pack of cigarettes by $1.10 in order to pay for programs to reduce youth smoking. Just before McCain's bill went to a vote, the Chamber spent $100,000 on television ads in Washington, showing clown cars of lobbyists descending on the capital and warning members of Congress that the money would just go to enrich the undeserving. "Taxing people like me to pay millionaire trial lawyers? What's next?" wonders a waitress.

The ads were effectively paid for by Philip Morris, which gave $100,000 in 1998 for the Chamber's "revitalization project" on top of its $50,000 in dues and another $30,000 for the National Chamber Litigation Center, its in-house team of lawyers who sue the government to block unwanted policies.

Flush with the Philip Morris money, the Chamber carried its message to Congress and the media. "Who is next?" asked Josten rhetorically. "The gaming industry? The beer and wine makers? Over-the-counter pharmaceutical companies? Fast food?" "One can only imagine which industry will be next," Donohue wrote members of Congress in 1998. Because the ads and media statements came from the Chamber and not from Philip Morris, they could be seen as something more than the agenda of the reviled tobacco companies directly affected by the popular bill.

In turn, the Chamber not only got its money but could also show other prospective donors that it was serious about delivering influence for big business. The tobacco campaign proved to be a crucial turning point in Donohue's quest to turn the Chamber into a money machine for lobbying on behalf of big corporate clients who preferred to stay behind the scenes. By the end of that year, he also had a $100,000 check in hand from R.J. Reynolds, which joined Philip Morris and more than sixty other companies in his high-rollers' "President's Advisory Group," and a request in for another $100,000 the following year.

The Philip Morris influence team would subsequently request $500,000 to pump into the Chamber as part of a larger $3.76 million campaign involving other proxy organizations, all of them conservative ideological shops such as Americans for Tax Reform, the government-shrinkage advocacy group run by Grover Norquist, and Coalitions for America, the lobbying arm of Paul Weyrich's Free Congress Foundation.

The Chamber's loyalties to the tobacco industry weren't new. R.J.

Reynolds had been a member since at least the 1960s, paying $10,000 a year back then, with a seat on the board of directors. Brown & Williamson was a dues-paying member until 1979, while the Tobacco Institute had bought an annual membership and sponsored projects and events in the 1980s.

Nor did tobacco companies just sit back and cut checks. Back in 1978 the National Chamber Foundation had produced an innocuous guide advising businesses on how to lower their health care costs: *A National Health Care Strategy* was a tepid effort to counter proposals for national health care programs. But it advised companies to help their employees quit smoking. It highlighted a documented link between smoking and worker absenteeism. And to hit the point home it included a heading in large type: "Smoking: an unhealthy and expensive habit."

The president of the Tobacco Institute, Sam Chilcote, fumed. "The relationship between the Chamber and The Tobacco Institute always has been one of cooperation and support," he wrote in a tense letter to Chamber president Richard Lesher, not subtly referring to his financial contributions—and those of the industry. "My hope is that this close relationship will continue in the future." The Tobacco Institute also enlisted the CEO of Liggett & Myers, Kinsley Van R. Dey Jr., to demand corrective action.

Donohue, then head of the National Chamber Foundation, assured him that a correction was coming. "I am certain that future revisions of *A National Health Care Strategy* will take special care to give a balanced analysis of this issue," he pledged in a letter, assuring Dey that "the United States Chamber of Commerce is very concerned about the issues you raise." He noted that the Tobacco Institute had already signed up to supply the Chamber with "additional data on the absentee issue."

Subsequent to the exchange, the Tobacco Institute inked an agreement to contribute $45,000 to the National Chamber Foundation. The institute then made annual contributions of at least $50,000 through 1993. "Assuming no one knows TI funded," one exec scribbled on meeting notes from discussions of one project.

Internally, Philip Morris CEO Hamish Maxwell called the company's $50,000 in annual Chamber of Commerce dues, split between the Chamber and its policy institute, a "membership investment." On the letter acknowledging the contribution for 1987, Maxwell scrawled, "Cld. we get more out of our membership? How?"

Soon afterward the National Chamber Foundation embarked on a study for Philip Morris that aimed to prove that no connection existed between employee smoking and absenteeism. It found no statistically significant connection between absenteeism and any other characteristic of a worker, other than income and physical activity. The Chamber subsequently publicized the finding, which even found its way into the ACLU's briefings on the pitfalls of "lifestyle discrimination" against smokers. (Not incidentally, the ACLU took $500,000 in contributions from Philip Morris in the same period.) To this day, the paper is cited in media coverage of the regulation of smoking in the workplace, as evidence showing no consequence. Yet it was written by a National Chamber Foundation staff person whose only credential was a Georgetown master's degree in economics. And nowhere in the report is its sponsorship by the tobacco industry disclosed.

A study attacking excise taxes; a journal (never published) debunking the trendy theme of "social costs" of business activity; a brief in a class action lawsuit against the tobacco companies—in the early 1990s, the formula played out again and again. The U.S. Chamber took money from tobacco companies, carried out projects in its own name, and then publicized them as Chamber findings, never mentioning the source of the funds.

But Philip Morris's patience with the Chamber's slim impact was clearly growing thin. It reduced the dues it gave to the Chamber, slashing its expected 1997 contribution to $25,000—a fraction of what it gave that year to New York City's local business association.

Donohue set out to rekindle the lucrative relationship. He visited

Philip Morris headquarters in New York City to meet with lobbyist Roy Marden, and he kept up a correspondence with Marden afterward. "It's been a wild four months, Roy!" Donohue wrote in January 1998. "If there's one thing I know how to do," he assured Marden, "it is to provide great value to those who really step up to the plate." He concluded with a promise: "You are absolutely right in sensing that a new chapter has begun at the Chamber. By agreeing to be such a strong supporter, you will always be heard here and always have a voice."

And so the Chamber of Commerce got to work. Philip Morris would contribute $180,000 to the U.S. Chamber in 1998, as Senator McCain introduced his cigarette-tax bill.

The Chamber urged Senator Spencer Abraham (R-MI) to block the bill, which Josten called "one of the largest tax and spend bills that Congress has ever considered." Donohue sent a letter to Senate majority leader Trent Lott (R-MS) and met privately with House Speaker Newt Gingrich as well as key senators with influence on the vote.

Alarmed by McCain's bill, the U.S. Chamber sent letters to every member of the Senate, and to the executives of every local chamber. It faxed out an "URGENT! action *CALL*" to its Grassroots Action Information Network, warning hysterically that the cigarette-tax bill would enrich trial lawyers by $190 billion at the expense of the poor and would create the world's largest black market in cigarettes. "Your help is needed IMMEDIATELY to ensure a strong vote opposing the legislation, which would impose over a half a trillion-dollar tax increase, and expand the scope and reach of the federal government." It urged members to call their senators and demand a vote against McCain's bill.

The political team of Josten and Chamber staffer Lonnie Taylor followed up with other members and held three press conferences with a constellation of tobacco-state legislators. Donohue sent letters to senators laying out a cascade of exaggerated predictions: that the bill would economically crush low-income people, create a vast new federal bureaucracy (seventeen bureaucracies, to be precise), and put "hundreds of thousands of jobs" on the line.

The Chamber issued an unambiguous threat to senators who didn't vote its way: even if the bill never came to the floor, they would be tarred in its *How They Voted* guide as having failed to stand up for American business. In his missive to Senator Lott, Donohue wrote: "We ask you to vote against any cloture measures to end debate—and we want you to know we will count this vote in our How They Voted ratings." In the end, the Senate blocked the bill in two procedural votes.

But the Chamber's service to the tobacco industry wasn't finished. In his 1999 State of the Union address, President Clinton promised that his Department of Justice would sue the tobacco companies to recover Medicare costs for the medical treatment of harmed smokers—a federal follow-up to the 1997 settlement that state attorneys general had made with the companies to compensate state treasuries for medical costs connected to the harm caused by the companies' products. The budget for the effort would be $23 million.

Philip Morris and other tobacco companies mobilized to block the president, by seeking to cut off the $23 million. Central to their project was an ad campaign aimed at members of Congress and Washington influencers—"a beltway buy targeted to opinion elites," in industry parlance.

By May, Philip Morris had settled on the U.S. Chamber as a vehicle of choice for the campaign. Planning a Roper poll on public attitudes toward the tobacco settlement, Philip Morris public policy chief David Sylvia coordinated with Josten by phone. "Chamber is the client, PM stays in the background, Chamber handles the day-to-day with Roper," Sylvia detailed to his colleagues. Philip Morris then edited and approved poll questions.

To proceed, they needed to get budget approval from Tom Collamore, the Philip Morris vice-president of corporate affairs—and part of that budget would be a payment to the U.S. Chamber. "Tom C can you work out contribution to Chamber on this matter?" wrote the tobacco company's top lobbyist that afternoon.

As it happened, Collamore had met with Tom Donohue in New York earlier that day. They were "close," in a colleague's estimation; Collamore served on the board of the National Chamber Foundation.

Philip Morris was already leaning on Tom Donohue for influence in the House and Senate as it sought to rally opposition to funding the White House lawsuit. "Chamber is doing good work," the company's government affairs chief, Beverly McKittrick, reported. "It would be helpful if Donohue would talk to Sens. Specter, Gorton, and Cochran."

Collamore's colleagues approached him for the financial contribution to the Chamber. Moments later Donohue "offered to call [Senator Orrin] Hatch if we really want him to," updated Collamore. "Please tell me our current wish list of who we'd like him to call."

The central idea of their campaign to head off Clinton's Justice Department from suing tobacco companies would be that the threat to the tobacco industry constituted a larger crisis for business in general—would booze be next? Philip Morris's pollsters honed and tested the message. "Research has identified several salient messages that can be leveraged to generate opposition to the federal lawsuit, among the most resonant is the 'slippery slope' argument, a major concern not just for the tobacco industry but for business in general," the pollsters' memo advised the Philip Morris executives, who then enlisted the Chamber to carry out the poll.

The Chamber's Institute for Legal Reform—the group that itself was taking no tobacco-industry money—put the stakes of the promised federal lawsuit in particularly histrionic terms. "This technique is a step toward totalitarianism, where government takes private property under a facade of due process," institute director Jim Wootton said in a press release. The Roper poll found (surprise!) that a plurality of Americans objected to tobacco industry–style lawsuits. A majority were in favor or had no opinion.

The Institute for Legal Reform shared its "privileged and confidential" poll results with the tobacco companies. Letters to members of Congress from the Chamber urging opposition to funding the Justice Department's effort were timed and coordinated with letters from other advocacy groups on the tobacco companies' payrolls, such as Citizens for a Sound Economy.

The Chamber put the Roper poll findings to work in Congress, in support of a bill sponsored by Senator Mitch McConnell (R-KY) to short-circuit future federal suits against corporations. In a letter to every member of Congress, the Chamber decried the Department of Justice's "step toward totalitarianism" and warned members threateningly—never mentioning that the correspondence had been bought and paid for by Philip Morris—that "the findings of the Roper-Starch poll relating to government lawsuits against business indicate that this is a dangerous strategy for politicians to pursue." If members of Congress were to believe the letter, a view held by a minority of voters, and hardly on their minds day to day, constituted a mortal political threat.

Tobacco companies carefully monitored the Chamber's actions to ensure that it was delivering on their investment. Like a political consulting firm serving a client, the Chamber supplied Philip Morris with a detailed rundown of its lobbying and media activities, and Bruce Josten faxed updates to Philip Morris lobbyist Roy Marden about its activities.

But the Chamber's frantic efforts on behalf of tobacco weren't enough to stop the tide of history that had shifted so inexorably against that industry. The president's promised lawsuit against tobacco companies, and the budget to support it, went through; parts of the case are still being litigated to this day.

Nonetheless, the Chamber continued to fight for the tobacco cause on Philip Morris's payroll. In 2000 it filed a brief urging the Supreme Court to eject the judge presiding over a landmark class action tobacco lawsuit against Philip Morris, claiming bias in favor of the plaintiffs. A jury would go on to assess $144 billion in punitive damages against the industry in that case; ultimately, it was overturned.

ONCE THE CHAMBER TURNED from friend of the Clinton administration to sworn enemy, the president could do no right in its eyes. A notable exception was NAFTA and other such pacts, the one major issue on which Clinton broke with his supporters in the labor movement. However consequential those free trade agreements were, they nevertheless marked exceptions. Labor and environmental groups were otherwise both strong allies and partners with Clinton—and they were the Chamber's mortal foes, the sources of laws and regulations that constrained the actions of business. Their causes, and the administration's support for them, quickly turned into wide-open targets for the U.S. Chamber.

The first juicy target for attack presented itself in 1997, as soon as Tom Donohue took the helm of the Chamber. That year Vice President Al Gore promised the AFL-CIO, the nation's largest labor federation, that the administration would act to bar companies found to have repeatedly violated federal laws from holding government contracts. Gore, in effect, committed to punish the scofflaws with the best weapon he had, taxpayers' own money.

This wasn't a case of labor groups trumping up a pet cause. The General Accounting Office determined that eighty firms, with $23 billion in federal contracts, had violated the National Labor Relations Act. The companies had threatened (and sometimes fired) workers who had tried to organize unions; or the companies had in some other way tried to stop them from exercising their right to band together and bargain collectively. Defense contractors—biggest among them, McDonnell Douglas, Westinghouse, and Raytheon—dominated the list.

And some companies killed. An investigation by *Mother Jones* magazine turned up a trail of destruction by government contractors in the years leading up to the Clinton administration's pursuit of a ban on federal contracts to corporate criminals. At a Phillips Petroleum chemical plant, twenty-three workers had died in an explosion that a subsequent investigation determined could have been avoided through safety measures. A shipbuilder, Avondale, left a trail of dead in its Louisiana shipyard. TRW illegally dumped chemical waste in landfills. General Electric had to be forced into environmental cleanups of its pollution at more than two dozen sites.

All those companies continued to get federal contracts, even though, technically, the government agencies were supposed to work only with companies that had "a satisfactory record of integrity and business ethics."

Already, the Chamber and the Trucking Associations had gone to court to shoot down President Clinton's 1995 executive order that sought to bar companies that permanently replaced striking workers from receiving federal contracts.

While Gore was promising labor that Washington would no longer bankroll businesses that maimed and killed, the Clinton administration also moved to police companies' behavior. Beginning in 1996, it advanced ergonomics standards from OSHA, requiring businesses to respond to worker complaints of pain or injury by altering working conditions and, where necessary, by providing medical treatment. OSHA predicted that the rules would prevent injuries for some 300,000 workers and save businesses $9 billion a year, while costing them $4.2 billion to implement.

Yet another second-term Clinton administration act of kindness to workers allowed states to grant unemployment insurance payments to those taking leave to care for newborn children. "Too many American workers," the president explained, "have been unable to take the leave they need because they simply cannot afford to go without a paycheck."

Environmentalists found traction with bold new rules curbing soot emissions and a set of environmental justice guidelines to steer review of industrial plant development in polluted urban areas.

All these acts drew lightning bolts from the U.S. Chamber: lawsuits, lobbying, cold mockery (its labor chief called the worker protections "political payback to unions"), and unsupported claims that the measures could doom businesses to insolvency. Most of the legislation managed to make it through the Washington regulatory process anyway—only to disappear into oblivion once George W. Bush took the White House in 2000.

NOW THAT IT HAD declared political war with the Clinton administration over any favor the White House might seek to do for labor, public health, or the environment, the Chamber had to show that members of Congress who joined the Chamber's fight would benefit, while those who didn't would face dire consequences. In 1999 Donohue announced that for the first time the Chamber would raise money to put into political races. No longer would the Chamber just wield the threat of a critical rating in its *How They Voted* guide—now members of Congress who played ball would receive material rewards, and as long as they remained in office, they would have to continue to deliver for their benefactors.

The campaign war chest started with $5 million, an astonishingly small figure in hindsight. To raise the money, Donohue hired Ted Welch, a professional investor and former RNC fund-raiser. Welch turned to big members for contributions, such as R.J. Reynolds, which chipped in $50,000. Added together, it all was enough to direct $100,000 apiece to forty House and ten Senate races, give or take—and to amp up the Chamber's leverage on those members who received the gold. Announced Donohue with typical bravado, "We've got a pocket full of cash, and we're getting into this deal."

A year before the 2000 election, the Chamber put the word out to Washington's political media that the $100,000 would be available to any member with the voting record and closely contested race to merit it. Just in case members weren't sure which votes counted, lobbyists spelled it out for them: a nay on a minimum wage hike and a yea on a measure to make it harder to impose trade sanctions on rogue governments would score points in the contest for the Chamber's election-year booty.

The Chamber ended up spending $21 million in the 2000 election season, more than quadruple its original goal, and four out of five of its picks emerged as winners. Among the freshmen who rode in with the Chamber's backing were Representatives Eric Cantor (R-VA) and Darrell Issa (R-CA). Another was Todd Akin (R-MO), who a decade later would lose the Chamber's backing in a hot Senate race after claiming that only "legitimate rape" can cause pregnancy.

Then Donohue upped the ante, promising to raise $30 million for 2002.

In 2000 the organization had a $70 million annual budget and 900 employees—which sounds impressive but was down from the peak of 1,400 employees in the early 1980s. And the Chamber still employed only ten full-time lobbyists. Donohue had the message down. He had the vision and many, many promises. He had his President's Advisory Group. He now needed the means.

Big donors had no shortage of needs that required the Chamber's attentions. In 2000 it was the auto industry's turn. Ford Explorers equipped with Bridgestone tires had seen a high rate of fatal failures, rousing Congress to press a vehicle-safety bill. To counter it, the Chamber rallied the auto industry around an influence strategy. General Motors ($250,000), Toyota ($200,000), Ford ($150,000), and DaimlerChrysler ($50,000) all contributed to the Institute for Legal Reform, just as it was pushing back against the bill, sponsored by Senator McCain, which would have subjected manufacturers of deadly defective products to criminal liability, including up to five years in jail for causing serious injury and fifteen for death.

Josten used their money to successfully persuade the House to introduce an alternative bill, without criminal liability for the manufacturers. The auto fight was a prime chance for Donohue's Chamber to prove it could deliver for its clients. McCain's measure never stood a chance.

As a matter of policy—in fact, it was spelled out in its bylaws—the Chamber did not take on industry-specific causes. And that made sense. After all, the Chamber was a federation of thousands of businesses in dozens of industries across the nation and wasn't in a great position to build consensus around big crusades. It usually left the lobbying on parochial issues, and the shaping of bills as drafts snaked through committees, to the trade groups.

But the industry-specific partnerships with the auto companies and, before that, the tobacco firms, were far from unique. As James VandeHei revealed in *The Wall Street Journal* (in an article that attracted little attention at the time because it was published on September 11, 2001), the Chamber routinely took funds from companies to lobby on specific legislation. Based on rare internal documents that he was able to secure, the price appeared to start at about $1 million. That's what Walmart, DaimlerChrysler, Home Depot, and the American Council of Life Insurers contributed to the Chamber's initial run at campaigns to sway judicial races in favor of business-friendly candidates.

In another fund-raising push, lobbyist Bruce Josten organized eleven pharmaceutical companies—including Merck, Schering-Plough, and Bristol-Meyers Squibb—to contribute $1.22 million each for a Chamber advertising campaign on a prescription drug bill that stood to save consumers billions at the expense of drug company profits. In another instance, VoiceStream gave $100,000 and received testimony against legislation that would have blocked its bid to merge with Deutsche Telekom. "The Chamber is not for sale," Donohue told VandeHei. He insisted these were causes that the group would have supported anyway.

Donohue amassed power as a member of corporate boards, including Union Pacific, Sunrise Senior Living, and XM Satellite Radio. Even as he pursued Qwest chairman Philip Anschutz for a contribution to the Chamber, and managed to secure $100,000 for lobbying against a bill that would have interfered in its business, he also secured a compensated seat on Qwest's board.

The Chamber's actions hewed in a literal sense to the IRS rules governing nonprofit trade groups, which state that earnings cannot "inure to the benefit of any private shareholder or individual." But

Donohue, and the companies on whose behalf his group advocated, benefited financially from the Chamber's tax-exempt and mostly undisclosed actions.

To fulfill his ambitions of creating Washington's most powerful lobbying machine, Donohue had little choice but to go where the money was: the big companies willing to part with funds in sums of $100,000 and up, to keep government off their backs. "It takes $2.5 million a week to run this place," Donohue told a Washington reporter. "I think about it every day."

But he wasn't just there to keep the institution above water. "We're only about a third of the way of where we are going to get before I get out of here," he vowed. He was wrong. By decade's end, the group's contributions, and spending, would grow five times over.

PART II

Government by Business, for Business

CHAPTER 5

Why Science Isn't Sacred

Clients: Defense, Coal, Oil, Salt

Whether you know it or not, if you live in the United States, you're a subject in a scientific laboratory. We all are (squeak), because even when it's known that substances can hurt the human body—or plants and animals, or ecosystems—regulating them to protect health is a lot harder than you might think.

Take perchlorate, which in high enough doses disrupts the functioning of the thyroid gland. Actually, you may already be taking it: perchlorate is in the drinking water of millions of Americans, especially in the Southwest—it can be found in about 5 percent of all large water systems. Generated in the production of rocket fuel, fireworks, and other explosives—and used in bleaching paper, perhaps for the very book you're reading—perchlorate shows up in crops as well: organic leafy greens carry twice as much as pesticided vegetables (though well below levels considered unsafe). Military and NASA contractors, a study for the Department of Defense concluded, are most likely the dominant source of perchlorate in drinking water and groundwater.

In 2011 the EPA sought to regulate perchlorate under the Safe Drinking Water Act. The question wasn't whether perchlorate was harmful but rather how much could be legally permitted in drinking water. When it started the process, the EPA projected it would have a regulation within eighteen months.

More than three years later, perchlorate in drinking water remains unregulated, following an attack led by the U.S. Chamber of Commerce. The Chamber demanded that the EPA withdraw the proposed regulation, which it claimed "improperly relied upon data that is not objective," and retract its findings. Cheekily, the Chamber assailed the EPA's proposed rule by invoking another EPA regulation, which said that water must be sampled at the spot where it moves into the local distribution system. In many cases in the EPA's study, it wasn't. It was therefore possible that, contra the EPA's claim, perchlorate didn't for practical purposes pose a health hazard in the first place. The Chamber helpfully cited a legal precedent for finding agency actions illegal when they violated its own rules—a precedent the Chamber's lawyers would no doubt invoke in court were the regulation to move ahead.

Europeans look at this state of affairs in bafflement. They have a perchlorate problem, too, seeped into greenhouse-grown fruits and vegetables. But the European Commission didn't dither waiting for a study. Instead, its regulators set strict caps on the permitted levels of perchlorate in produce, while scientists took on the time-consuming research to figure out precisely what levels consumers could safely tolerate.

Such preemptive action in the face of likely environmental hazards is standard operating procedure for the European Union. Enshrined in the EU's constitution, the "precautionary principle" doesn't stop progress or industry—dozens of genetically modified organisms are legal (and labeled) in European food, and after a years-long ban, the EU now even imports some hormone-boosted U.S. beef. But much as Americans require that medicine go through review by the FDA before it's consumed by the public, Europeans review the fruits of bio- and chemical engineering with care.

Just as the Europeans made their big commitment to the precautionary principle, in the late 1990s, the United States galloped in the opposite direction. Even when American scientists warn loudly of likely consequences and costs—when evidence suggests harm is not just a hypothesis—government regulations seeking to protect health and the environment are wide open to attacks that delay action, sometimes indefinitely, through technical challenges to the scientific research underlying them.

The Chamber has played a pivotal role in making it much, much tougher for U.S. regulators to crack down on environmental health hazards. A decade before the perchlorate challenge, with help from friends in Congress, it changed the ground rules for federal regulation in a way that made the assault on the drinking water regulation possible, and paved the way for even more consequential attacks on research on climate change.

The agents behind these changes were Jim Tozzi and Teresa Gorman, a pair of enterprising Washington lobbyists whose clients included Philip Morris. Gorman, a former congressional energy committee staffer working for the Republican minority, had been an environmental adviser to the first Bush administration.

Tozzi describes himself, in his gravelly drawl, as "a simple ex-musician from New Orleans" who just happens to have a Ph.D. in economics. At the invitation of President Nixon, Tozzi also pioneered the use of White House reviews to alter or block federal agencies' regulations—in other words, undermining regulation from inside the government itself. Enshrined by Congress in 1980 as the Office of Information and Regulatory Affairs, with Tozzi as its first director, this wing of the White House budget office has long functioned as the abattoir where regulations affecting business have gone to die. One pending rule, which would allow the EPA to regulate toxic coal ash left over from power plants, has been stuck in the works for four years, slowed to an agonizingly cautious crawl cowering before warnings from the Chamber that the EPA has overreached its legal authority. The not-so-subtle message conveyed there to the White House: *Expect a lawsuit if this rule goes through.* One undotted "i" in the new regulations, one clause insufficiently rooted, could cause the whole endeavor to implode in court.

Jim Tozzi left government service during the Reagan administration, in a bid to make enough money to send his kids to college. The companies that had once urged his agency to go easy on regulating them could now hire him as their own private consultant. In their service, he and his team came up with a one-two punch that would make it much more difficult for federal agencies to advance rules regulating harmful corporate behavior.

The first step was to expose scientific research to outside attacks. And the second step was to open government regulations to challenges should any questions linger about the science and data that undergird them.

One of Tozzi's first targets was a study of the effects of second-hand smoke, which OSHA had used to justify proposed rules on indoor air quality in 1994. The regulation would have required employers either to ban smoking in the workplace or to provide a fresh air–ventilated room in which it could take place. Tozzi and Philip Morris, which funded his activities, each hounded the study's lead researcher—Elizabeth Fontham, who would later head the American Cancer Society—for the underlying data and got nowhere.

If he couldn't get scientists to cough up their data, Tozzi would force them. The Chamber was a crucial partner in putting to work his chosen tool of coercion: a one-sentence amendment inserted into the four-thousand-page 1999 budget bill, which required all scientific data generated through government grants to be made available to the public. At Tozzi's urging, the Chamber's lobbyists quarterbacked the amendment into the final budget bill, making sure key members kept the provision in the mix.

Never mind that such scrutiny is not required in any other area of government funding, or that in 1980 the U.S. Supreme Court had decided that research data did not count as a government record that had to be shown on demand. More significantly, the amendment, introduced by Senator Richard Shelby (R-AL), would undermine peer-reviewed scientific research by opening it up to second-guessing and challenges to its conclusions—exactly as intended.

After Congress approved the Shelby amendment, it fell to the

White House Office of Management and Budget (OMB) to decide how agencies had to respond to data requests, and what information, if any, would be off limits to outsiders. Reviewing publicly available submissions to the agency that formerly employed him, Tozzi kept a close eye on the thousands of comments flooding into OMB, and by his count those opposing the release of research data outnumbered supporters by ten to one. Scientists and research institutions, outraged at the invasion of government into their work, were particularly outspoken.

That's where the Chamber came in, in collaboration with Tozzi, to shift the results. Its chief on regulatory policy, Bill Kovacs, called to arms members of his organization's policy committees with a memo headlined PRIORITY ISSUE REQUIRING IMMEDIATE ATTENTION. The new rule, he explained, "will allow the public, for the first time, to challenge the [EPA] based on the facts as determined by the research, not just on the information the agency selects." The economic impact of signing the Kyoto Protocol to rein in greenhouse gas emissions; the health consequences of secondhand smoke; the epidemiology behind the Superfund program; breast implant safety—Kovacs's list of regulations present and future that could now be more aggressively challenged went on and on.

Firing up the Chamber's grassroots fax list—"In the Regulatory Reform Arena, There May Never Be a More Important Issue!" the missive screamed—Kovacs implored members to flood White House regulators with comments supporting tough rules requiring disclosure of government-funded research, and to write, e-mail, and call the White House official in charge of putting the Shelby amendment to work.

The Chamber needed the voice of business to scream loudly, because the forces of free inquiry—not least the National Academy of Sciences and the nation's major research universities—sought to prevail on the EPA and other agencies to ignore the Shelby amendment to every extent possible. Kovacs warned ominously that the EPA had already signaled its intention to refrain from enforcement.

In the end, the Chamber's rally in support of releasing the data appeared to have paid off: 55 percent of the comments submitted supported the data release, and the majority of input came from correspondents whose affiliation was unidentified. OMB issued just what the Chamber wanted: a strict and inescapable requirement to disclose all scientific data from public government-funded research, with exceptions only for trade secrets or privacy-violating information.

The Shelby amendment in hand, it was now the Chamber's turn to hound researchers to share their data. With the secondhand smoke rule safely stalled over at OSHA—it never saw the light of day, ultimately euthanized by the George W. Bush administration—the Chamber sought and found a fresh, well-fortified target: a peer-reviewed Harvard study, published in the *New England Journal of Medicine* in 1993, that was on its way to becoming the most-cited paper ever on the health effects of air pollution. The EPA used the research to undergird new rules, required by the Clean Air Act, to cut back on tiny, deadly soot particles in the air. They were to go into effect in 1997.

For more than fifteen years, the Harvard public health researchers had tracked the health of more than eight thousand people in six cities and concluded—after controlling for smoking and other factors that might cloud the results—that tiny soot particles in the air increased death rates. The subjects in the most polluted cities, St. Louis and Steubenville, Ohio, were 26 percent more likely to die of lung afflictions than those in cleaner Portage, Wisconsin, and Topeka, Kansas. Overall, people in the dirtier-air cities died two years earlier than those in the cleaner ones. Coal-burning power plants, automobile exhaust, and home heating turned out to be the main killers.

This was dangerous information to utility and coal companies. The energy industry is an important bloc of the U.S. Chamber's membership—how important, we can't precisely know, because unlike tobacco companies, they have been able to shield their internal records from public view.

Yet energy's influence was indisputable. A half-dozen energy and power-generation companies sat on the Chamber's board, which in the early 1990s had been helmed by the CEO of Phillips Petroleum, C. J. Silas, who then went on to chair the American Petroleum Institute, the trade group representing the industry.

The Chamber, with an Exxon lawyer on its advisory committee, prepared legal action in federal court to block the EPA from imposing rules on ozone and soot emissions. Exxon, along with the Edison Electric Institute and chemical and real estate trade groups, would soon join Kovacs to press federal agencies not only to release their scientific data but to open that research to challenge by outsiders who disputed the results.

Coal and power companies were particularly keen to kill the newly proposed EPA rules. The potential costs to energy companies if the rules went into effect—for retrofitting power plants, reengineering cars, and everything else—were significant, but under the Clean Air Act, those costs were ultimately not allowed to be a factor in shaping regulation. And the benefits to the public of government action were clear. A required EPA cost-benefit analysis showed that thanks to the toll of shortened lives—each worth millions of dollars in the calculation—the potential gain from the regulation outweighed its cost by at least a factor of five.

The White House had decided that under the Shelby amendment, only future research would be open to public scrutiny—excluding the 1993 air pollution study data from its reach. Kovacs demanded it anyway.

The EPA refused to force the Harvard research team to produce its data. The dean of Harvard's public health school instead turned it over to the Health Effects Institute—an independent arbiter funded by the EPA and the auto industry to referee such disputes. Their review confirmed the original findings.

But a Chamber of Commerce lawsuit to block the new air quality rules—unanimously rebuffed by the U.S. Supreme Court in 2001—delayed their going into effect until 2006, during which time, by the

EPA's count, another fifteen thousand people (at least) died unnecessarily each year.

Now that Shelby's rule was in play, the stage was set for part two
of Jim Tozzi's regulatory revolution: finding a mechanism to deploy
the data, forced from the hands of scientists, to attack the regulations
themselves. Tozzi once again used an appropriations bill as a friendly
host, with the help of Representative Jo Ann Emerson (R-MO), who
until her husband vacated his seat by death had been a lobbyist with
the American Insurance Association.

In coordination with Tozzi, the Chamber made sure the new measure, called the Data Quality Act, wormed its way up from committee
and onto the House floor, by lobbying individual members it decided
were persuadable. Kovacs and Tozzi met and talked frequently as the
campaign pressed on.

THE DATA QUALITY ACT, passed in 2001, allowed anyone to challenge information disseminated by the government, in any form, and
demand a correction. It didn't only preempt the precautionary principle, were federal agencies tempted to follow the lead of their European counterparts. It also demanded an extraordinarily high level of
scientific proof, publicly disclosed, before government could promote
any regulation. Even well-established science became vulnerable to
attack, if other sources raised questions about it. Under the Data
Quality Act, regulators would have to weigh detailed evidence presented by petitioners, even if it contradicted established findings, or at
the very least justify their refusal to do so.

Staffers in the White House Office of Information and Regulatory
Affairs—where Tozzi used to work—were now supposed to weigh
the body of scientific (and not so scientific) evidence before signing
off on each of the hundreds of new regulations that flooded in during
a given year. It was a close-to-impossible task. In the interest of barring overreaching regulation, business won one of the most sweeping
federal laws ever enacted.

The U.S. Chamber's hard-line demand that government rules

spring from absolute certainty about the science justifying them placed it well to the right of the George W. Bush administration's new EPA administrator, Christine Todd Whitman, who would have to put the Data Quality Act to work. Whitman, as governor of New Jersey, had, shortly before Bush's election and her own appointment to the post, made a firm, impassioned case for the precautionary principle.

"I believe policymakers need to take a precautionary approach to environmental protection," she told a gathering at the National Academy of Sciences in the fall of 2000. "By this I mean we must (1) acknowledge that uncertainty is inherent in managing natural resources, (2) recognize it is usually easier to prevent environmental damage than to repair it later, and (3) shift the burden of proof away from those advocating protection toward those proposing an action that may be harmful."

She offered two guiding aphorisms: "Environmental policy should always be based on the soundest information available at the time" and "The absence of certainty is not an excuse to do nothing."

President-elect Bush appointed her as EPA administrator weeks later. Whitman for the next two years would endure relentless pressure from the White House to weaken clean air standards, in the face of hazards that were indisputable—demands that eventually forced her resignation.

Along the way the Chamber shielded the energy industry from scrutiny for its role in influencing the Bush administration's energy policy. That role was substantial, to say the least. Vice President Dick Cheney, a creature of the oil industry—most recently as CEO of energy services giant Halliburton—had arrived at the White House in 2001 determined to pump up U.S. fossil fuel supplies, and by his second week in office had the go-ahead from President George W. Bush to launch an energy task force in cooperation with industry.

Good-bye, Al Gore and any hope for U.S. ratification of the Kyoto treaty to curb greenhouse gas emissions. Hello, Cheney and fellow extractors dearly hoped, drilling in the Arctic National Wildlife Refuge—perhaps even Iraq.

Despite demands from journalists and others, the White House resolutely refused to provide the identities of companies and individuals that met with Cheney's task force. Meanwhile the Chamber played a very public role in advancing and legitimizing oil and power companies' objectives as the task force met behind the scenes.

Energy Secretary Spencer Abraham, formerly a Michigan senator, had close ties to the Chamber. The previous year Donohue's group had spent mightily to help him keep his Senate seat, $1 million by one calculation. Both as energy secretary and as senator, his spokesperson was Joseph Davis, who had previously performed the same job for the Chamber.

Now the Chamber would cash in on its investment, bringing the energy secretary into sync with its resistance to regulate greenhouse gas emissions. On February 23, 2001, Donohue visited Abraham in his office, while the CEO of BP waited for the energy secretary's next appointment. A day earlier the head of the CSX railway had come to talk coal—one of the biggest commodities it shipped. And Abraham had already heard from a roomful of electric utility executives, operating coal-burning facilities, about what they wanted from the White House.

Their impact quickly resonated. Bush had made a campaign pledge to reduce carbon dioxide emissions from power plants. Two months into his term, after a review by Abraham's agency, the administration backed off. The Department of Energy concluded that "significantly higher electricity prices" would result were the administration to act on Bush's promise, the president wrote to four senators. "We must be very careful not to take actions that could harm consumers," Bush added.

That same month Abraham chose the Chamber as his venue for his first major public speech, to lay out his vision for supercharged energy drilling and the uninhibited burning of fossil fuels. The oil giant Chevron had initially suggested that the Bush White House itself hold the event, called the National Energy Summit.

Donohue, introducing Abraham at the Chamber energy summit,

primed the pump with his usual dramatic but unfounded predictions of catastrophe. Should the White House fail to unleash fossil fuels—at oil fields, in power plants, in gas tanks, and wherever else demand called for—Donohue told the crowd, the American economy was doomed. Such failure "poses the single biggest threat to our economic prosperity in the first decade of this new century," he warned. "Without action, the outlook looks grim."

Secretary Abraham's speech that followed might as well have been written by the same hand. "The failure to meet this challenge will threaten our nation's economic prosperity, compromise our national security, and literally alter the way we live our lives," he warned. ". . . The United States, and our North American and hemispheric neighbors, are blessed with a rich abundance of natural resources. It's political leadership that's been scarce." Front and center in his "environmentally responsible" exploration of domestic resources was the Alaska National Wildlife Refuge, which had been protected from oil drilling for decades.

"Spence, we thank you for your participation," wrote Donohue in his thank-you note. "We know that in the near term you will be further developing a national energy policy. We look forward to deploying the Chamber's many resources to help you form and carry forward that vital policy."

The drumbeat sounded by the Chamber and its members in the energy industry echoed two days after the summit, when Tom Donohue had warned of a time in the not-distant future when "lights go out and gas tanks go empty." Rolling California blackouts, which had reached Orange County for the first time that week, made for a suitably apocalyptic backdrop for the call to extract.

Senators James Inhofe (R-OK) and John Breaux (R-LA) delivered the message of doom in a letter to Vice President Dick Cheney, in his role as head of the White House energy task force, sounding the alarm about "a potential energy supply shortage of significant dimensions" and demanding swift action to unleash new energy production.

Two months later, the Cheney task force issued its much-anticipated report: a love letter to fossil fuel drilling whose passions didn't stop at the long-impenetrable border of the Arctic National Wildlife Refuge. The possibility that oil rigs could breach the refuge sent environmentalists into high alert, and from there seized public attention easily moved by threats to foxes and seals.

But more immediately, and less photogenically, the Chamber and the coal interests on its board of directors and in its membership sought to unshackle power plants from the clutches of the EPA. Their target was the Clean Air Act rules known as "New Source Review," which required new power plants and those going through upgrades to install pollution controls to limit their impact on the environment. In 1999, the Clinton administration and eight northeastern states suffering from environmental fallout from midwestern coal-burning power plants had sued power companies that didn't comply with the rules, including American Electric Power, a Chamber member and the country's largest electricity generator.

Utilities would pay a high price for breaking the law. Those that settled quickly with the Clinton administration EPA committed to spending more than $1 billion each on pollution controls for their plants. American Electric Power would end up fighting the feds for another seven years, only to end up with a $4.7 billion bill to clean up its belching smokestacks.

The industry's pain moved Inhofe and Breaux—representing the oil-producing states of Oklahoma and Louisiana—in their letter to Cheney, to point accusing fingers directly at the EPA, blaming New Source Review for slowing the rollout of oil refineries. They asked Cheney to suspend the EPA's activities to control power plant and oil refinery pollution until the program could be reviewed.

In its final report in May, Cheney's task force asked the EPA to reconsider its power plant reviews. But vice president or no vice president, such a request had no force of mandate. EPA Administrator Whitman showed no sign of moving swiftly to pull the plug.

Worse, Whitman dared to examine the science before acting—if for no other reason than to bulletproof the administration's actions in order to stand up to an inevitable legal challenge. In June, the EPA sought to assess the known facts about New Source Review's impact on the cost of producing energy.

Evidence just didn't exist that New Source Review deterred fresh sources of power generation. To the extent the doomsday scenario peddled by the Chamber on behalf of the coal industry was even close to correct, the greatest culprit appeared to have been the broader deregulation of the power industry, which had made profit in erecting new plants less certain.

Indeed, as the coal advisory group to Secretary Abraham had already pointed out and the EPA had previously noted, new coal-burning plants with the technology required by New Source Review were actually cheaper and more efficient to operate than the old ones. The problem, from the industry's point of view, was one of cost: the substantial up-front expense of installing the new technology into existing power plants.

WHITMAN'S DECISION TO TAKE the time to study the facts brought down the wrath of the White House. By August 2001, Cheney demanded to know why her agency hadn't taken swifter action to roll back New Source Review.

Even as Cheney hounded Whitman, the Chamber hounded Cheney. Come November, Donohue wrote to Cheney demanding "immediate" action to roll back the EPA pollution-control program, which supposedly posed "a severe impediment to increasing domestic energy supply." "National energy policy, indeed national security," he insisted, "requires the removal of every administrative and regulatory obstacle to increased domestic energy and fuel production."

Whitman showed no signs of being convinced of a connection between pollution controls and the nation's ability to produce sufficient electricity. After all, her agency's review had found none. She was cc'ed on the letter, along with Abraham and the head of Cheney's energy task force, Andrew Lundquist.

More than a year after the Chamber and the coal industry first pressed their case to Abraham and Cheney, Whitman and her agency held firm to the facts. "EPA finds that the NSR program has not significantly impeded investment in new power plants or refineries," the EPA's June 2002 report to President Bush concluded. It did seize on some scraps of evidence that the regulations had discouraged upgrades to existing facilities—allegedly because of uncertainty over whether projects would have had to go through headache-inducing EPA reviews—and advised that a cap-and-trade program would keep the air clean at lower cost and with fewer complications. How many plants had failed to expand because of the supposedly onerous regulations? How much electricity failed to come online as a result? No one, least of all the EPA, could say.

Adrift on this flimsy premise, the rules that came out of Whitman's agency later that year, instead of recommending cap-and-trade, excluded at least half of power plant upgrades from review and did nothing to encourage improvements to advance air quality. Someone had forced Whitman's hand.

A federal appeals court would later slap down the Bush administration's rules because the EPA had not acted based on actual data about the impacts to human health. (So much for the Data Quality Act.) Instead, as the General Accounting Office noted, "EPA relied primarily on anecdotal information from the industries most affected."

In the end, the power plant pollution curbs survived (and presumably your reading device or light bulb is still working). Whitman didn't. In mid-2003 Whitman resigned. She later pointed to the New Source Review battle, and relentless pressures from industry to roll back the Clean Air Act, as the reason.

THE BUSH ADMINISTRATION OFFERED the Chamber a precious window to roll back regulations, and the Chamber jumped right through the plate glass. Kovacs considered advancing the Data Quality Act and other regulation busters as "fall on our sword issues" for the

Chamber. Now that the law was in place, the next step was to get judges to use it to block the federal government from interfering in business. Once the right precedent was set for having courts enforce the Data Quality Act, any company would be able to jump in and claim it had been harmed by purportedly faulty information.

Since the Bush administration wasn't in the habit of advancing regulations that were objectionable to business, finding a test case was no simple task. But in 2003 the Chamber at last found a great cause that merited forceful action: it sued the Department of Health and Human Services (DHHS) for suggesting on its website, and in pamphlets and press releases, that Americans should lower their salt consumption.

The advice from the government health agency might sound about as uncontroversial as suggesting that getting enough exercise and sleep is a good idea. But the science of salt was (and remains) unsettled enough to expose this seemingly banal advice to attack. The government's dietary recommendations largely rested on a 2001 study, published in *The New England Journal of Medicine,* that tracked the blood pressure of hundreds of subjects, half of whom were prescribed a low-fat diet rich in fruits, vegetables, and whole grains, then capped their daily sodium intake at levels controlled by the researchers.

The so-called DASH study found that the lower-sodium diets reduced blood pressure and that "results should be applicable to most people in the United States." That was enough to prompt the DHHS to relay the advice to the general public—and the salt industry to fight back.

In tandem with the Salt Institute, "the world's foremost source of authoritative information about salt," which was bankrolled by $1.3 million in annual dues from the industry, the Chamber fired off a petition to the National Heart, Lung, and Blood Institute, the DHHS division that relayed the sodium study's findings to the public. The groups demanded that the researchers produce detailed information about the study's participants. But even without that additional information, the Chamber and the Salt Institute contended that the dietary advice was not supported by the research, and they proceeded to demand that the federal health agency pull the recommendation from public view.

Rebuffed by DHHS, the Chamber and the Salt Institute sued the government. The Chamber charged in their federal court petition that the group of subjects studied "appeared to be greatly skewed toward persons with salt sensitivity, and was not a representative sample of adult Americans." Somehow, even though the researchers had never released details about who was in their study group, the Chamber and the Salt Institute were able to divine the subjects' vital statistics. Based on assumptions about data it had failed to get, the Chamber told a judge that the "claim that all persons should limit salt intake regardless of their pre-existing cardiovascular risk is unsupported by sound science . . . and, quite simply, wrong."

It all boiled down to a basic question of public education: could the government give broad advice as a matter of public health and safety, even if it had not been proven to be literally true for every single American?

High salt consumption is well established to be associated with increased blood pressure for people already afflicted with hypertension—chronically elevated blood pressure, a condition that affects about one in three American adults. For them, excessive salt consumption is deadly—a stepping-stone to strokes and heart attacks. The DASH study went further and also found benefits for people with lower blood pressure.

Drawing directly from the conclusions of this peer-reviewed and -verified study, DHHS was telling every American to reduce salt consumption to less than 2,400 milligrams a day. And the Chamber, along with the Salt Institute, put their own interests in front of that urgent communication.

The courts didn't buy it. The Chamber and the Salt Institute could not prove that they had been harmed by what at that point was ubiquitous and true-enough health advice. It would be harder in the future to challenge government regulations on the facts, at least through the Data Quality Act. Kovacs's attempt to wield the Data Quality Act to block government action ended in failure, never to be revisited by the Chamber.

WHEN THE DATA QUALITY Act turned out not to be the magic bullet they'd hoped for—it only crippled but did not kill the role of disinterested scientific research in formulating policy—the Chamber and its sponsoring industries had to move up the food chain of federal power. Rather than merely slowing or preventing the enactment of new regulations through the courts, their new strategy moved to block unwanted laws from taking hold in the first place. This approach was well suited to their battle to conquer the forces massing to take on the defining science-versus-business battle of the dawning century: action to rein in global warning. The Chamber's passion for transparency and truth would soon dwindle as strongly as it had flared during the salt fight.

Alarm bells had burbled for years through the scientific community, but in 1988 they clanged loudly in Washington, when NASA climate scientist James Hansen told a Senate committee that the so-called greenhouse effect was real, man-made, and destined to put life on earth into a state of upheaval.

Thereafter the heat intensified. In 1990 the UN Intergovernmental Panel on Climate Change concluded that global warming existed. By 1995 the 2,500 scientists who made up the panel warned that the burning of fossil fuels—primarily coal and oil—had moved the earth into an era of climate instability, one that was likely to provoke environmental, economic, and social upheaval.

As the devastating findings kept coming from a steady stream of scientific papers, the Chamber joined an angry chorus of industry groups that made strenuous efforts to shout them down. The Burson-Marsteller public relations firm coordinated a campaign dedicated to sowing continued doubt over the existence of global warming. As part of that effort, headquartered out of the rival National Association of Manufacturers, the Chamber lobbied members of Congress against bills, amendments, and U.S. ratification of the Kyoto Protocol, which would have signed the United States up for a rollback to 1990 levels of carbon emissions.

And for a few years, with the fossil-fuel-industry-friendly Bush administration in the White House and Republicans leading the House of Representatives, the regulations crew at the Chamber could move on to other urgent priorities, like pouring salt into the American diet.

Then in 2007 Democrats took over the House, and the political sands shifted again. As soon as the new majority took the gavel, a core of leading Chamber members broke ranks to urge federal action to reduce U.S. greenhouse gas emissions.

The companies that formed the United States Climate Action Partnership were motivated, mostly, by their usual spur: profit. Their executives could see oh so clearly that Congress was poised to rein in greenhouse gas emissions. If a cap-and-trade carbon crackdown could yield a money-making opportunity or competitive advantage—well, that was something these companies could get behind.

Caterpillar, Duke Energy, General Electric, PG&E, Dow Chemical, Alcoa, DuPont—the inaugural membership of the Climate Action Partnership had much in common with the list of Chamber board members past and present. The partnership debuted with a promise to deliver a cap-and-trade program "limiting global atmospheric GHG concentrations to a level that minimizes large-scale adverse climate change impacts to human populations and the natural environment." The pledge, realistically, entailed serious and in some cases costly changes to how U.S. companies did business, not least partnership members. The equipment manufacturer Caterpillar, for one, could suffer mightily if coal mining scaled back. BP stood to suffer cost burdens on its U.S. operations not borne by competitors that refined their oil elsewhere. The arrival of this corporate climate action brigade would appear to put the Chamber in a treacherous position astride a divided business community, much as it had been in the fight over the Clinton health care bill more than a decade earlier. But the reality was that what most of its members wanted really didn't matter anymore, if a large contributor or two had different priorities. The Chamber still nominally ran major policy positions through committees of members and then the membership itself, and Chamber leadership insisted that its members went through "internal debate" on its climate agenda. But climate activists on the board would later charge that the specifics of hard-line attacks on cap-and-trade never went to a board review.

In 2008, the year battle in the climate war broke out on the Senate floor, the Chamber received one-third of its $140 million in contributions from just nineteen donors, which each gave $1 million or more. The largest—like all of them, anonymous—gave $15.3 million. There's no way to know if that money came from a member with a dog in the climate fight or, if so, which it was. But the contribution, and a parade of other multimillion-dollar donations that year, was a sure sign of how successfully Donohue had positioned the Chamber as a front group for hire for companies that did not want to publicly be seen as supporting politically unpopular positions.

At that moment, doing nothing on climate change was one of the least popular stands a company could possibly take. Even 60 percent of *Republican* voters polled said they agreed that immediate action was needed to halt climate change; among Democrats, 90 percent agreed. Across all polled, three in four said that to counter global warming, they would be willing to pay more for energy derived from renewable sources like the sun and wind.

The other thing clear by then was that it was possible, at least theoretically, to take cost-effective action to reduce the concentration of carbon dioxide in the atmosphere. In a report for the Conference Board, a research institute supporting effective business practices globally, the consulting firm McKinsey & Company had found that cost-effective action by the United States could feasibly reduce greenhouse gases in the atmosphere by some four billion tons at a cost of roughly $50 a ton.

With key members of the Chamber and a public majority in favor of firm and sensible regulation, the Chamber, fueled by anonymous donations, sped in the opposite direction. Many signs pointed to the coal industry as the funder behind the Chamber's efforts. Coal still accounted for more than one-third of all the power generated in the United States. But more to the point, the United States consumed 25 percent of all the power generated by coal in the world, second only to China. And coal, in all its uses, accounts for some 40 percent of emissions of carbon dioxide, which is the most prevalent greenhouse gas and the one driving global warming.

The Chamber's board of directors included executives from Peabody Energy, Southern Company, Massey Energy, Duke Energy, and CONSOL Energy, all of whose business depended on the mining and burning of coal. Donohue himself had joined the board of rail giant Union Pacific, which counted on coal transportation for one-quarter of its business. Between 2004 and 2011, Union Pacific gave $600,000 to the Chamber's leadership fund. In total, its statements to investors reveal, it gave the Chamber more than $1 million.

In the months before a climate bill came into play in the Capitol, Donohue made vague statements of principle in support of action, tempered by warnings of lost jobs, a stampede of business overseas, and cripplingly high energy prices back home. As a concept, he said, he supported cap-and-trade as a means of controlling carbon emissions. But the practical reality was that no bill could satisfy one of the Chamber's key demands: that any solution also involve developing nations. That condition had already derailed American participation in the Kyoto Protocol, under which wealthier nations agreed to abide by carbon caps, but competing developing countries—including economic behemoth China—got away without obligations or costs to reduce their emissions.

On December 5, 2007, the carbon cap-and-trade bill written by Senators Joe Lieberman (I-CT) and John Warner (R-VA) vaulted from a congressional committee onto the national stage. By March 2008, the Chamber had teamed up with the National Association of Manufacturers and other pro-fossil-fuel groups to sound the alarms at local "dialogues," panel discussions and such with local business leaders in states with the most to lose. Up to four million jobs would be lost, they warned. Gas and electricity prices would double or more, with a loss to each household of thousands of dollars every year. Just to make sure the message got across where it counted—to the constituents of senators who would be voting on Lieberman-Warner—the Chamber provided breakdowns of the calamitous consequences for every state.

It was true that the costs of Lieberman-Warner would not have been borne evenly—and the coal-mining, transportation, and coal-burning industries would unquestionably have paid for much of that hit. So would electricity customers in coal-burning states. But environmentalists challenged the math: how could the Chamber, for instance, assume no meaningful increase in use of wind energy, and no solar to speak of at all? Other studies that didn't impose such constraints found that cap-and-trade would inflict much milder hits on the economy.

The National Association of Manufacturers study that the Chamber retailed also neglected provisions in the bill that were specifically designed to lower the cost of cap-and-trade to businesses, such as the ability to store up carbon credits for future use as their price, under an increasingly strict cap, continued to rise. Even the hyperideological Heritage Foundation, which sent an economist to speak at some of the dialogues, came up with less severe estimates for cap-and-trade's economic hit, using its own set of skewed assumptions.

Surreally, until March 2008, the Chamber officially had no position on climate change itself, never mind a particular bill; nor could it, since so many of its leading members in industries with the most at stake had taken strong stands in favor of action. Even when Donohue did at last reveal that the Chamber supported some kind of effort to reduce greenhouse gas emissions, he declined to get behind cap-and-trade, a tax, or any other specific strategy.

But the Chamber's opposition to Lieberman-Warner was clear and undeniable. In the spring of 2008, as the bill's supporters sought a supermajority of sixty Senate votes to bring it to the floor for a vote, the Chamber sponsored an apocalyptic TV and Internet ad campaign aimed at the senators who would decide. On the screen of one ad, a man bundled in a scarf and coat prepared his morning eggs in a pan held over burning candles, before he joined a pack of commuters jogging down the highway to work. "Climate legislation being considered by Congress could make it too expensive to heat our homes, power our lives and drive our cars," warned the voice of God in the ad. "Is this really how Americans want to live? Washington politicians should not demand what technology cannot deliver. Urge your senator to vote no on the Lieberman-Warner climate bill."

The ads were designed to shift public sentiment, but their ultimate aim was to influence the members of the Senate who would have to vote on a climate bill. As the Chamber's Bruce Josten explained to *Roll Call:* "You're always better off if you can get constituents talking" to their elected officials.

The bill fell twelve senators short of the sixty Senate yeas that it needed to go to a vote. It didn't help that on the eve of the cloture vote, ten Democrats, most of whom voted for the go-ahead, wrote a letter to Barbara Boxer (D-CA), chair of the Senate's environment committee, and Majority Leader Harry Reid expressing grave concerns about the bill, many of which could have been torn from the Chamber's own talking points. All were from states that would likely have seen costs to businesses or households rise disproportionately.

Having succeeded in undermining the bill, the Chamber went on to attack the losing side. Claire McCaskill (D-MO) and Sherrod Brown (D-OH), two of the letter's signers, were among the senators who voted for the bill even though they could expect to face blistering campaigns from the Chamber and local businesses for doing so. In the 2012 election they were, predictably, slimed in ads by the Chamber as big-government monsters, but both survived. Jim Webb (D-VA) and Evan Bayh (D-IN) voted for the bill and retired rather than seek reelection under threat of such attacks. Alone in immunity stood

Blanche Lincoln (D-AR), who had already proven herself such a Chamber loyalist—a member of the "Spirit of Enterprise" club for having voted with the Chamber at least 70 percent of the time—that in 2010 she had earned a TV ad campaign on her behalf from the Chamber. Unlike most candidates the Chamber supported that year, she lost to her Republican rival.

THE SITUATION SHIFTED AGAIN with the 2008 presidential election. Within months of the election of Barack Obama as president, the new chief executive opted to take strong action on his own, without waiting for Congress. The EPA moved to classify greenhouse gases as pollutants, subjecting them to regulation under the Clean Air Act. The move was a prelude to planned emissions restrictions for fossil-fuel-burning vehicles and could have ultimately reached far deeper into the economy. The Chamber and the fuel extractors and burners could challenge it all they wanted and would try to delay and destroy it in court. And the House and Senate would continue to debate cap-and-trade bills for the next two years, without reaching the necessary sixty votes in the Senate. But the power to make or break members of Congress, arguably the Chamber's most important weapon, didn't entirely matter in reckoning with an Obama White House determined to go it alone if it had to.

The Chamber would now have to pull off an illusionist's trick: it would have to deliver for the fossil-fuel-industry patrons that expected it to block tough action on carbon emissions, while also representing its own broader membership and respecting its internal process of deliberation through member committees. After all, the Chamber's tax-exempt status, and its ability to raise funds without disclosing their sources, depended on fulfilling the mission "to advance human progress through an economic, political, and social system based on individual freedom, incentive, opportunity and responsibility"—not to carry out campaigns on behalf of individual, deep-pocketed sponsors. As it was, the Chamber's political operation was the subject of a complaint to the IRS from Public Citizen, demanding an investigation into its declaration as tax-exempt millions of dollars in campaign-connected spending.

In late April 2009, the Chamber's environment and energy committee organized a three-hour private pseudodebate between advocates of cap-and-trade (Dow Chemical), a carbon tax (Exxon), and technology incentives (Chamber board member Fred Palmer of Peabody Energy, who once justified his company's anti-climate-action stance by declaring, on camera, that burning coal and emitting CO_2 was "doing God's work"). Some hundred members were in the room for what Kovacs called "quite a spirited discussion," of which he later observed: "At the end of the debate, there were no members asking to change our policy."

But in the days leading up to the meeting, Tom Donohue had received a stinging complaint from the VP of government affairs at member firm Johnson & Johnson, a player in the Climate Action Partnership, informing Donohue that "we would appreciate it if statements made by the Chamber reflected the full range of views, especially those of Chamber members advocating for Congressional action." Just a few hours after the "debate," Kovacs snubbed Johnson & Johnson's request. He went before Congress to rip apart the latest cap-and-trade bill, mostly on the untested premise that renewable energy sources couldn't develop fast enough to fill the gap left as fossil-fuel burning declined. The ambassador for American business was asking Congress to believe that U.S. companies didn't have the ability to forge ahead and build a new market or compete globally.

Representative Edward Markey (D-MA), one of the sponsors of the bill, couldn't help but point out that back in the 1980s the Chamber had also fought his Telecommunications Act, which deregulated the phone industry and thereby made possible the digital communications revolution. Then and now, Markey said, the Chamber's interest in protecting incumbent corporate powers got in the way of what was best for the nation's society and economy. Then Markey asked a burning question: the committee had just heard from Chamber board members Alcoa and Duke Energy, speaking in support of cap-and-trade, so what in the world was Kovacs doing speaking in opposition?

Kovacs smiled meekly and made a brief argument against cap-and-trade that sounded more like a threat: that any action on its behalf was bound to become ensnared in crippling lawsuits. His written testimony launched into talking points about the Chamber's internal policy decisions being based on "core principles" and a "transparent democratic process." No one was fooled, but the Chamber could maintain the pretense that it favored climate action in principle.

Just two months later the Obama administration's move to regulate greenhouse gases as pollutants forced the Chamber's toxic climate change denialism out into the open. In a technical and at first obscure briefing submitted to the EPA, the Chamber called for a public proceeding in which the science of climate change—which it called "hugely controverted"—could be openly debated, by participants who would be sworn under oath and could be cross-examined, just as in a court proceeding. In a Hail Mary play, trying to catch a ball thrown by misinformation campaigns promoted by companies and industry groups with mammoth greenhouse gas footprints, the Chamber was openly demanding the trial of science that its instigators had been previously denied when the subject was soot or salt.

There was little doubt what side its leadership was arguing. Eight years earlier Bill Kovacs had told a CNNfn interviewer that while global warming exists, "there's no link between greenhouse gases and human activity." But by the time of its summer 2009 petition to the EPA, the Chamber was forced to acknowledge that "climate change is to some extent influenced by anthropogenic GHG emissions." The question that the Chamber was now pressing the Obama administration to open for public debate was not whether global warming was real, or at least partly caused by humans, but whether these confirmed shifts in the environment posed a threat to life—the basis on which the EPA moved to take action.

Rather than leave its arguments to the imagination, the Chamber's petition spelled out supposed evidence that global warming was not an imminent threat to human health. In fact, the Chamber argued in almost comical detail, climate change was poised to be a boon. Crops would grow faster and stronger as temperatures rose, while the number of illnesses and deaths attributed to heat would be outnumbered by illnesses and deaths that didn't happen in the cold.

While the petition was pending, in a highly unfortunate but not accidental choice of historical reference, Kovacs told the *Los Angeles Times* that such a hearing would be the "Scopes monkey trial of the 21st century." "It would be evolution versus creationism," he insisted. "It would be the science of climate change on trial."

The Scopes trial, as anyone who has seen the classic movie *Inherit the Wind* will remember, pitted legendary attorney Clarence Darrow against William Jennings Bryan in a showdown over Darwin versus biblical creationism. Science won. Here Kovacs was suggesting, with no small measure of hubris, that science would reveal the harms of global warming as mere superstition and legend.

Kovacs's declaration of combat served its intended purpose of attracting media attention to the Chamber's crusade against the Obama administration's greenhouse gas action. But once environmentalists started looking at what the Chamber was actually saying in its case to the EPA, they were flummoxed. It wasn't just calling for a showdown over issues where scientists hadn't yet reached consensus or where there was a case to be made for the benefits of rising temperatures. The Chamber was literally demanding that settled science be opened for debate, with testimony from industry consultants contending that the oceans were not, in fact, turning more acidic or rising as polar ice melted. Kovac wasn't proposing a debate—he was setting up what could have been an embarrassing rout for himself.

THIS WAS NOT WHAT many of the Chamber's board members had signed up for and certainly not what they wanted to put out in public. Increasingly, the Chamber was out of step with its leading members. Of its 122 board members, the Natural Resources Defense Council

(NRDC) counted twenty-three that had a public position on climate change—and just four of those lined up with those the Chamber was so strenuously advocating, in the face of scientific consensus.

The list of companies represented on the Chamber's board of directors that publicly sought action against climate change included some of the biggest, most trusted brand names in American industry, including IBM, Nike, PepsiCo, and Xerox. Also on the list were energy producers PNM, Southern Company, Duke Energy, and Entergy.

The NRDC put that scorecard in an understated but explosive report that gained traction in media coverage. Companies suddenly faced questions from shareholders and customers about their membership in the Chamber. The report forced them to confront the gulf between their own public positions and actions, and those of the organization that spoke on their behalf.

Not only were some of the Chamber's biggest members in open disagreement with its position and unable to change it; they were also unable to find out which members and contributors were, in fact, calling the shots.

The first to step out and renounce the Chamber was Peter Darbee, CEO of PG&E, the California electric power giant, who informed Donohue that his group's "extreme rhetoric and obstructionist tactics" made his company's continued membership impossible. "We find it dismaying," Darbee wrote Donohue in September 2009, "that the Chamber neglects the indisputable fact that a decisive majority of experts have said the data on global warming are compelling and point to a threat that cannot be ignored. . . . We have come to the difficult conclusion that our fundamental differences over this issue have grown so significant that we will not renew PG&E's Chamber membership next year."

As a member supportive of the Chamber's advocacy for free enterprise, Darbee could not help but add: "I'm struck by the irony, as we try to restore public trust in business on the one hand, on the other the Chamber's behavior on the climate issue only reinforces stereotypes that erode that very same confidence."

The dam broken, other members promptly stepped up to declare their resignations. The next two, energy companies Exelon and PNM Resources, both sat on the Chamber's board of directors. The nuclear generator Exelon would be among the winners of a climate bill, since the bill would make atomic power cheaper relative to coal, but Exelon also owned a small yet powerfully symbolic stake in the climate fight: among its holdings was a Pennsylvania coal plant that burned 3.7 million tons a year, putting it in the top ten nationally among greenhouse gas belchers.

Nike also resigned from the Chamber's board of directors—though not from the organization itself—and charged that staff was setting policy without consulting the board.

Apple, a member that was not on the board of directors, saw no reason to continue to work with the Chamber. "We would prefer that the Chamber take a more progressive stance on this critical issue and play a constructive role in addressing the climate crisis," wrote Apple's chief lobbyist. "However, because the Chamber's position differs so sharply with Apple's, we have decided to resign our membership effective immediately."

A COUPLE OF WEEKS later journalists were called to the National Press Club for a surprise announcement: the Chamber would drop its opposition to the climate bills in Congress and work toward comprehensive legislation to fight climate change. "U.S. Chamber of Commerce Announces Free Enterprise Survival Strategy," began the press release.

A Chamber spokesman elaborated at the press conference, declaring that the Chamber had resolved to act to prevent "destruction of food and water supplies worldwide with the result of mass migrations, famine, and death on a scale never before imagined. Needless to say, that would be bad for business." Cap-and-trade wouldn't suffice; only a carbon tax, a potentially more draconian solution, could give business the predictability it needed.

Reuters and National Journal both ran with the stunning news.

So did Fox Business Network. Before the "press conference" was over, an actual Chamber public relations staffer interrupted to declare it a hoax, and indeed it was, the work of the satirical duo the Yes Men, who found in the Chamber's bloated rhetorical style a ready-made target for one of its stunts. ("Who are you really, sir?" the Chamber's fake flack deadpanned to the real one who had just barged in indignantly.) But the deed was done, and the humiliating point made: the Chamber's obstructionist position on climate action had made it a laughingstock.

For the record, the Chamber responded: "Public relations hoaxes undermine the genuine effort to find solutions on the challenge of climate change. These irresponsible tactics are a foolish distraction from the serious efforts by our nation to reduce greenhouse gases."

As high-profile companies jumped ship, the Chamber was increasingly in no position to hold back from taking a firm position in the climate fight. Bruce Josten wrote Senators Barbara Boxer and James Inhofe, whose committee held the keys to climate legislation, to let them know that his organization was ready to meet with Senate leaders to craft a bill.

Senators John Kerry (D-MA) and Lindsey Graham (R-SC) had just coauthored a *New York Times* op-ed detailing a business-friendly climate bill, one that would expand oil drilling and nuclear energy, make the United States "the Saudi Arabia of clean coal," and cut the EPA out of the greenhouse gas regulation business.

Donohue soon after met with Kerry, Graham, and their third amigo, independent Senator Joe Lieberman, who sought the Chamber's blessings for their project. Their irresistible offer: immunity from regulation of greenhouse gases by the EPA. "We'll start working with you guys right now," Donohue is said to have responded.

But Senate politics, and the Deepwater Horizon oil spill disaster in the Gulf of Mexico, conspired to make the deal—so appealing to the Chamber—a nonstarter. Expanding oil drilling now was politically dangerous business. Graham pulled out, and Senate Democrats gave up on getting sixty supporters to force a vote. In a highly partisan Senate, not a single Republican could be persuaded to join, a turn of events that Senate majority leader Harry Reid called "terribly disappointing."

Its deal with Congress denied, the Chamber returned to attack mode. The EPA had officially determined that greenhouse gases were pollutants that the agency could regulate, as a danger to human health; the Chamber marched into court to block it.

In the meantime, the Chamber informed members of Congress that in this election year, 2010, it had a $50 million campaign war chest that it was prepared to spend to annihilate vulnerable members who fell out of line. It would be "the most aggressive voter-education and issue-advocacy effort in our nearly hundred-year history," Donohue vowed.

In the end, the Chamber spent nearly $33 million on the 2010 elections—more than any other group in the country. Climate wasn't the only issue on which it judged potential candidates; financial reform and the health care overhaul competed for attention. But among the votes it tallied in its *How They Voted* guide for 2010 were nays on a symbolic Republican-sponsored resolution that would have merely expressed disapproval of the EPA's move to regulate greenhouse gases. Democrats from high-carbon Indiana, Louisiana, West Virginia, and Nebraska supported the statement, after receiving a letter from the Chamber reminding them that their vote would be noted on its scorecard.

And this pit bull was not letting go. The Chamber would spend the next three years in court challenging the EPA's CO_2 rules. Suing alongside Peabody Energy and the National Association of Manufacturers—who were protecting their own aging industries in the face of innovation—the Chamber lost, over and over and over.

The courts were particularly unimpressed with the Chamber's contentions that the science of global warming remained unsettled and that the EPA improperly mingled research findings from multiple sources. "This is how science works," an appeals court judge wrote with palpable condescension. "The EPA is not required to reprove the existence of the atom every time it approaches a scientific question." The reports the EPA used as the basis for its rules *were* their evidence. The Chamber appealed the appeal and lost again.

It also continued to lose members. Amid the defections and the growing public scrutiny of the Chamber's climate stance, Duke Energy had decided to stick it out on the board of directors in the hope of pushing positive change. Like some other power companies, Duke had reckoned it could turn cap-and-trade into a boon for business, a way to get paid for building new clean-energy plants the company was going to have to construct anyway as old ones became obsolete. But Duke, too, ended up resigning in 2010.

If the Chamber couldn't win against the EPA, or against the growing tide of public concern over global warming, there was one court fight it could pursue to the bitter end. The Yes Men snowed business reporters with their phony Chamber climate change press conference and smeared humiliating footage all over CNN, MSNBC, Fox, and beyond; a week later the Chamber sued the duo in federal court, accusing them of "commercial identity theft masquerading as social activism."

The movie *The Yes Men Fix the World* was being released that week, and the hoax was, the Chamber informed the court, nothing more than an exploitative publicity stunt. The Chamber, claiming trademark infringement, cyberpiracy, and damage to its reputation, demanded that the Yes Men pull all the video of the phony press conference from circulation.

Parrying, the Yes Men put together a special short video commemorating the event, tweaking an "organization that pulls off some of the world's biggest hoaxes. . . . Since they spend so much money on their hoaxes, many people believe them." Then they put the video on peer-to-peer Internet file-sharing networks to ensure its propagation and survival.

Three years later the case still had not gone to trial—and the Chamber showed no signs of dropping it. The Electronic Frontier Foundation mounted a free speech defense of Yes Men Andy Bichlbaum and Mike Bonanno, who went on with their satirical careers, rather surprised that the Chamber kept the case alive in the courts for so long.

"This case has not affected us at all," says Bichlbaum, who posed as Chamber official "Hingo Sembra" at the fake press conference. In the end, he says, the Yes Men have lost money on their supposedly profiteering stunt. "Except we get to talk about it and make fun of the Chamber of Commerce some more. So we mock them even more than we were mocking them before. It makes for good mocking."

So much so that when the Chamber finally abandoned its unwinnable case in 2013, the Yes Men threatened—satirically, of course—to sue back. "This lawsuit gave us a chance to help reveal the U.S. Chamber's many hoaxes to the public," explained Bichlbaum. Now the Yes Men would seek justice for that which had been denied—a chance, through a trial, to expose the Chamber's hoaxes to the world.

SO MUCH FOR SCIENCE—or economics, for that matter. For the sake of a generous and anonymous cluster of carbon-centric donors, the Chamber of Commerce threw away the business opportunity of the century.

Imagine for a moment, hard as that might be, if the Chamber's lobbyists had fought for the other side, had sent the signal to key members on the Hill that climate change demanded a break from business as usual—if only because business itself had much to gain in a cap-and-trade marketplace and a whole lot to lose, too, as flooding, drought, and other extremes wiped out assets and profit in the United States and across the globe.

What if the Chamber had pushed cap-and-trade as the right move for American industry, without insisting on the poison pill of new oil drilling unleashed in the Gulf of Mexico?

What if the Chamber had sought to build a new-energy economy instead of protecting a dead-end one centered on fossil fuel?

In whatever business and political calculus led Kovacs, Donohue, and their colleagues to double down on a strategy of questioning and delay of the need to act on climate change—and whoever their mystery donors actually were—ideology dead-set against government intervention weighed heavily on the scales.

Indeed, the same absolutism against environmental and health regulation that had driven the Data Quality Act—and driven Christie Whitman out of her post at the EPA—held firm even once it made no sense whatsoever. But to admit and act otherwise would be to puncture the hard-line credo that motivated the Chamber's every move: that any regulation with costs to businesses had to be defeated. (Footnote: if some of those businesses were moved to write large checks to that end.)

After years of relentless, creative attempts to sabotage government regulation on health and the environment, right down to its DNA, they certainly were not about to let Congress and the Obama administration march in and open an entirely new front in the regulation wars by bringing greenhouse gases into play.

Blind absolutism in the face of contrary information about the best interests of business was more than willfully foolish, and more than ignorant of the crushing cost of climate change. It betrayed the very premise of an organization founded to advance free enterprise, by deliberately tilting the political environment in favor of a few favored players—those who had the most to lose and would pay generously to cling to their position of primacy.

Those fossil fuel addicts won the showdown. And the rest of the world lost.

CHAPTER 6

How Consumers Lost
in the Courts

Clients: Insurance, Tobacco, Auto Manufacturers

A long time ago, in a nation far, far away—1990s America, to be exact—swaggering lawyers identified individuals who had been harmed by businesses' products and practices, and reached sizable settlements on their behalf in class action lawsuits. Like X-wing fighter pilots tilting at the Death Star, they targeted vulnerable spots in the armor of business operations and detonated for explosive results.

A tobacco settlement redirected billions of dollars to help states pay for the medical care of those sickened by cigarettes. Bausch & Lomb had to make restitution after marketing identical contact lenses under multiple brand names, at wildly varying prices. Shell had to, yes, shell out $1 billion to customers who bought pipes the company had manufactured, which turned out to leak.

Class action lawsuits like these don't just cost companies cash. They can turn into public relations and political debacles that cause consumers to lose faith in a company's products or even an entire industry. Think of the diet drug fen-phen, linked to heart damage and billions of dollars in settlements with harmed plaintiffs; its manufacturer, American Home Products, changed its name to Wyeth the same month a judge approved the settlement. Or recall the $2.1 billion Toshiba and NEC paid to settle a suit over defective floppy-disk drive controllers, which corrupted and destroyed users' data.

When businesses get speared by a major, headline-grabbing class action suit like that, they not only have to pony up the settlement cash, they also have to publicly take responsibility for the harm their operations have caused. In theory, such accountability incentivizes businesses to take care of problems before they have a chance to reach the public.

Until recently. These days it's a lot harder for consumers to bring and win a class action lawsuit than it used to be. A bill championed by the Chamber and signed into law in 2005 by George W. Bush, the Class Action Fairness Act, forces most big civil cases into federal courts, where judges tend to be friendlier to business defendants. Remember, the U.S. Senate, ushered into office on the wings of corporate campaign contributions, has to approve nominees, and in federal courts juries usually aren't there to be swayed. Without the prospect of big paydays, lawyers are less likely to bring class action cases in the first place. President Bush called the act "a critical step toward ending the lawsuit culture in our country."

BUT ACTION BY ALL three branches of federal government to undo the power of plaintiffs in the courts wasn't enough. To make sure that business kept the upper hand in showdowns with consumers, the Chamber went to a place it never had before: the elections to pick judges on state courts. And in no election were the stakes so high as in the 2004 race for state supreme court in Illinois.

Even by the low standards of Illinois elections, the combat was brutally ugly. Voters opening their mailboxes that fall had to endure a lurid true-crime tableau: "A plot to murder a pregnant woman with a steel pipe and hatchet was meticulously planned. . . . A Grave was even dug in advance! And Thanks to Judge Gordon Maag, THE PLOTTER IS OUT ON THE STREET TO *TRY IT ALL AGAIN*."

The bloody mailer, and television spots like it, were the handiwork of the U.S. Chamber of Commerce. Officially, the advertising came from the Illinois Republican Party. But behind the scenes, the Chamber had given the state GOP more than $2 million. And the state Republicans, in the days and weeks following the Chamber's contributions, had spent almost the same amount of money on ads and payroll for the campaign of Lloyd Karmeier, a Republican candidate for an open seat on the state's highest court.

A state judicial race might seem like an unlikely place to spend millions of dollars on pulp horror media, but the Chamber needed to win a state supreme court spot at all costs—billions of dollars were on the line. The Illinois campaign blitz was part of a national court-cleansing campaign driven by corporate America's desire to weaken the hand of plaintiffs harmed by their products and practices.

Indeed, the fight for the seat on the Illinois bench, savage and record-breakingly expensive as it was, was just one of two dozen state-level elections for judge and attorney general where the U.S. Chamber weighed in. Its instrument of warfare was the Institute for Legal Reform, a 501(c)(6) organization that was separate from the Chamber but under the same roof. Founded in 1998, the institute concentrated the considerable financial firepower of a core of sponsors into a single, coordinated, and highly anonymous effort to rebalance the scales of justice. In many cases, the money it injected into campaigns proved decisive. In 2004 alone, the Institute won 12 of the 13 state high court races where it did battle. By then, it had succeeded twenty-one times in all, spending more than $144 million along the way and claiming a win rate upward of 80 percent.

The Institute for Legal Reform had started with an investment of $500,000 and a steering committee chaired by Steven Hantler, a lawyer who had defended DaimlerChrysler against class action and other lawsuits. They included oddball cases, like one from a teenager who had been rolled over by his own Dodge Caravan after a passenger stuffed a hot Carl's Jr. french fry down his back and a second passenger threw the car into reverse. In another, an Alabama jury awarded $225,000 because the front passenger seat on a decade-old Chrysler New Yorker vibrated at high speeds.

But others were deadly serious. In one suit, Texas lawyers sought $2 billion from Chrysler, after four children died in the crash of a

Dodge Neon. Their mother had told police that their father had fallen asleep at the wheel and the car rolled over when he jolted awake and tried to regain control. The lawyers sought to document for the court a different story: that the steering system, which had been the subject of a voluntary recall, was defective. The steering turned out to be just fine, but the legal encounter was too close for comfort for Hantler.

"I can't tell you the number of times Chrysler was accused of putting defective products on the road," Hantler laments.

Even so, Hantler, who had started his career representing plaintiffs, could see worse threats on the horizon. He watched warily in 1999 as competitor General Motors got hit in California with a record-setting $4.9 billion jury verdict, to compensate six passengers in a Chevy Malibu whose fuel tank had exploded six years earlier. All but $108 million of that sum came in punitive damages.

Hantler and the founder and chief executive of Home Depot, Bernie Marcus, had been helping fund another organization, Citizens for a Sound Economy ("The Voice of Consumers for Free Enterprise"), to limit the damage to their companies from consumer lawsuits. That group had been launched with additional funding from Koch Industries, which had incurred massive liability for environmental pollution. Even as Donohue announced the formation of the Chamber's Institute for Legal Reform in the spring of 1998, Marcus teamed up with New York Stock Exchange chief Dick Grasso to hold an exclusive luncheon on the same subject with Citizens for a Sound Economy, attended by the CEO of Philip Morris and by other executives eager to squelch lawsuit payouts.

Citizens for a Sound Economy had sunk much of its energy into a failed bill in Congress that would have drastically limited punitive damages in lawsuits. Its focus and message were clouded by tobacco companies seeking to surreptitiously influence federal laws and policies, which made generous donations and in return enjoyed lobbying campaigns by the group conducted brazenly on their industry's behalf. But it was a 501(c)(3) nonprofit organization, barred by the IRS from significant involvement in political action. It could merely "edu-

cate" members of Congress, not overtly seek their election to or ex-
pulsion from the Capitol.

Meanwhile, firmly planted on the bench in some of the most generous states for juries were judges whom business lawyers saw as
sympathetic to plaintiffs. Hantler's contribution, he recalls, "was suggesting to the Chamber that they look at state tort reform, because
that's where ninety-five percent of the lawsuits were filed."

The campaign Hantler suggested was a fight to win not only elections but also public opinion more broadly among citizens who sat
on juries. "I think that windfalls and hundred-million-dollar verdicts
are abhorrent to the American public," explains Hantler. "So this really was a communications effort to take our case to the court of
public opinion, which really had not been done before. The Chamber
was an excellent vehicle to do that."

That would take money, a whole lot of it. At the time, the Institute
for Legal Reform board had more former U.S. attorneys general
(Edwin Meese and Richard Thornburgh) than high-roller industry
players who were prepared to make hefty financial contributions.
The board chair was a sociologist who advised corporate clients on
the art of winning over juries. The institute was still a think tank, in
a town packed with them.

THAT WOULD QUICKLY CHANGE. In 1999 Lawrence Kraus, who had
been heading the institute, retired after little more than a year on the
job, and consultant Jim Wootton took the reins. When he started, this
former Reagan and Bush justice official was still running an organization, Safe Streets Alliance, that pressed states to keep prisoners behind bars for their full sentences. He would now turn his expertise in
the opposite direction, to lessen the courts' power over defendants.
Wootton would team with Chamber chief Donohue to turn the institute into a $46 million-a-year organization in just three years.

Wootton and Donohue had a can't-say-no pitch to potential
funders. They would take the Citizens for a Sound Economy model
and raise it to a whole new level because, as a trade association, they

would face fewer restrictions on political advocacy. Like the Chamber itself, the institute would be sanctioned by the IRS to pump anonymous money into politics. As Wootton recounts it now, "You could sort of show the corporate leadership that you could reach parity with the plaintiffs' trial bar in these judicial races, that there would be an appetite for engaging in those races, with enough resources to be competitive." Business had to band together to get the job done.

It worked. By the turn of the century, Bernie Marcus—who saw lawsuit costs creep into the price of every light bulb and ladder he sold at Home Depot—and other corporate leaders looking to limit their liability had decided that the Institute for Legal Reform offered a worthwhile investment—an opportunity to realign the state courts as well as federal law.

On their coattails came other sponsors—GM, Toyota, and Ford from the auto industry, Walmart and other retailers, insurers State Farm and AIG, and corporate giants like FedEx and Johnson & Johnson. Companies had to contribute a half-million to a million dollars a year to participate seriously in the Institute for Legal Reform, and to this day the identities of all but a few of the sponsors remain secret. Together they looked to step up and deliver a knockout blow—not just to one judge but to a dozen or more of them, in multiple states.

"Prior to 2000, business was using minor-league dollars against the plaintiffs' lawyers' major-league funding," Hantler recounts. Within three years, fueled by $68 million in anonymous contributions, the Institute for Legal Reform would transform into an operations base for a multistate war. The institute would also proceed to work in Washington to change the rules of the civil justice game, so that billion-dollar verdicts would no longer come to the state judges inclined to approve them and such claims would instead go to federal court.

For insurance companies and their clients operating in the shadow of lawsuit liability, the spending made familiar sense. The Chamber was, in effect, selling them a policy on which they could file claims when the weather turned stormy in the courts, state legislatures, and

Congress. As Donohue put it in an interview a decade later: "We're the reinsurance industry for individual industry associations and state chambers of commerce."

They wouldn't just have the advantage of a critical mass of coordinated spending around targeted races. Companies buying this innovative form of insurance would also be able to avoid the kind of bad publicity that is anathema to household brand names. Imagine if the companies were publicly identified with such political assaults: "This attack ad against the state's top judge brought to you by Home Depot," or "Chrysler presents: We hate the guy you elected last time."

One very good reason companies didn't want to be public about their campaign spending was that, by and large, the system for sorting out liability for defective products and harmful actions was actually working well, for plaintiffs and defendants alike. Complaints from business about the burdens of costly jury verdicts weren't new—a previous panic had set in during the 1980s, as insurers warned that they were not collecting enough in premiums to cover a surge in payouts and blamed greedy trial lawyers and overly generous state laws, judges, and juries for their grief.

But soon after the premiums rose, they declined again, in keeping with the economic cycle. Insurance costs for U.S. businesses dropped every year between 1993 and 1996 and dropped more than 12 percent in 1996. And while class action lawsuits were a costly fact of life for companies, consumer plaintiffs accounted for only about one-quarter of cases.

Even at the peak of the first panic, most companies in one representative survey of corporate America said that the so-called crisis wasn't much of one. Their premiums had increased, sure. But insurance companies usually paid what needed to be laid out when claims were there to be made. If anything had changed, the companies reported, it was that their products were better made, their services more safely delivered, because lawsuits encouraged preemptive behavior by wary companies.

Only 3 percent of corporate counsel at companies surveyed said they had agreed to court settlements of $1 million or more in liability lawsuits, and just 6 percent of all cases ended up with a company on the losing side of a verdict. In two-thirds of product-liability settlements, the companies agreed to pay plaintiffs $50,000 or less. Usually consumers lost.

Those weren't the cases Walmart and Philip Morris—or their insurers—were worried about. What the deep-pocketed donors feared was jackpot justice, in which attorneys found soft and vulnerable spots in the legal system, friendly hosts for costly class action suits. Tobacco companies and other killers felt themselves especially vulnerable. The late 1990s saw a rise in the still-small number of big-ticket awards, won by increasingly bold trial lawyers and signed off on by cooperative judges.

Where other organizations had failed to tip the balance, the Chamber's Institute for Legal Reform assured contributors it would surgically strike and take out the jurists who got in the way of caps on jury awards that lobbyists had worked so hard to win.

THE OHIO SUPREME COURT justice Alice Robie Resnick certainly qualified. In 1999 she wrote the four-to-three decision striking down as unconstitutional a law that would have capped punitive damages in lawsuits at as low as $250,000 and noneconomic damages at $500,000. Her court had struck down similar caps before, and her decision railed against the state legislature for trying again nonetheless—"brushing aside a mandate of this court on constitutional issues as if it were of no consequence."

As far as the state's business powers were concerned, Justice Resnick had failed them many other times. The Ohio Chamber of Commerce rated each justice based on their history on nearly two hundred rulings; on a hundred-point scale, Resnick scored just eighteen. Of all the players on the slim majority who had thrown out so-called tort reform and frequently ruled against business in environmental and other costly cases, Justice Resnick was the ripest for removal in 2000.

"The Ohio Supreme Court is a significant threat to Ohio's economic well-being," warned the president of the Ohio Chamber, Andrew Doehrel, who proceeded to declare: "It's high time that Ohioans take action to adjust the political leanings of this Court." The Ohio Chamber and its political operation, Citizens for a Strong Ohio, then poured $4.2 million into a campaign attacking Resnick. Even Governor Bob Taft—great-grandson of the U.S. president who had helped found the Chamber—reportedly made calls to raise funds.

With little more than a week to go before Election Day 2000, they got backup from Washington. "She's taken over twenty thousand dollars from one influential contributor," screamed the TV ad paid for by the U.S. Chamber. "On one important vote she cast after that same contributor sent a letter of complaint, Alice Resnick was the only Supreme Court justice to reverse her own vote. Justice Alice Resnick—voting with her contributors and even changing her vote after they complain."

The ad showed the statue of blind Justice—Resnick, by implication—leering from behind her blindfold as contributions from special interests tip the scales. The ad concluded with a chilling question that suggested a criminal conspiracy: "Alice Resnick. Is justice for sale?"

Ironically, in the case in question, Justice Resnick had sided with a retirement home that argued it was not required to pay construction workers a state-set wage—exactly the kind of defendant the Chamber usually sided with. And the ad itself was a lie. Resnick had never in fact reversed her position. She ruled in favor of the employer, ruled against an attempt by the state to rehear the case, and then once again voted to uphold her original decision.

"The particularly tough ad we ran in Ohio was a difficult ad to decide to run," Wootton acknowledged later. But it was not so difficult, in that none of the sponsors had to make their identities public. Or so they thought. The state elections commission later determined that Citizens for a Strong Ohio was a political action committee—not an education group—and in 2005 a court forced it to divulge its funders. The U.S. Chamber, at $200,000, was the biggest. Also pitching in were Procter & Gamble, AT&T, Ford, Enron, Honda, Whirl-pool, DaimlerChrysler, Exxon, Philip Morris, Anheuser-Busch, and Sprint. Even IAMS and White Castle threw in some spare change. The insurance industry was the biggest backer of all.

Aside from the Ohio campaign, that year the U.S. Chamber also targeted races in Alabama, Indiana, Michigan, and Mississippi. In all, it endorsed fifteen candidates for judge and attorney general, and twelve of them won. By Wootton's estimate, the Chamber spent between $6 million and $7 million in 2000, its first year of picking judges. In the Ohio campaign alone, Citizens for a Strong Ohio spent an estimated $4.2 million to dislodge Resnick—to this day, the most money the U.S. Chamber or affiliates have ever put into a judicial race.

BUT ITS BIG PREY got away. Justice Resnick survived the attacks, winning 57 percent of the vote to hold on to her spot on the bench. Also losing were two of the Chamber's favored candidates in Mississippi, where the Chamber of Commerce sponsored a positive TV ad campaign, cheering on three sitting judges and one newcomer. As in Ohio, the Chamber ended up with a second headache in Mississippi: state officials demanded to know who had *really* been paying for the aggressive ad campaigns, so clearly intended to decide who sat on the bench in their state. Who was paying the Chamber and its affiliates?

The Mississippi attorney general, Mike Moore, a Democrat, contended that the ads were not merely "educational," as the Institute for Legal Reform claimed, but political, which meant the Chamber would have to register as a political committee—and that meant it would also have to disclose its sources of funding. The state also demanded the ads be pulled off the air. Even Mississippi's chief judge—one of the beneficiaries of the ad campaign, which ran on thirteen stations—agreed that the Chamber should pull the plug on ads that, in his words, prompted "concern for the integrity of both judicial elections and the judicial system in our state."

The Chamber appealed to a higher power. On the eve of the election, it obtained an order from Supreme Court justice Antonin Scalia dictating that the commercials continue to run. Just two days later Scalia would head the majority that blocked the Florida vote recount and ultimately handed the 2000 presidential election to George W. Bush.

Even after the Chamber's ads were aired and over with, its fight to protect its sponsors from exposure had only begun. The group filed suit in federal court, where a judge ruled that the Mississippi judge race ads were, in fact, political—they clearly told voters exactly whom to cast their ballots for on Election Day. Two years later an appellate panel flipped the decision. In their unanimous view, the ads may have made a rather strong hint—"A fair and independent voice for Mississippi" went the pitch for reelecting Judge Lenore Prather— but could not be regulated because they didn't give an explicit order to viewers, like "vote for" or "elect." It was an outcome that the panel dryly admitted "may be counterintuitive to a commonsense understanding of the message conveyed by the television political advertisements."

The Chamber's fight for secrecy wasn't over yet. As the 2002 elections drew closer, Mississippi, backed by twenty other states, pleaded with the U.S. Supreme Court to reconsider the decision to block disclosure of donors, which the states' lawyers said "emasculated" their ability to monitor campaign spending.

Hence the Chamber faced the very real possibility that the sponsors of any campaign ads that it or its affiliates aired in the 2002 election season would ultimately be exposed under states' campaign finance disclosure laws—and not just in Mississippi.

Wootton, who was in charge of the institute in that election year, denies that the looming Supreme Court decision changed the Chamber's strategy. "I think everyone was aware of the issue, but I don't think it affected anyone's behavior in terms of campaign efforts," he says. But just as suddenly as the Chamber had landed on the stage of state elections in 2000, with its judge-bashing and -boosting ads, by 2002 its presence had vanished.

Or so it seemed. Clearly, the Chamber was spending money—just not in ways that were outwardly visible. Donohue opened 2002 vowing to spend $20 million or so to decide state races for judge and attorney general, an extraordinary and probably unprecedented wave of cash. By the end of that year, the Institute for Legal Reform had raised more than double that, topping $46 million, and spent $43 million of it.

Where was it spending that money? The Chamber used an array of different conduits. It handed $2.6 million to the American Taxpayers Alliance, a political influence shop headed by Republican operative Scott Reed, who deployed slightly more than that to pick off judgeships in Illinois and other states.

Mississippi was another obvious target of interest. That year the Chamber released a Harris poll survey of corporate lawyers that found that Mississippi had the most hostile legal environment of any state in the nation; its judges ranked dead last for impartiality and competence. In a poor state, lawsuits against big corporate defendants headquartered elsewhere served as a perverse sort of economic stimulus, generating big paydays for attorneys' firms—and political contributions that kept friendly judges in place.

After the survey's release, the U.S. Chamber took the extraordinary step of calling for a boycott of Mississippi businesses to protest the state's legal climate, and it sponsored a newspaper ad campaign urging state residents to demand change.

Mississippi Supreme Court justice Chuck McRae was surprised to find that he was being targeted by a Virginia group called the Law Enforcement Alliance of America. McRae was a zingy populist whose appeal was best embodied by the Harley-Davidson he rode to work, in full leather. He claims that he never even wanted to be a state supreme court judge—the money in private practice was much better— and had run only because a candidate he'd recruited dropped out at the last minute. But more seriously, he's a former trial lawyer who had persistently thwarted efforts to make his state a tougher place for plaintiffs. He possessed plenty of campaign cash contributed from plaintiffs' trial lawyers, who were evidently unconcerned about the ethics or the appearance of giving funds to a judge who weighed in on their lawsuits.

The Law Enforcement Alliance of America had already run judge-busting ads in Pennsylvania, mostly paid for by the Chamber of Commerce and the National Rifle Association (NRA).

The alliance—a spin-off of the NRA that nominally advocated for police safety—was drawn to the Mississippi contest because of a proposed law it supported that would block anyone but the state from filing product liability cases in state courts against gun manufacturers. In the 1990s the state's attorney general had leaped into action just before a similar law that protected tobacco companies went into effect, and launched a lawsuit against the tobacco industry over the costs it had imposed on the state health care system. By the time he and other attorneys general were finished with the industry, the tobacco companies had reached an agreement that committed them to paying a staggering $246 billion to forty-six states.

McRae thumbed his nose at the tobacco industry too, arguing in a ruling against the now-dissolved American Tobacco Company that companies like Philip Morris and R.J. Reynolds should have to pay for the mass destruction they've inflicted. "Mississippi should erect billboards at all state lines which read, 'Welcome to Mississippi, where cigarette manufacturers need not pay the price for the damages their products cause.'" It was, he lamented, "cost-effective for tobacco companies across America to maim, injure and kill in Mississippi."

Now Miami, Bridgeport, New Orleans, and Chicago all filed lawsuits against gun companies, modeled on those that had conquered Big Tobacco. The gun industry was going to do everything it could to avoid the tobacco companies' costly fate, and the U.S. Chamber stood by its side. "We felt an obligation with tobacco to stand up and speak out," Kraus had said with the passion of principle when he was at the helm of the Chamber's Institute for Legal Reform. "We did it there, we'll do it with guns, and we'll do it with every target until we can put a stop to it."

The Law Enforcement Alliance and the Chamber certainly put an end to Justice Chuck McRae's tenure on the court. By one count, the Chamber put up more than $1 million through third parties to remove him from the bench. In its determination to unseat him, the alliance was not above using the homicide of a preschooler as fodder for its cause, and it worked. The ads screamed: "Chuck McRae? He was the only judge to vote to reverse the conviction of the murderer of a three-year-old girl." McRae's successor, Jess Dickinson, was a local attorney who defended lawsuits on behalf of General Motors and decried "the trial lawyer agenda."

McRae believes the Law Enforcement Alliance—and behind it, the U.S. Chamber—targeted him on the belief that he would have voted to strike down the proposed Mississippi bill preempting lawsuits against the gun industry. "I don't know if I would have ruled against them," he suggests. "I would have to see the facts." But McRae has made no secret, now or then, of his views on laws capping jury awards: not on your life. "People don't even realize that they're losing their constitutional rights," he pronounces, "trial by jury, their rights of being redressed for an injury caused by someone else, with these caps and everything else."

More than a decade after spending big on its Pennsylvania, Texas, and Mississippi legal campaigns, the Law Enforcement Alliance of America is today under a court order in Texas to divulge its funding sources, the result of a lawsuit from former Austin mayor Kirk Watson. In 2002, as Watson and a second candidate, also a plaintiff in the case, made bids for the office of state attorney general, the alliance attacked Watson with $1.5 million in ads focused on his past as a personal injury lawyer, who "made millions suing doctors, hospitals and small businesses." (McRae recalls seeing the same actors in the Texas ads as in the ones slamming him back home, thinking, "These guys look awfully familiar.")

The alliance has aggressively fought the court order to reveal its funders; it was rebuffed by an appeals court and the Texas Supreme Court, but as of this writing has not produced the demanded information. Neither the U.S. Chamber nor the Law Enforcement Alliance has ever denied reports that the Chamber, along with the NRA, used the alliance as a funnel for pouring money into judicial races. "I wouldn't comment on that," declares Jim Wootton, who left the Chamber shortly after the 2002 elections.

In all, the Institute for Legal Reform reported spending $12.5 million on "contributions" in 2002—funds that flowed to other groups, all unnamed. Another $12.5 million went to consultants, while advertising—destinations unspecified—accounted for another $8 million.

Just after Election Day 2002, the Supreme Court declined to hear Mississippi's case seeking to reveal the Chamber's secret donors. The coast was now clear for ads that, without risk of exposure, pointedly persuaded voters to put business-friendly judges on the bench.

To PREPARE FOR THE next election cycle, a dozen or so Institute for Legal Reform members gathered by conference call on a regular basis to discuss strategy for their attacks on candidates for judgeships and state attorneys general, from Washington to Mississippi to West Virginia. They decided which were vulnerable and which they shouldn't bother with.

As the effort moved ahead on full firepower, Illinois was an obvious candidate for what the institute called "tier 1": states that offered cause for concern and that had a climate receptive to action.

A handful of Illinois counties had a reputation as hot spots for plaintiffs' lawyers looking to make a kill—to generate massive, national class action settlements that would generate big fees for them along with modest awards for members of the suing class who stepped forward to claim them. The verdicts arrived tens of millions, a billion, and even ten billion dollars at a time, often starting in rural, downstate Madison and St. Clair Counties, across the Mississippi River from St. Louis. They were won by survivors of dead smokers; by tens of thousands of consumers who had been misled by their insurance companies; by victims of medical malpractice; and by sufferers of mesothelioma, the deadly consequence of asbestos exposure.

Two cases in particular, decided in Madison County, would not stand. In 1999 a Madison County jury had awarded $10 billion in a product liability case against Philip Morris; the plaintiffs were smokers who said that the packaging and marketing of "light" cigarettes had deceived them into thinking they were less harmful than standard smokes. In fact the opposite was true: smokers tend to drag extra hard on lights, in order to get the desired dose of nicotine. Philip Morris had appealed the verdict to the state supreme court.

The U.S. Chamber took a swing at nixing the $10 billion payout using conventional means, submitting a brief to the state supreme court on behalf of Philip Morris. Decrying "abuse of class action litigation," Chamber attorneys argued it was untenable to sue on behalf of the 1.4 million living smokers who had ever bought a pack of Philip Morris–made lights in Illinois, because "a cigarette's tar and nicotine yield depends on an individual's smoking behavior." And at least some smokers, the reasoning went, didn't inhale light cigarettes in ways that are any more dangerous than how they might drag on a Marlboro Red.

The other case had delivered a $1.05 billion judgment against State Farm Mutual Automobile Insurance, a division of the industry giant and also a Chamber member. State Farm had routinely slapped generic auto body parts onto auto policy customers' vehicles after crashes, which were cheaper but not made to manufacturers' specifications. Policyholders—who, ironically, are also stakeholders in the company—were led to believe they were the real deal. A county jurist had decided to award plaintiffs $456.6 million in compensation— barely one hundred dollars per affected customer. The bulk of the award came in the form of punitive damages. The jurist had issued the judgment in the face of "overwhelming evidence of State Farm's calculated deception of its policy holders." Those words were part of an opinion issued by the appellate court judge Gordon Maag, upholding the verdict.

Both the Philip Morris and the State Farm cases were now heading to the Illinois Supreme Court for a final verdict. A seat on the court was up for election; whoever won it would cast a deciding vote on State Farm's and Philip Morris's appeals. Judge Maag was running for that seat and would cast that vote, unless someone managed to stop him.

That someone would be Judge Lloyd Karmeier. As a political consultant who turned down a job in the campaign would later tell the Illinois Supreme Court, Karmeier was recruited by a State Farm lobbyist, who handed the reins of the campaign to the Illinois Civil Justice League—a tort reform group heavily funded by State Farm and the Chamber. "You've passed all the tryouts we need," the league's director e-mailed the Republican judge.

The race between Maag and Karmeier was bloody; they spent a total of $9.3 million—a record amount for a judicial race anywhere. More than two-thirds of those funds financed a blizzard of TV ads in St. Louis. Trial lawyers helped Maag raise a $2.8 million war chest.

If Maag was tainted by that relationship, however, Karmeier was toxic. Some of Karmeier's donations came from attorneys representing tobacco companies or through an Illinois political action committee to which Philip Morris contributed. More than $350,000 of the pro-Karmeier political action committee's cash came from executives, lawyers, and others associated with State Farm insurance.

As much as anything, the campaign was propelled by the U.S. Chamber and its Illinois affiliates. The U.S. Chamber spent more money on the race than any other group: $2.3 million in all. The Illinois Chamber pitched in with $245,000 of its own, and still more funding came from the Chicagoland Chamber. The president of the Illinois Chamber served on Karmeier's finance committee. State Farm's CEO Ed Rust Jr. sat on the board of the Chamber's Institute for Legal Reform, which meant that his company contributed at least $500,000 to the institute. Board members weighed in on the selection of political targets—and for State Farm, the Illinois judge race was the big one.

Rust followed in the footsteps of his father, Edward Sr., who had served not only as chief executive of State Farm but also—for a brief and tumultuous term—as president of the U.S. Chamber, in the early 1970s. Like his son, Edward Sr. had inherited the company from his father and enjoyed certain patrician pastimes—he bred horses and smoked a pipe.

But that was where the similarities ended. Edward Sr. had put consumers and their interests at the center of his worldview. After all, they were the ones who paid the premiums on household and auto insurance, and it was State Farm's job to protect policyholders. The company was and remains a mutual insurer, which means that policyholders are all part owners of the company.

Even so, Chamber staff and members were stunned when in 1973 Edward Sr. boldly told a conference of life insurance underwriters in Chicago that consumer crusader Ralph Nader was not their enemy but in fact their secret ally: a challenge to business to be more responsive to customers.

They should get used to Nader, he declared—and learn from his example. "He has been described in some quarters as an enemy of the system, but I think we are forced to the conclusion that his commitment is to make the system work," Rust told an audience accustomed to cursing and raging at the consumer advocate. "If we look at the other side, we see a clear community of interest that Nader has with American business."

One reason he admired Nader so, Rust explained, was that the advocate worked within the system, toward the same goals held by business—"on products that work as they are supposed to, on warranties that protect the buyer at least as much as the seller, on services that genuinely serve." Nader was channeling genuine discontent among American consumers, and business, Rust opined, would do well to heed the message.

The next day, in full freak-out mode, the Chamber rushed to issue a press release clarifying that Rust spoke for himself alone and not for the Chamber. The group's spin didn't deter the *Wall Street Journal* editorial page from heralding Rust's great insight that Nader was not an enemy but an ally of business. "This is wise counsel," declared the item, headlined RALPH NADER, CAPITALIST. Rust Sr. even invited Nader, the author of *Unsafe at Any Speed*, to make a film for State Farm agents. He lasted at the Chamber's helm barely a year.

Edward Rust Jr. had a dramatically different take from his father on the value of consumer warriors to State Farm. In the 1990s, after Rust Jr. took over, jury verdicts and settlements against the company accumulated with alarming force, and the cases revealed troubling practices at the giant insurer.

After State Farm refused to settle a claim and embroiled a policyholder in a costly and unnecessary trial, an appellate court in Utah found "systematic destruction of documents" and "systematic manipulation of individual claim files to conceal claim mishandling." The jury awarded $145 million in punitive damages, an amount upheld by the state supreme court.

Another $200 million had gone out the window for a settlement of a case in Idaho alleging misleading sales practices. "The insured's medical records were not examined and reports were not prepared by doctors or even reviewed by doctors," wrote Idaho judge D. Duff McKee in upholding $9.5 million in damages awarded by a jury. "[T]he evidence was overwhelming that the utilization review company selected by the claim examiner was a completely bogus operation." The state supreme court upheld the verdict three to two on first crack.

In 2000 an unprecedented big-money (for Idaho) campaign largely funded by business interests sought a more favorable Supreme Court. One of the judges who had backed the verdict against State Farm lost his reelection. With a new judge on the bench, State Farm sought a new ruling, and this time it won. The Idaho experience showed the easiest path to winning: if State Farm's attorneys couldn't persuade juries, then it would just change who sat on the bench. Hence its focus on the Illinois race between Karmeier and Maag.

On the night of his victory, Karmeier publicly denounced to a reporter the money war that had made it possible. "That's obscene for a judicial race. What does it gain people? How can people have faith in the system?" But once he was in office, he immediately paid off his campaign financers' investment in him. Before he was even sworn in to the supreme court, the Illinois justices heard oral arguments in the case against Philip Morris and voted to reverse the $10 billion Philip Morris judgment. Karmeier then cast the deciding vote that relieved State Farm of its billion-dollar burden, after refusing to recuse himself from the case.

INSURANCE COMPANIES DIDN'T BENEFIT just from getting friendly judges on the bench. They also needed to keep law enforcement off their backs, and the Institute for Legal Reform offered its services there too, coordinating "education" campaigns designed to block unfriendly candidates for state attorney general.

Like the campaigns to remove judges, the 2002 and 2004 efforts to turn voters off to unwanted aspirants for attorney general were run by the institute's political affairs director Rob Engstrom, a former staffer for the Republican National Committee. Institute consultant Tom Cole, who was preparing to run for Congress from Oklahoma, had recruited Engstrom in 2002.

In Washington State in 2004, Engstrom and his colleagues delivered $1.5 million to a group called the Voters Education Committee, whose sole reason for being appeared to be to prevent a former insurance commissioner named Deborah Senn from becoming the state's attorney general. Like the U.S. Chamber in Mississippi, the group had failed to register with the state as a political committee. The Institute for Legal Reform also backed up the campaign with polling and other services.

During her tenure as Washington insurance commissioner, Deborah Senn had certainly been no friend of the industry she regulated. She was the kind of commissioner who, after ending up in the hospital after breaking her arm snowboarding, not only argued with the insurance company because it decided to bill her for out-of-network care; she pushed to change the law on emergency care so that wouldn't happen to anyone else. Once the law was in place, she demanded that four insurers, including Aetna and Blue Cross, reimburse hundreds of emergency room claims that they had denied.

Senn had also roundly punished insurance companies that got out of line. One prominent target was Prudential, the largest insurer in the nation. It had been the subject of a massive national case seeking to compensate consumers who were ripped off by deceptive life insurance sales practices. As states sought a national consent decree from the company, Senn was one of six attorneys general nationally who held out for stronger assurances that customers would get aid. She also hit the company with $1.3 million in fines and other costs, separate from the court settlement that benefited consumers.

Senn had been doing her job—just not the way that Aetna, Prudential, and other health and insurance companies wanted her to. Ten days before the primary, she was stunned to turn on the *Today* show, *Good Morning America,* and any other morning show—to see ads from a group she had never heard of, accusing her of cutting a deal with an insurance company to lower a fine in exchange for funds to be sent directly to her office.

Well, yes, she had done that—it had been part of the Prudential deal, to make sure her office was staffed to enforce it and to pursue further investigations. And there was nothing sinister or uncommon about a legal settlement providing funds for such a purpose. The ad was attacking her for her success in advocating for the public interest.

"I was swiftboated," says Senn. "They take your positive attributes—and this is [Karl] Rove's MO—and turn it into a negative. They basically said that I was not a consumer advocate, and people believed it, even though I was really well known."

In Senn, the Chamber had found an adversary who did not go

quietly. She later joked, speaking of a college-era dalliance with the theater, "I left acting because I couldn't stand the rejection of auditioning. So I entered politics, where I could be rejected by a million people all at once."

In between her early run as a performer and her race for attorney general, Chicago-born Senn had been a peripatetic legal advocate: for the environment as a regulator for the state of Illinois, as a plaintiffs' attorney in Alaska, and as a women's advocate in Olympia, Washington. She had taken a running leap to win election as Washington's insurance commissioner in 1992 and established herself as a friend to consumers, one who didn't play the games lobbyists were used to.

Now in 2004 she won the Democratic primary despite the wall of ads against her—and then demanded a state investigation into who had bought $1.25 million in airtime specifically to get rid of her.

As in Mississippi, a state commission concluded that the ads were not, as the Voters Education Committee claimed, merely "educational." As is plainly evident, they had been part of a political campaign only days before an election, which meant that the committee would have to disclose the donors behind the ad campaign. The then-attorney general, Christine Gregoire, who was running for governor, threatened to go to court to demand the names. Before she could do so, the Voters Education Committee disclosed its one and only funder: the U.S. Chamber of Commerce.

"We were like, the who? The what?!" recalls Senn. "We could never get behind who the real donors were."

Having won the primary, Senn faced even more vicious ads, blaming her for chronic ills in health insurance: under her watch, consumers were paying more for health insurance and receiving less coverage for their money. (Who wasn't?) The ads, sponsored by the Republican State Leadership Committee, ran in the weeks between the primary and the general election. The Republican group received $1.1 million in contributions from the U.S. Chamber—more than any other group that year. Senn lost the election.

In total, the U.S. Chamber had spent nearly $3 million to prevent her from becoming Washington's chief lawyer. It never even alerted its local members, including the Seattle, Tacoma, Kelso, and Bellevue Chambers, or the statewide Association of Washington Business, which signed a letter of protest. "Continuing our good working relationship is jeopardized by the recent revelations that the U.S. Chamber's Institute for Legal Reform dumped $1.5 million into the 'Anti–Deborah Senn Ad Campaign' without our prior knowledge and, more importantly, without any attempt to consult us about the wisdom of such an effort." The Washington groups nonetheless decided to retain their Chamber memberships.

The Washington spend was just a tiny fraction of the 2004 judicial campaign blitz. The same year it went after McRae, Maag, and Senn, the Institute for Legal Reform targeted another thirteen races, and won all but one. Rob Engstrom would ultimately confirm that the Chamber had spent roughly $100 million on its "voter education" efforts in just five years.

As the Chamber revved up its court realignment project, one sponsor was especially determined to crack down on juries: the American International Group, or AIG. A blitz of jury awards against companies that AIG insured was, the company resolved, a cancer on the value of its stock.

Back in the 1990s, CEO Maurice Greenberg had vocally pressed for an overhaul of state laws governing lawsuits. Punitive damages? Make them uninsurable—or better yet, have state legislatures get rid of them. Greenberg and his lobbyists had also been leading advocates for an overhaul of the federal Superfund law that would have relieved a company of liability for pollution if another company—even one that no longer existed—could be blamed. (Greenberg wanted to see taxpayers pay for cleanups instead.) That push failed in Congress, and Greenberg complained bitterly that a lack of unity and militancy within the insurance industry would continue to thwart his Superfund project. "The industry will do what it always does and not speak with one voice," he lamented.

Greenberg was instrumental in turning that "one voice" into a chorus. Not only did he sit on the Institute for Legal Reform's board of directors, he was also board chair of the Starr Foundation, a tax-exempt repository for AIG's surplus funds. Normally, Starr trafficked in the standard do-gooder fare of major New York City philanthropists, distributing scholarships, sponsoring cancer research, making grants to the ballet, BAM, and Boy Scouts. It even granted $3 million to help the Environmental Defense Fund reduce greenhouse gas emissions.

In this apolitical mix, one recipient stood out. Between 2002 and 2006, Greenberg's foundation doled out more than $24 million in contributions—all tax-deductible—to the National Chamber Foundation, the U.S. Chamber's tax-exempt research arm.

The foundation, controlled by the Chamber but legally barred from getting involved in elections, lent money to the Chamber at the very time when the Chamber was financing judge-removal campaigns in state after state. As late as 2010, the foundation reported it had $18.8 million in outstanding loans to the Chamber. They were reported as designated for a capital campaign and were restricted for use only on education and research in keeping with the foundation's mission. Had Greenberg written a check to the Chamber and asked it to spend the funds on elections, the funds—and their source—would have had to be reported to the FEC, under strict campaign finance rules that slammed down in 2002.

What was Greenberg buying? In his antipathy to trial lawyers and the judges who enabled them, he had made no secret of his quest to get Congress to clamp down on lawsuit payouts. "Irrational jury awards and liability inflation," he reported to analysts in early 2003, had forced his company to set aside $1.7 billion in extra funds. With Republicans in the White House and controlling both houses of Congress, the feds were bound to sympathize.

One important lesson for the insurance companies and clients defending megalawsuits was that federal courts tended to be friendlier to their interests than state ones. In 2004, when the Supreme Court weighed in on the $145 million Utah judgment against State Farm, six of the nine justices decided that the punishment was excessive and slapped the award down to a fraction of that size.

So from the beginning, the Institute for Legal Reform set out to short-circuit the state courts and steer class action suits to federal judges, in cases where plaintiffs came from more than one state. In 2005 it won a partial victory with the Class Action Fairness Act, which requires major cases with plaintiffs in multiple states to go through the federal courts. It was as if Congress had agreed to build a highway bypass around the state judges strung along the Mississippi River.

In just the first two years of the Chamber's push to rein in trial lawyers, one count found that insurance and other companies had put 475 lobbyists on the case; nearly one in ten of them was working for the U.S. Chamber of Commerce or Institute for Legal Reform. Retailers, automakers, pharmaceutical companies, and more joined ranks to force class action lawsuits out of state courts and into the hands of federal judges, in cases that didn't go before citizen juries.

Among the lobbying firms on the case for the Chamber was Mayer Brown, where Jim Wootton had gone after his turn at the helm of the Institute for Legal Reform. Since then class action cases have increasingly shifted away from state courts and into federal ones.

The fight against trial lawyers also took the national stage in the 2004 elections, when Senator John Edwards (D-NC) ran at the bottom half of the Democratic ticket. Before serving in the U.S. Senate, Edwards had been a plaintiffs' lawyer and a wildly successful one at that.

That fall a political committee called the November Fund, with the Chamber of Commerce as its primary funder, spent most of its $3 million in contributions on ads and mailings boosting the Bush-Cheney ticket, targeting in eight states women with children. It aimed to block any chance that a Kerry-Edwards White House would take charge of Supreme Court and other federal judge appointments. After Kerry-Edwards's defeat, Tom Donohue told his board of directors:

"We believed that the prospect of having a trial lawyer a heartbeat away from the presidency would influence our legal, judicial, and regulatory environment for years to come."

Following a complaint from a Washington ethics group, the FEC by a vote of four to two found preliminary evidence that the November Fund had improperly failed to register and divulge its activities as a political committee, and that Donohue had violated federal law by steering corporate campaign contributions directly to a federal campaign committee in order to influence an election. In the end, though, the Chamber and the November Fund got off the hook with the FEC, just as the Coalition had in 1998. They reached an agreement with the FEC to settle the case, only to have three commissioners reject the agreement in 2008. Appointed by the Bush administration shortly after the FEC reached the deal with Donohue and the Chamber, the trio declared the entire proceeding invalid. With the six-member commission deadlocked, the November Fund and the Chamber were in the clear.

Much of the money spent on the 2004 election was not openly reported. As Public Citizen pointed out in a complaint to the IRS, Donohue told his own board that the Chamber had spent "up to $30 million" on campaigns that year, for everything from judicial seats to members of Congress. Yet in their filings to the IRS, required of all nonprofit organizations, the Chamber and the Institute for Legal Reform had reported spending only $18 million that year on elections.

Where was the rest of the money? The IRS never responded to the Public Citizen complaint.

Four years later—with the Democratic Party in the White House and in hope of a different result—the union-sponsored U.S. Chamber Watch tried to raise basic questions with the IRS about the Starr Foundation's contributions to the Chamber. Nothing ever happened. Again and again, in state elections and in federal ones, including presidential races, the U.S. Chamber and its affiliated organizations were operating as political organizations and effective ones at that. But as far as the IRS was concerned, they remained educational groups, free to do what they would with their funds. And in the case of the Starr Foundation, that $24 million was tax deductible for whoever supplied it to the National Chamber Foundation—for AIG, or even for Maurice Greenberg himself.

WITH THE CHAMBER'S HELP, Greenberg, Marcus, and their partners succeeded in making U.S. courts far less friendly to consumers seeking to bring corporate wrongdoers to account.

Some of those turned away at the courthouse door—the plaintiffs' lawyers who'd made sport of winning staggeringly large settlements with the help of friendly judges, and claiming much of the loot in fees—deserved a firm rebuff. And big-ticket class action lawsuits still press on, now in federal court, like the one resulting in a $1.6 billion settlement in 2013 for owners of Toyotas prone to sudden acceleration.

But no longer can wronged individuals count on top state legal officials to fairly weigh their interests. Voters in twenty-two states have the power to pick their top judges, and in forty-three to select their attorneys general. Their choices in state after state have indelibly narrowed to those acceptable to corporate counsel—candidates who know far better than to stray out of line.

CHAPTER 7

How Business Bought Congress

Clients: Insurance, Pharma

Anyone who followed the 2012 midterm elections for Congress could be forgiven for thinking that the U.S. Chamber of Commerce was a spent force in politics. It unleashed $33 million in ads to influence dozens of House contests and to take over the Senate for Republicans, who began the election season in the minority, with forty-seven senators out of one hundred. Out of thirty-six House races, the Chamber's candidates prevailed in just twenty-three. And it snagged just one Senate seat, out of fourteen contests that it spent money to win. By the time the votes were counted, the Chamber was two steps farther from its goal of a Republican Senate majority than it had been at the start, with the GOP holding just forty-five seats.

By the calculation of the Sunlight Foundation, which tracks campaign spending, the Chamber's $33 million in spending on the 2012 congressional showdown had yielded a 6.9 percent return on investment. Put another way: its win-loss record resembled that of the 1962 Mets.

But that doesn't tell the whole story. The Republican hold on the House remained secure—and that owed much to the Chamber's numerous victories in 2010. And the seeming disaster of its senatorial campaign appeared so mostly because the bid the Chamber had made was so bold: to put the Republican Party back in charge of the Senate—preferably with a sixty-vote, filibuster-protected supermajority—just as it had already captured the House, and to do it during the reelection campaign of a popular Democratic president. The truth was that the Chamber, even in a down year, had been a prime player in the American electoral circus. And come 2014, Republicans would succeed in taking over the Senate. The Chamber poured in $36 million to make it so, ensuring the defeat of Democratic incumbents Kay Hagan of North Carolina, Mark Udall of Colorado, and Mark Begich of Alaska.

A strong American political consensus once held that no business is supposed to be in the business of influencing federal elections. A century before the U.S. Chamber of Commerce reinvented itself as a political assault weapon, a corporate syndicate had bankrolled the election of a president. The resulting scandal had inspired a flat-out ban on corporate funding of campaigns for Congress and the White House.

The candidate was Republican William McKinley; the bagman, mining magnate Mark Hanna. In 1896 the populist Democratic presidential candidate William Jennings Bryan rallied voters with a promise to move the nation off its "cross of gold"—the precious-metal standard backing every dollar of U.S. currency. Business owners dreaded that expanding the money supply would set off a storm of inflation destructive to their holdings, and McKinley's campaign quickly recognized that it could capitalize on their fear and outrage.

Hanna didn't just collect corporate donations. He systematically assessed funds from major companies, like a tax, for the campaign. Standard Oil—where the Rockefellers had made their fortune—contributed $250,000. J. P. Morgan, Henry Frick, Andrew Carnegie—they, too, were generous donors. A railroad handed over fifty thousand-dollar bills in an envelope. A slew of other industrialists did much the same.

Hanna's camp estimated the total take at $3.5 million—the equivalent of an astounding $95 million today. But the truth was that no one knew, because no record-keeping system for political contributions even existed. Whatever its size, that fortune paid for the 1896 equivalent of wall-to-wall ads in prime time.

While McKinley held court on his front porch in Ohio, his campaign stayed in the public eye with 250 million pamphlets, in a rainbow of languages. Speakers and literature flooded Pullman, Westinghouse, Carnegie Steel, Standard Oil, and other factories, reaching workers right at their machines. The Republicans' fortune even paid for the first-ever Flag Day, supplying millions of stars-and-stripes for a national frenzy of patriotic standard waving.

One poster circulated by the Republican Party shows a stylish family happily basking "in the sunshine of protection," and prosperous bees buzzing around a hive, in contrast to the depressing life endured by the same trio living "under the cloud of free trade," dressed in rags and condemned to idleness. The platform printed below called tariffs "the foundation of American development and prosperity."

It's hard to fathom today, when unfettered global trade is a religious credo of the GOP, right up there with opposition to abortion and the evils of taxation. But in the age of the robber barons, industrialists insisted that the exact opposite was true, that the U.S. economy would wither unless high tariffs kept foreign competitors out.

The cash infusion bought McKinley the presidency and a reelection, but he was assassinated by an anarchist shortly into his second term. After McKinley's death, vice-turned-president Theodore Roosevelt found himself forced to reckon for the sins of the GOP and its corporate finance binge. The new chief executive was no friend of Hanna, who had tried to block Roosevelt from the vice-presidential nomination. But the president also was deeply implicated: the Republican National Committee had taken massive donations from companies and business leaders for his 1904 reelection campaign.

Under pressure from newspaper editors and progressive members of Congress, Roosevelt backed a bill to eliminate corporate contributions in elections—drafted "in the interest of good government and calculated to promote purity in the selection of public officials." Officially, as of 1907, corporate contributions were banned.

But there was no way to enforce the law, and companies could easily disguise their contributions as individual donations. Later, they began to shovel cash through political action committees. It took six decades and a lawsuit from the reform group Common Cause against both the Democratic and Republican National Committees to goose Congress into passing a law in the 1970s, requiring real disclosure of donations. The newly created Federal Election Commission was empowered to enforce strict limits on spending to influence elections that came from outside candidates' committees.

That didn't last long. In 1976 the Supreme Court ruled in *Buckley v. Valeo* that organizations could spend money to influence elections— protected by the First Amendment of the U.S. Constitution—as long as they didn't explicitly instruct voters to pull a lever for or against a named candidate.

More than any other single organization, the U.S. Chamber of Commerce has taken the Supreme Court's blessing of corporate political spending and mined it for political influence. Josten, Donohue, and a by then former aide to Senator Mitch McConnell (R-KY) named Steven Law built the Chamber into a campaign-spending machine with the power to swing elections, acting on behalf of unnamed business sponsors. Along the way, it pushed to rewrite the rules of political spending to amplify big business's power over the polls.

Business isn't the only player at the track. Labor unions spend big on elections too, with ready access to funds assessed from member dues—all reliably spent on Democratic candidates. In 2012, unions showered $115.6 million in independent spending to influence federal races, the watchdog Center for Responsive Politics calculated. Yet that impressive sum amounts to less than 14 percent of the more than $800 million in disclosed outside money that descended on the races—almost all of it from business. The transformation of election laws, and the sheer amount of money spent on races, have in the last decade thrown a tremendous advantage to business, which has the power to dominate the airwaves with attack ads.

Usually—though not always—those ads succeed in wounding their targets. They also serve as a kind of nuclear deterrent, keeping members of Congress who might think of crossing the Chamber from casting votes they might regret come election time.

Representative Jim Matheson (D-UT) was on both sides of the pain. In 2000 he suffered $1 million in withering attacks from the Chamber, the NRA, and other groups, as he sought, and ultimately claimed, an open congressional seat. Matheson got the message. He phoned the Chamber a week after he arrived in Washington to broker a truce.

"Look, I realize you went after me," Chamber political director Bill Miller recalled the congressman told him. "I realize you don't want me to be here. I am here. I am going to be a pro-business vote for you on the Democratic side. I want to form a partnership whereby you tell me what you need on the votes that are significant votes to the business community, and I'll be there for you." Matheson now has a 77 percent lifetime score on the Chamber's *How They Voted* guide, one of the highest of any Democrat. In 2002 and ever since, he got the Chamber's endorsement.

Much of Washington sang "Kumbaya" when Republican Senator John McCain and Democratic Senator Russ Feingold teamed up to pass serious campaign finance reform in 2002. Not the Chamber of Commerce. The McCain-Feingold bill banned so-called soft money contributions to candidates and parties, customarily made by companies and labor unions and until then totally unregulated. Also verboten were corporate- or union-funded outside ads that purported to "educate" voters about candidates in the months leading up to election day—exactly the kind of fare that the Chamber's Coalition project had cooked up and shared with John Boehner and other congressional Republicans during the 1990s.

The Chamber sued to block McCain-Feingold. "This is a country founded on free speech," inveighed Tom Donohue, "and the government cannot tell us that we have the right to speak on issues at the beginning of a campaign, but not at the end, when public debate matters most."

But the truth was that while the ad blackout was a blow to Donohue's ambitions of influence, other parts of McCain-Feingold proved a boon to the Chamber, by giving it a unique advantage in the political marketplace. As a nonprofit trade group, it could still collect and spend corporate money on campaigns, as long as it cast the efforts as merely "educational." The four Supreme Court dissenters in 2006's *Wisconsin Right to Life v. FEC* who sought stronger campaign finance regulation would later call the distinction between these so-called issue ads and banned campaign commercials "a patent fiction."

The GOP and Democratic Party committees had collected nearly half a billion dollars in soft money in 2000—influence-seeking funds that would now need a new home. U.S. Chamber political consultant Tom Cole accurately forecast: "We'll start having political shops inside the business groups. They will be full-service combat shops. I think you will ultimately see more soft money in ways that are more difficult to trace."

And when the Supreme Court upheld McCain-Feingold in 2003, the losing plaintiff Senator Mitch McConnell warned, "This law will not remove one dime from politics. . . . Outside interest groups have become modern political parties. Soft money is not gone—it has just changed its address."

For much corporate spending on elections, the forwarding address became 1615 H Street. Other groups could also take corporate donations and run ads. Most were known as 527s, for the section of the IRS code that allows political education committees to operate without paying taxes. But one crucial difference separated 527s and the Chamber: as an established trade organization that did plenty more than boost candidates, the Chamber was free to run ads in campaigns without ever disclosing its sources of funds.

Companies cut off from soft money that did not want to have public exposure could count on the U.S. Chamber to keep their secrets and combine their money into a critical mass of firepower.

The Chamber found the perfect test case to prove its mojo in a campaign against Senator Tom Daschle (D-SD) who was—until the Democrats lost control in 2002—Senate majority leader.

Daschle happened to be a tight ally with trial lawyers, who were an important part of his donor base. In the year leading up to his re-election bid in 2004, the U.S. Chamber and the Institute for Legal Reform spent millions lobbying him and other senators trying to push through their legal reform agenda—in particular, to move state class action cases to friendlier federal courts.

Daschle was also an obstacle to passing a proposed $250,000 cap on punitive damages in medical lawsuits—he insisted on keeping asbestos manufacturers liable to their cancer victims. In 2004, as Senate minority leader, he had the power to use the filibuster to block votes his party caucus didn't want.

The insurance industry and the Chamber's other big clients wanted Daschle gone. Their candidate was Republican nominee John Thune, a party player whose political mentor had ejected *über*-liberal Senator George McGovern (D-SD) from office. Thune had lost his 2002 run against South Dakota's other senator by just a few hundred votes and had a clear shot at victory. "If we had the ability to replace one with the other, absolutely we would," Chamber political director Bill Miller said frankly. "John Thune is a friend of the Chamber, very helpful. Tom Daschle is helpful about half the time."

Actually, Daschle voted 75 percent of the time with Republican President George W. Bush, but that wasn't enough. Only cooperation with a crackdown on lawsuit payouts would redeem Daschle, and he wasn't budging.

Within South Dakota, Daschle had a tight alliance with local chamber affiliates. He reliably supplied the Sioux Falls Area Chamber with A-list speakers for its annual meeting—Treasury Secretary Robert Rubin, astronaut John Glenn. In 2002, at the local chamber's request, he himself delivered the keynote.

None of that intimacy mattered once the national Chamber parachuted in for its electoral assault. Miller jokingly called the 2004 reelection campaign a "mayor's race," because by his tally just thirty thousand votes had been up for grabs. To capture those, the U.S. Chamber would spend $400,000 on a radio and TV ad blitz, scaring voters about "doctors driven out of rural America by skyrocketing insurance rates, leaving the sick nowhere to turn."

Under the McCain-Feingold campaign finance law, all such ads had to stop sixty days before the general election. What the Chamber could and did do after that point was to barrage South Dakota voters with mail, e-mails, phone calls, and visits to their front doors. The Chamber paid for ten statewide mailings, accusing Daschle of "losing touch with our South Dakota values," targeted at independents and young voters. "We're not in the TV business anymore," Miller summed up. "We're in the turnout business."

Being forced by McCain-Feingold into a ground game turned out to have unexpected advantages. After the Chamber's intensive direct campaign, even Hutterite colonies that had never allowed their members to vote made an exception and turned out blocs of ballots for Thune.

With help from another $3.2 million in spending, mostly on radio and TV ads, from the National Republican Senatorial Committee, the Chamber won its mayor's race. Tom Daschle went down to defeat, the first Senate party leader to be removed from office in fifty-two years.

WITH DASCHLE OUT OF the way, the bill to block big multistate class action lawsuits could move forward. Donohue felt compelled to apologize to his board of directors for not getting the class action bill passed immediately after election day, before Daschle had even left the Capitol. "Let me be clear that we tried very hard to get the class action bill completed, but Congressional leaders determined they could not open up a narrowly-focused lame duck agenda to include contentious matters," he wrote. "However, they agreed to strongly support an effort to move this legislation early in the New Year."

Despite the new limitations on its broadcast ads, 2004 had been a good year for the Chamber. After that year's elections, Donohue took stock for his board of directors: the Chamber had put 215 people on the ground in thirty-one states and contacted voters through 3.7 million pieces of mail, 5.6 million phone calls, and 30 million–plus e-mails. It hadn't been wall-to-wall TV, but it had worked: of the twenty-eight targeted House seats, the Chamber won twenty, along with seven out of nine Senate races.

How much the Chamber actually spent remains something of a mystery. Early in the year, execs floated record-breaking numbers to D.C. journalists, suggesting it was about to spend $40 million to take out Daschle and other targets. After the fact, Miller reported the total as $25 million; Donohue told the board in his memo "up to $30 million."

Spending records tell a different story. The Chamber's filings to the IRS and Senate for that year showed less than $4 million for "direct and indirect political expenditures." The Institute for Legal Reform spent far more on the state judge and attorney general campaigns that year, including those against Gordon Maag in Illinois and Deborah Senn in Washington—all told, $14 million. That's a grand total of $18 million—not nothing. But the amount disclosed as spent to hit members of Congress was a pitiful one-tenth of the amount the group publicly boasted it would spend at the beginning of the year. Its own accounting suggests the Chamber was taking credit for election victories mostly financed by others. It may have done so in order to save face—that, or else it had failed to tell the IRS in full about its political contributions to proxy attack-ad groups.

The show of money in 2006 was more forceful, with $19 million from the Chamber and another $13 million from the Institute for Legal Reform. The trove paid for an ocean of early TV ads, efforts that did not have to be registered with the FEC. Some ads praised members of Congress who had voted for the Medicare prescription drug plan, using funds supplied by the pharmaceutical industry. (The Chamber was so effusive that it hailed two members who had not even been in Congress when the costly prescription program went up for a vote.) The Chamber also spread some of its spending to business-friendly Democrats, like Representative Melissa Bean of Illinois.

By 2008 the media blackout before election day was a crippling thing of the past. Opponents of campaign finance restrictions had finally prevailed on the Supreme Court to dislodge a pillar of McCain-Feingold: the part that blacked out ads at the height of election season. Armed with the power of TV advertising, the Chamber could take on more races in more states, getting much more bang for its political bucks.

It then got an assist from the FEC, which added a mere eight words to the rules on when groups must disclose their donors—only in the case of funds given "for the purpose of furthering electioneering communications"—thereby creating a vast loophole for political fund-raising by nonprofit organizations. As long as donors didn't specify how their cash was to be used, the Chamber and other groups would not have to publicly report their identities or gifts.

But donors have ways of making their desires known—especially through the Chamber's lobbying of members of Congress already sitting in office. Lobbying money faces no limits. The Chamber is the all-time record holder for lobbying spending in Congress, laying out more than a billion dollars between 1998 and 2013—more than runners-up General Electric, the American Medical Association, and the American Hospital Association combined.

The Chamber spent $145 million on it in the session leading up to the 2008 elections, including a fierce blitz of lobbying against the labor-backed Employee Free Choice Act (EFCA), which would have made it easier for unions to organize workplaces.

Not coincidentally, stopping EFCA was the driving issue behind the Chamber's 2008 campaign spending. Labor leaders thought it less than coincidental that after their Coalition for a Democratic Workplace had sought to devote $20 million to Senate races to improve the chances of EFCA's passage, the Chamber came out and said it would spend exactly that much.

First with Nader, then with the trial lawyers, and now again with labor unions, the Chamber confronted the political power of an opponent by mimicking and outdoing it.

The Chamber poured the bulk of its campaign cash, nearly $14 million, into protecting seats of allies in the Senate. "From the business community's perspective, a focus on the Senate makes sense," Miller explained that summer. EFCA had passed the Democrat-controlled House but was blocked in the Senate, where in practice any bill needed sixty filibuster-busting votes in support, out of one hundred, to move ahead. Keeping Democrats short of that magic sixty was the goal.

That stretch to deflect a momentous but unlikely result meant the Chamber spent most of its money that year on long-shot races and losing candidates. In New Hampshire, its $3 million outlay failed to protect Senator John Sununu from an upset by Jeanne Shaheen. In Minnesota, it spent nearly as much trying to block liberal radio host Al Franken from unseating the incumbent Republican senator, Norm Coleman. In North Carolina, another $1 million in attack ads wasn't enough to keep Senator Elizabeth Dole from displacement by moderate Democratic upstart Kay Hagan. And in Oregon, the two-term Republican incumbent senator Gordon Smith went down to defeat. All were helped along by the sweeping coattails of Democratic presidential victor Barack Obama.

The races where the Chamber was able to help protect its friends cost it dearly—$900,000 alone for Senator McConnell, who got by with 53 percent of the vote. In all, the Chamber spent more than $23 million on elections that year.

The Chamber may have been the biggest of the dark money spenders on congressional races, but the parties' own fund-raising, most spectacularly the Democratic Senatorial Campaign Committee, massively outgunned it. Stewarded by Chuck Schumer (D-NY), the committee raked in $163 million in contributions in 2008, much of it donated by other members of the Senate who had more cash than they needed to hold on to their seats and from bankers at booming firms like JPMorgan Chase, Goldman Sachs, and Citigroup, who were based in Schumer's home state and subject to the Banking and Finance Committees, where Schumer was assigned.

So while the Chamber spent $2.4 million attacking Al Franken in some memorably nasty ads—"High taxes aren't very funny," ran the refrain—the Senate scrum and more than $257 million in campaign spending by the Democratic and Republican committees drowned out the voice of business.

But the Chamber would soon have a shot at not only deciding a handful of targeted races, but capturing majority control of the entire House or Senate. The week after Election Day 2008, the U.S. Supreme Court agreed to hear the case of Citizens United, a flamethrowing conservative group that had been determined to broadcast a ninety-minute attack movie on Hillary Clinton during the presidential primary that year. What Citizens United didn't want to do was reveal who had paid for the screed about the "socialist" former first lady, which it was required to do under McCain-Feingold.

The Chamber rallied to the Citizens United cause, informing the justices in a friend-of-the-court brief that they should pay heed because the Chamber had just spent more on election-year issue ads than anyone else in the country. (In reality, the Chamber was outspent in 2008 by an outfit called Freedom's Watch, a project heavily funded by GOP mega-donor Sheldon Adelson.)

The Chamber's brief to the Supreme Court was stunningly candid in just coming out and announcing that its members wanted to influence elections, and they sought to do it without anyone knowing who they were or how much they were spending. Disclosure of donors "puts member interests at risk" and encourages "retaliation," because companies' customers might lash back if they learned of their spending. Look no further, justices, than the consumer boycott of ExxonMobil after it lobbied to open the Arctic wildlife refuge to oil drilling. Companies should be shielded, the Chamber insisted, from that kind of public accountability.

The Chamber complained that the nearly $17 million it spent in 2008 was but a fraction of what it could actually get out there if it were able to solicit donations for specific campaigns without having to reveal donors. Because its donors wished to remain anonymous, the organization's free speech was being "suppressed."

It was an absurd argument, as all justices except Clarence Thomas recognized. Citizens United won—and the Chamber, contrary to popular belief, lost an important battle. The Supreme Court majority rejected its logic and upheld the part of McCain-Feingold that required political donors to show their faces to the public, even if they tried to push their money through laundries like the Chamber.

After the ruling was handed down, tellingly, the Chamber made only a perfunctory, terse statement to the media. It came not from Donohue but from Robin Conrad of the U.S. Chamber Litigation Center, whose argument against disclosing the identities of donors had been eviscerated by eight of the justices: "Today's ruling protects the First Amendment rights of organizations across the political spectrum, and is a positive for the political process and free enterprise."

As THE JUSTICES DELIBERATED on Citizens United in the wake of Obama's victory over McCain, the Chamber turned its focus to one industry above all others: health insurers.

The Chamber hasn't always been rabidly opposed to having the federal government involved in health insurance. In fact, it long ago acknowledged the obvious truth that markets may not adequately meet public needs.

In 1944 the Chamber's membership voted on a series of recommendations to enhance social security in the broadest sense—not only old-age insurance but also health and other protection. It's astonishing now, but back then more than 69 percent of the Chamber membership approved of a resolution declaring that "if, after a reasonable period of time, the private effort of employers to provide protection against non-industrial and non-occupational disabilities and sickness still leaves substantial gaps in coverage, only then should public action be taken." Members passed this resolution under the proviso that such action not take the form of socialized medicine, in which doctors become government employees. Explicitly on the table for discussion was some form of government compulsion, under which employers would have to provide insurance.

As a matter of course, the Chamber more recently claimed to speak for three million businesses across the country, most of them small. But in fact most of those companies were members of their local chambers of commerce, which are in turn affiliated with the national organization. Take those away, and the picture altered considerably. In 2009 the Chamber proper had just fifteen hundred contributors who gave $5,000 or more.

Most stayed within six figures. But one astonishing (and anonymous) sum stood out that year above all others: a single donation of $86.2 million—42 percent of all the money the Chamber took in. Whoever supplied that had both the means to write a check that big and something they sought to buy that was worth that much. The obvious suspect was the health insurance industry, which the Obama administration's drive to bring coverage within reach of almost every American was poised to transform.

The donor, as word on the Hill had it and as IRS filings later confirmed, was America's Health Insurance Plans (AHIP), which spent $89.5 million on "advocacy" that year. Its members were insurers with much to lose in the upheaval of health care reform; reported backers of the Chamber contribution included Aetna, WellPoint, Cigna, UnitedHealth, and Humana. As the group explained, coyly, to the IRS: "Expenses were incurred to organizations that generally aligned with AHIP's views on health care reform."

AHIP is a nonprofit trade organization, just like the Chamber. So why would it give such a massive sum to a sibling, instead of going on its own influence spending spree? Two words: brand protection. Hundreds of health plans are openly members of their trade association, which had made no secret in Washington of its opposition to the so-called public option creating a new government-run health plan as one alternative to private insurance. (*Politico* estimated that health players spent $1 million a day on their Washington lobbyists during the health care fight.)

But as the debate on the Hill heated up in the summer of 2009, so did the attacks from Democratic leaders on the insurers that stood in the way of the public option. In July, House Speaker Nancy Pelosi let loose savage invective against the industry.

"They've been immoral all along in how they have treated the people that they insure," Pelosi railed against health insurers. "They are the villains. They have been part of the problem in a major way. They are doing everything in their power to stop a public option from happening."

INSURERS COULD CONTINUE TO prove their enemy Pelosi right—or they could find a better way. The industry's giants couldn't afford to have Americans associate them with opposing better, cheaper, more accessible health care.

Many insurers and AHIP itself were on the record as supporting health care reform, in principle. "You have our commitment to play, to contribute, and to help pass health care reform this year," its chief Karen Ignagni promised President Obama at a White House summit in early 2009.

It didn't pan out that way. The White House demanded concessions from different parts of the health industry, and the insurers weren't in a generous mood. Worse, that summer President Obama called out the industry on its rabid opposition, vented daily by lobbyists, to the so-called public option of a government-sponsored health plan to serve customers outside the private insurance market. "If private insurers say that the marketplace provides the best quality health care," the president taunted, "then why is it that the government, which they say can't run anything, suddenly is going to drive them out of business?"

Obama's question was entirely fair and logical. But the health care industry had grown accustomed to a White House, under President George W. Bush, that lavished billions of dollars in subsidies on private health care companies—not on government-run competition. The industry fled across Lafayette Park, where the Chamber of Commerce gladly proffered itself as a lightning rod—the same job it already had performed for the coal industry on the climate change fight in Congress.

In August, equipped with a mountain of funds from America's Health Insurance Plans, the Chamber escalated what had been a frenzy of private meetings on the Hill into open political warfare in American living rooms. It aired TV and radio scare ads in twenty states, with a special focus on the districts of members deemed persuadable.

The first rounds of ads ran in districts with vulnerable members of the House and Senate, warning of a trillion-dollar bill and endlessly swelling deficits—represented by a red balloon that bursts at the end of the thirty seconds.

If any big insurers were Chamber members, they didn't advertise the fact, which meant that the Chamber could lead its anti-public-option ad campaign without any taint rubbing off on the firms.

In exchange for heaps of money, the health insurers would get to hide out of the public eye while the Chamber inserted itself into the midst of the storm. In addition, they would also be able to recast their own self-serving, industry-protective agenda as advancing the best interests of all businesses, and to enlist the companies who were their customers as allies in the fight.

With or without the public option, health care reform was undoubtedly going to force the industry to be more consumer-friendly than it had ever been. The proposed legislation was full of land mines for the insurance business. The exchanges would compel the plans to compete with one another on a level playing field. Insurers would not be able to reject customers because of preexisting medical conditions, and their rates would be subject to review. All plans would have to provide a minimum level of coverage. One of the most painful items capped administrative costs to no more than twenty cents out of every dollar customers spent on premiums; anything spent over that would have to be refunded to customers.

Even before all the specifics of the plan emerged, the U.S. Chamber stood out among business groups as especially hostile to reform. When the process started, the Business Roundtable and the National Federation of Independent Business both made it clear to Senate leaders that they were open to some kind of federal health law. They had even been part of a coalition, alongside AARP and the Service Employees International Union, to push positive reform that helped business and workers alike. But the Chamber, having learned its lesson in 1994, spurned even mild scenarios, like creating high-risk insurance pools for people with preexisting conditions.

Through the summer of 2009, the Chamber nonetheless sought influence over the final result, in case killing a bill wasn't possible. Its health care team participated in two dozen meetings with the White House, with a working group convened by Senator Ted Kennedy (D-MA), and with the Senate Finance Committee. The Chamber also descended on the offices of at least a dozen influenceable senators, alongside reps from some of its more prominent members, among them Xerox, U.S. Steel, IBM, and Halliburton.

In a city of vocal and well-funded demands, the U.S. Chamber's voice screamed the loudest. In 2009, together with its affiliates, it spent a record $145 million on Washington lobbying.

At the height of the health care battle, the Chamber spent a small portion of that money hiring outside firms. On health care, it brought on Quinn Gillespie, a lobbying shop cofounded by former RNC chair Ed Gillespie. On the team was Kevin Kayes, former counsel to Senate majority leader Harry Reid (D-NV). In the event Democrats reached sixty seats in the Senate, securing a filibuster-proof supermajority, Reid would wield extraordinary power. Of the nearly $124 million the U.S. Chamber spent on lobbying and influence in 2009, nearly half went to a single ad firm, National Media and Public Affairs, to produce a chilling series of TV commercials on the consequences for the national economy of the proposed health care package, to run in states with vulnerable members of Congress.

It spent another $16 million on the advertising and consulting services of APCO Worldwide—the same public relations firm that the health insurers' trade group had brought on to do damage control on Michael Moore's 2007 industry send-up *Sicko*. Now APCO would turn its spin control to the health care reform bill, paid that year by both the Chamber and the health insurers.

As the House vote neared, the advertising assault grew more urgent. In one spot, factory workers watch somberly as one of their colleagues gets called into the boss's office—in order, it appears, to be told he's getting laid off. The soundtrack delivers a terrifying prediction: "Millions of lost jobs. The highest unemployment in twenty-five years. And Congress' latest health care bill makes a tough economy even worse. Billions in crushing tax increases, mostly on small business. But nothing to control rising health care costs."

And then, the sell: "Call Congress. Tell them that the new health care bill is a bill America can't afford to pay."

In November the Affordable Care Act passed the Democratic-majority House 220 to 215. The Chamber redoubled its media assault to ensure that the Senate did not get on board with health care reform. It worked with Senate Finance Committee chair Max Baucus on drafts of the Senate's health reform bill and made sure that the Senate version did not include the public option.

The Senate bill also did not come with a mandate for employers to provide health insurance. When Senator John Kerry sought an amendment that would require all companies with more than twenty-five employees to provide coverage, the Chamber beat it back too. In the end, the mandate was limited to companies twice as big, and the Chamber continued to push for its abolition.

But Congress wasn't quite done with the Affordable Care Act yet. While it approved the package 60–39, along party lines, in November 2009, the Senate still needed to align its version of the bill with the one earlier passed by the House, which unlike the Senate's included the public option.

THE DEATH OF SENATOR Ted Kennedy, reform's leading champion, in the midst of the Affordable Care Act's journey had opened up a Senate seat—one that could, if its occupant so chose, vote to block reform entirely, because of Senate rules that effectively require a sixty-vote supermajority to bring a measure to the floor. The opportunity to decide the January 2010 special election in Massachusetts was too delicious for the Chamber of Commerce and the health insurers to pass up.

The Chamber put its money behind Scott Brown, a former model and *Cosmo* magazine "America's Sexiest Man" contest winner who rocketed out of obscurity to a competitive place in the polls.

Massachusetts had had a government-enhanced health insurance system since 2006—affectionately known as Romneycare, after Governor Mitt Romney—and polls consistently showed that between three-fifths and two-thirds of state residents favored the program. So the Chamber couldn't use health care as a bludgeon against state attorney general Martha Coakley. Instead it hauled out a coded version of the same: less spending on public goods, more freedom for private industry.

The Chamber's ads incanted Brown's name repeatedly, to make sure the endorsement stuck in voters' brains: "Scott Brown believes in fiscal responsibility. Scott Brown supports measures that hold spending, cut taxes, and help businesses invest in new jobs. Scott Brown's plan empowers businesses, not politicians."

Like previous Chamber election ads, these ran under the pretense that they were merely educating voters on the issues, not endorsing a particular candidate. They barely fit within the letter of the law and ranged far from its spirit.

The nude *Cosmo* photos, his wife's music video role as a femme fatale who gets white toothpaste squirted at her face, his revelations of childhood sexual abuse—the very, very public life of Scott Brown suggested that his triumph over Coakley was a victory of TV culture and of good-looking, goofy pluck over creaky Democratic machine politics. But in the final calculation, the Chamber's ads played an important role, countering big spends by the Service Employees International Union and the Democratic Senatorial Campaign Committee. The Chamber health care lobbyist Jim Gelfand called Brown's victory "the January surprise."

The election of Scott Brown to the Massachusetts Senate seat formerly held by the late liberal Ted Kennedy marked the arrival of the U.S. Chamber as an undisputed kingmaker of congressional campaigns—not just a helping hand to a candidate and the Republican Party's committee, but the deciding reason for victory. Brown learned in his January special election what dozens of inexperienced Republicans would discover that November: that the Chamber and affiliated election funds would bankroll campaigns big enough to crush well-established opponents, and they were willing to push the limits of campaign spending laws to do it.

Twisting the law would not even be necessary anymore, because two days after Brown's election, the Supreme Court's decision in *Citizens United v. Federal Election Commission* remade the political landscape. In 2010 the Chamber could continue with its "educational" ads, into the tens of millions of dollars, targeted at tight races where its spending could make a difference. But if it wanted to, it could now also baldly urge voters to vote for or against a candidate.

So, for that matter, could anyone else. A piece of paper to the FEC, and a thousand dollars in a bank, was all it took to form a Super PAC entitled to spend unlimited sums on election ads. If a group was really ambitious, it could hybridize the two life-forms—combining a Super PAC with a Chamber-style tax-exempt "social welfare" organization. That way one group could raise money without disclosing its donors, if it was clever about how it asked, then donate the funds to the Super PAC.

That's what Republican strategist Karl Rove did, in partnership with former U.S. Chamber chief counsel Steve Law. While Law was still the Chamber's top attorney, he sat down with Rove to brainstorm a new force in conservative politics—freed from the albatross of member businesses, with their inconveniently diverse ideas about the needs of the nation. American Crossroads, established in early 2010, would be the Super PAC, while Crossroads GPS would raise much of the money—its sources undisclosed—as an IRS-blessed nonprofit "social welfare" organization.

Law had been working for years to beat back proposals to restrict corporate campaign spending, starting out at the right hand of Senator Mitch McConnell in the 1990s. McConnell was a creature of Kentucky's pivotal tobacco industry, which donated generously to his campaigns and regularly met with his office to advance its interests in Congress.

Steve Law, who served as McConnell's chief of staff, was a loyal soldier. When a bipartisan coalition in the Senate proposed that the FDA regulate tobacco as a drug, Law helped beat it back. Philip Morris's CEO, William Campbell, led the anti-FDA fight and preposterously testified, alongside other tobacco CEOs, that he did not believe nicotine was addictive. Campbell afterward praised Law, and Law later jotted a handwritten note thanking him for a holiday gift. "I look forward to an increasingly close and productive relationship this year," he wrote at the beginning of 1996. "We've got a lot to do!"

Law also helped the tobacco company navigate campaign finance rules so that it could siphon funds from its national PAC into Kentucky state races. He even accepted, on behalf of McConnell's office, tickets to a Washington Bullets basketball game and a Ringo Starr show, proffered by the industry's trade association, the Tobacco Institute. "I had no idea there were so many Beatles fans in the office; I was besieged!" Law handwrote back in gratitude.

At the Chamber, fresh from a top post in the Bush administration Department of Labor, Law dove in to beat back unions in their quest to make it easier for workers to join them via the Employee Free Choice Act. He also led the push to overturn the McCain-Feingold campaign finance law, helping, through the Chamber's brief to the

Supreme Court, win the transformative decision that his mentor Mc-Connell had failed to achieve in an earlier lawsuit against the FEC.

The Supreme Court's *Citizens United* ruling was in some sense a setback for the Chamber: no longer would it readily dominate as a funnel for corporate political spending. But while *Citizens United* would give the Chamber fresh competition from a proliferation of Super PACs, it also threw into sharp relief the unique advantages of the influence machine that Tom Donohue and his team had built.

First of all, companies that went the Super PAC route to political influence quickly found themselves burned. In July 2010, just months after the Supreme Court ruling, Target and Best Buy faced a torrent of consumer rage after campaign filings for a Super PAC backing Minnesota congressional candidate Tom Emmer revealed that the companies had given $250,000 for ads bolstering Emmer, who had come out against gay marriage. Some gay rights advocates called for a boycott against Target, which was forced to state publicly that "Target's support for the GLBT community is unwavering."

Chamber of Commerce contributions would remain, always, completely confidential.

The other key to the Chamber's political strategy was the Hill squeeze. While American Crossroads could finance ad blitzes to sway voter sentiment, that was pretty much its sole reason for being (notwithstanding Law's insistence to the IRS in its application for Crossroads GPS that politics "will not constitute the organization's primary purpose"). American Crossroads and other Super PACs would amass heavy artillery, then let it loose at targets.

The Chamber played an equally aggressive but substantially different game. It spent big on elections—but it also lavished even more money on Washington lobbying, targeting members of the House and Senate who could expect to face the wrath of attack ads if they didn't get in line. It could not only pick members; it also told them how to vote while they were in the Capitol. As one Hill aide confidentially described the squeeze: "How do I say no to a K Street lobbyist, realizing that they have all the money they need to defeat my boss in the next election?"

The heat was now on members of Congress to step in line. Those who rated 70 or higher on the Chamber's *How They Voted* scorecard automatically got an endorsement from the group. But if their scores were low, and they represented a district where they were vulnerable to replacement by a challenger, they could expect to become the target of attack ads right up to election day.

The Chamber would spend $133 million on lobbying in 2010—four times as much as it did on its record-busting blitz of TV attack ads that year. The fear campaign was on, even before the 2010 elections began in earnest. Donohue fanned the panic by spreading word around Washington that the U.S. Chamber was amassing a war chest as big as $75 million. In the final tally, it would spend not even half that much.

But the notion of the $75 million monster stuck. Even a month after the election, *Politico* would continue to refer to "its hard-hitting $75 million ad campaign to elect a Republican House." (Donohue would later repeat the same move in 2012, announcing in a January appearance on CNBC, "I would suspect we'll be a little more vigorous than—no, I'll tell you. We'll be much more vigorous. Much more vigorous meaning closer to a hundred million." Chamber spending hit just one-third of that.)

Even so, its $33 million made it the largest force in the campaigns for Congress outside the Republican and Democratic Party committees, which could take funds only from individuals and even then only up to about $30,000 each—and, of course, they had to disclose who gave the money.

Thanks to *Citizens United*, the Chamber wasn't the only player at the secret-money game in 2010. Crossroads GPS was right there with it, as was American Action Network, a nonprofit/Super PAC combo organized by ex-senator Norm Coleman of Minnesota. Meeting at Karl Rove's house in Virginia, the three groups decided to join forces—to coordinate their spending, much as labor and other Democratic allies already did—so that they weren't duplicating efforts or leaving critical races undercovered. Together they would pile on more than $97 million in ads—more than the Republican Party's own congressional committees spent.

They shared more than strategy—the organizations also had sponsors in common. The following year, as the U.S. Chamber and its partners pressed Congress to repeal health care reform, the insurance company Aetna would accidentally reveal to its regulators that it had given $4.5 million to the Chamber and another $3 million to the American Action Network. Most other funders of the health care attacks remained anonymous, but their contributions were felt in blistering ads.

Of the Chamber's $33 million piece of the 2010 congressional combat trove, just $4.2 million went into ads supporting its strategic allies, all of them Republican. The other $29 million financed a nonstop advertising machine that targeted Democrats and independents—and not incidentally provided a major source of funding for the television stations whose news operations might have offered some counterbalance.

A fresh blitz of ads leading up to the March 2010 House vote on health care reform doubled as a kick-off to the Chamber's midterm campaign agenda, targeting the districts of dozens of vulnerable members of Congress in seventeen states.

The saturation of the paid ads—and of aligned attacks on Fox News and talk radio—showed up clearly in public opinion. In March, just after President Obama signed the Affordable Care Act into law, 49 percent of Americans polled by Gallup said they thought it was a "good thing." By the end of the year, just 42 percent agreed—and 47 percent said they didn't approve of the law.

And no wonder. By early October in the midterm election season, the Chamber of Commerce had sponsored an astounding 27,500 TV ad spots around the country, the watchdog group Media Matters tallied, and in many states most or all of the commercials slammed incumbents for their health care votes. The Chamber's attacks served to punish Democrats who'd stood on the wrong side of the health care fight—and, by removing them, ensure the takeover of the House by a Republican majority.

Attack ads have long confounded political scientists. Research has shown that they usually don't work; while they raise the profile of a campaign, they are just as likely to generate a backlash against the attacker as hurt the candidate under attack. But independent spending is different. As in its fights on the Hill over climate change or health care, being the source of a negative attack can't hurt the Chamber. If anything, the group's willingness to absorb body blows makes its services quite valuable indeed. Between the Chamber and its partners in spending, the sheer volume of negative ads had its intended effect.

Representative Chris Carney (D-PA), who had been an interrogator at Guantánamo, was known as a reliably conservative Democrat, but the only credential that mattered to the Chamber was his vote in favor of the Affordable Care Act. In a heavily Republican district, where President Obama did not get a majority of votes in 2008, the Chamber lavished $400,000 on attack ads that accused Carney of having "voted for a reckless Washington takeover of health care and [House Speaker] Nancy Pelosi's reckless budget."

"You would turn on the television, and each commercial break, there would be not one, but usually two, negative ads about me," recalls Carney. He lost his bid for a third term.

First-term representative Mary Jo Kilroy (D-OH) had not only voted for the Affordable Care Act and cap-and-trade; she also dared to introduce a bill building on the "Say on Pay" amendment to the Dodd-Frank financial reform bill, which gave shareholders an advisory vote on executive compensation. Kilroy sought to require disclosure of how institutional investors like pension funds voted too. Another bill would have created an investor advisory committee to the SEC. She lost after the Chamber spent more on the race than any other outside group, including the Democratic and Republican Congressional Committees. Its ads terrified Ohio senior citizens into thinking that Kilroy was personally responsible for robbing them of their government health insurance.

"The seniors defected from voting Democratic that year," sums up Kilroy. "And I think in large measure [it was] because of the scare tactics that the Chamber used, telling seniors over and over that they're going to lose their Medicare. That the bill that I voted for was going to slash their Medicare. It would push them off. They would lose their benefits. You heard this throughout this campaign in the fall."

Paul Hodes, running for an open New Hampshire Senate seat, got the triple attack: from the Chamber, the American Action Network, and American Crossroads. ("Money—it's a five-letter word," he quips.) The Chamber alone spent nearly $2.4 million, half of what Hodes raised for his entire campaign. He lost too.

But it didn't take a track record in Congress to invite fatal Chamber attack ads. In the Ohio race for Senate, Lieutenant Governor Lee Fisher presented himself as a pro-business Democrat—he formerly headed the state's economic development agency—and a friend of local chambers. To his fury, Chamber attack ads assaulted him without even a voting record as an excuse. The ads started so early, in June, that they did not have to be reported to the FEC. "Their attacks on me were completely and totally based on one thing and one thing only. That was my political affiliation—my party," says Fisher. "It had nothing to do with my views on issues."

Health care scare ads were not the only bludgeon deployed to push members into compliance. In April 2010 Representative Chris Van Hollen (D-MD) introduced the DISCLOSE Act (the acronym stands for Democracy Is Strengthened by Casting Light on Spending in Elections), a bill with 114 cosponsors that would have banned political spending by companies that did business with government and required others to supply detailed information about their contributors on behalf of campaigns. It passed the House handily in June and headed to the Senate.

But in the Senate, a bill needs sixty supporters to move to the floor for a vote, and supporters of DISCLOSE had fifty-nine. Senator Scott Brown dashed their hopes when he came out in opposition. As the Chamber reminded senators, in boldface, in letters sent when sponsors tried to move DISCLOSE forward: "The Chamber will include Senate votes on this legislation in our annual *How They Voted* scorecard."

A vote for DISCLOSE, lest anyone be fooled by its sponsors' justifications, was not in the Chamber's view a vote for fair and consistent transparency for all money that went into political campaigns or to bolster "the public's trust and faith in the rules and the integrity of the electoral process." Tom Donohue lambasted DISCLOSE as a self-serving fraud, an effort by enemies of business in Congress to protect their own jobs by silencing their critics. "The fact that this assault to the First Amendment is being considered as millions are desperately looking for work is a complete outrage," he railed. "Despite their best efforts, there is no back room dark enough, no partisan motive strong enough, and no cynicism profound enough to barter away Americans' freedom of speech."

Energy and drug companies—including ExxonMobil, Glaxo-SmithKline, and Novo Nordisk—sent lobbyists to school members of Congress who might be tempted to support DISCLOSE. So did media companies Clear Channel, Cox, CBS, and Viacom, which stood to lose massive revenues that they counted on from TV and radio campaign ads.

Virtually all the ads on the Chamber's end were vicious, often truth-bending attacks. The sheer scale of the assaults, targeting fifty-nine races and mostly crushing Democrats, had their effect. In 2010 the Chamber's candidate won 57 percent of the time.

The GOP gained control of the House back from Democrats, denying President Obama the alliance he needed in Congress to move his legislative agenda. The new House leader would be John Boehner, who in 1998 had collaborated so closely with the Chamber on its campaign to protect the seats of Republicans in Congress.

Coordinating with Crossroads, the American Action Network, and other groups, the Chamber also made gains in the Senate, bolstering the supermajority blockade—the difference between the Democratic majority and the magic sixty yeas needed to bring a vote to the floor—to seven seats, up from one.

In Florida, the Chamber took the lead with $2 million in attacks on GOP-turned-independent governor Charles Crist, who had committed the crime of saying that had he been in Congress, he would have backed health care reform.

One of the Chamber's biggest spends went down the toilet: it dumped nearly $5 million into the disastrous quest of former Hewlett-Packard executive Carly Fiorina to unseat Senator Barbara Boxer in California. But most of its Senate picks won their races.

The Chamber had made strides in state politics too. Far less recognized than its role in Congress, but every bit as important in changing the political playing field, is its place as the top sponsor of the Republican State Leadership Committee, a fund that seeks GOP control of statehouses, to which it contributes nearly $4 million a cycle. In 2010 the Chamber's efforts helped the GOP not only capture the U.S. House of Representatives but also gain or hold twenty houses of state legislatures across the country, including the senate in New York, where it threw $100,000 into the Republican Party fund.

Among much else, those legislatures draw the district lines for Congress in each state, commonly using gerrymandering to skew more districts to GOP candidates than would be elected if district boundary lines were drawn without regard to party preference. That year eleven state legislatures switched to GOP-majority control, giving members effective power to decide congressional races through redistricting, which took place after the 2010 Census. By 2012 just seventeen of the fifty state legislatures were Democratic-controlled, versus twenty-seven held by the GOP.

Donohue's board rewarded him with a hefty raise in 2010—his compensation totaled $4.7 million, up from $3.7 million the previous year, most of it in incentive bonuses. As long as he kept donors' identities secret, the funds would continue to flow in, and Donohue and other Chamber executives would personally reap the benefits.

MANY OF THE BIGGEST contributions to the Chamber of Commerce are brought in by rainmaker-in-chief Agnes Warfield, a former RNC fund-raiser. In the 1990s she had helped pull in millions for a non-profit organization run by Senator Lamar Alexander (R-TN), the Republican Satellite Exchange Network, that bolstered his visibility and Republican prospects in the run-up to his presidential campaign.

Warfield has been so successful in pulling in money for the Chamber that in 2009 her pay in incentive bonuses ($1.1 million) exceeded her $720,000 salary. She makes more money than anyone at the Chamber other than Donohue. By 2012, her incentive-pay bonus reached $2 million a year.

Donohue, Warfield, and other fund-raisers were not about to let some Democrats slay the golden goose by outing the identities of the Chamber's donors. Representative Van Hollen, thwarted in his fruit-less two-year quest for a Senate vote on the DISCLOSE Act, sued the FEC, looking to close that little electioneering communications loop-hole that allowed the Chamber and other groups to keep contributors secret.

In March 2012, just as election season was getting under way, a federal court ruled in Van Hollen's favor. Judge Amy Berman Jackson, an Obama appointee, found that the bipartisan FEC had over-reached by stifling disclosure of donors that had been mandated by the McCain-Feingold law. The ruling meant that the Chamber and other groups could keep broadcasting those supposedly educational "electioneering communications" all they wanted, but they would have to promptly disclose the funding sources for every ad to the FEC and the American public, just as McCain-Feingold prescribed.

Secrecy was everything to the Chamber—the commodity it could offer at a high market price, in a district with no shortage of compet-ing industry lobbyists and political hit shops. It was hardly going to stop airing attack ads, not when Donohue had gone on CNBC and vowed to spend $100 million to decide what Congress would look like from 2013 on.

There was only one thing it could do now: drop the painfully bogus pretense that its campaign ads were merely an educational service, on the order of *Schoolhouse Rock!* Instead, during the 2012 campaign it went into full-frontal direct political advocacy and attacks, instructing voters to cast ballots for specific candidates—or more often, against them. Under the arcana of federal election laws, the Chamber of Commerce could simply reveal itself—not its donors—as the source of the funds.

Plunging directly into politics violates a prime directive of any nonprofit organization: that partisan activity not constitute the group's primary purpose. As it was, campaign finance reformers had a complaint pending with the IRS, arguing in great detail that the U.S. Chamber was plainly a political organization, not a social welfare group, and therefore was not entitled to nonprofit status.

Now, to save its own supremacy, the Chamber was coming out and admitting that it was, in fact, a political machine. It was proving its opponents right. Unrestrained, it proceeded to invest $32.6 million in spots that specifically told Americans how to vote, almost all in the form of attack ads. That was on top of the $3.4 million already sunk into February campaign spots that supposedly just educated voters. "This whole fraudulent pretense that their campaign spending was just issue advocacy just entirely goes out the window," marvels Craig Holman, on the team at Public Citizen that made the case to the IRS. The agency has never responded to the complaint.

CHAPTER 8

Why Bankers and Boards Get Richer, and Workers Don't

Clients: Wall Street, Agribusiness, Energy

Medicine has microbes: tiny particles, invisible to the human eye, that carry life-or-death power over their foreign hosts. And so it is in the politics of business, where minuscule details of the legal code determine just how far companies can stretch in pursuit of profit.

We tend to think of laws as being made in Congress, springing to life from the womb of the Capitol dome. But most of their power takes shape through the crafting of rules by government agencies. Federal regulations harbor the power to make or cost billions for companies, to permit or ban high-risk corporate behavior, to decide who wins and who loses in the economy. That's why Chamber of Commerce lobbyists have spent, collectively, hundreds of years helping write those rules—and with increasing fervor and success, they have gone to court to block ones that don't suit its members.

Next time you're at work, look for the poster explaining the rights you have as a worker to join forces with your colleagues to form a union and bargain collectively with your employer over wages and benefits. You won't find it. The National Labor Relations Board (NLRB) tried to change that: in 2010 the federal regulator called for employers to put an eleven-by-seventeen poster someplace where workers could see it. The cost to each business, by the board's estimation: $62.04 during the first year. Human resources departments would even be able to download the poster for free from the NLRB website.

There's plenty of precedent for such posters. The sign telling workers they're entitled to a minimum wage has been on the office bulletin board, in one form or another, since 1938. Other employee rights get their exposure too—in small type, but still. Thanks to President Richard Nixon, occupational health and safety notices instruct workers to report any suspected environmental hazards promptly to OSHA. Fellow Republican George H. W. Bush signed off on the posting, assuring workers that they can take a leave of absence when a family member is born or needs care and still come back to a job.

Equal opportunity regardless of gender, race, or age; the right to come back to work after a stint in the armed forces; even (thanks to Reagan) the right to refuse a lie-detector test: none of these pieces of paper, all of which are required by law to be on display in most workplaces, has damaged democracy.

But workers' rights to bargain with their employers have no such status, even though federal law ensures them, and decades of union organizing have kept them alive.

A proposed 2010 NLRB regulation aimed to fix that gap and affix signs to workplace walls. Employees clearly needed the information. By that year, the rate of union membership in the United States had plummeted to 11 percent, and less than 7 percent in the private sector. While many forces account for that decline, it certainly hasn't helped that most workers don't even know that they can join a union and be assured—theoretically at least—that they won't face retaliation.

But the nation's seven million private-industry union workers— earning on average $150 more a week than their nonunion peers— were too many for the Chamber of Commerce. With its South Carolina affiliate, the U.S. Chamber headed to court to file a lawsuit, arguing that the NLRB did not have the power to force unwilling employers to promote unionization.

All the sign did was inform workers of a right that they have had, in one form or another, since 1935. That was when the National Labor Relations Act established their power "to organize and bargain collectively with their employers"—in other words, to join a union, something millions of Americans did in the decades that followed, an era when levels of union membership and middle-class prosperity went hand in hand.

The act wasn't designed just to help workers. As Congress noted when it passed the law, collective bargaining improves the flow of commerce. In the decades before the landmark labor law, Americans had been all too familiar with the alternatives—strikes, pickets, slow-downs, mass firings, and other actions that had, along with speculative booms and busts, chronically thrown the economy into chaos.

The NLRB's poster rule, like all such actions from federal agencies, had to go through an open review. That was when the circus began. Of the six thousand–plus public comments on the NLRB's proposed poster, nearly nine hundred used phrasing suggested by the Chamber of Commerce: "I do not support the NLRB's attempt to force nearly every business in America to post a biased notice of labor rights." One letter was submitted by one "I. M. Forfriedem," another by someone who purported to be a former union official. Thousands more originated with an association of human resources executives.

Cut-and-pasted talking points were a start, but they weren't nearly enough to stop the poster rule from advancing, which is why the Chamber then sued the government. The outpouring of outrage in the open review sufficed to give the appearance of widespread alarm among small business. Any judge who decided to block the NLRB would have plenty of cover to say that the obligation to put up a poster posed genuine potential for harm.

The national and South Carolina Chambers sued under an obscure 1946 federal law called the Administrative Procedure Act, which governs every step by which U.S. government agencies like the EPA or FDA develop the detailed rules through which they wield their ample power. That law has been around almost as long as the labor act, and rarely had anyone had a bad thing to say about it.

But the law gave the Chambers a candy store full of ways to block the signs. One was to convince a judge that the posting rule was arbitrary or capricious—a point all those letters got across. The commenters' script noted, for instance, that the signs didn't spell out for workers their right in many states *not* to join a union.

Or a judge could simply find—as one in South Carolina did, in a ruling invalidating the NLRB's move—that Congress had never authorized the board to draw up posters in the first place. Three dozen members of Congress piled on as the NLRB appealed the decision. With seeming powers of spiritual channeling, the representatives insisted that their predecessors, decades ago in the Capitol, had never wanted employers to notify workers of their right to organize. Their congressional members' legal brief was written by the same law firm that the Chambers had hired to wage the case.

In the end, the posters were never printed. The NLRB suspended the rule, while the national and South Carolina Chambers fought it in court, and in 2013 the board lost its appeal of the judge's decision.

What's important here is not just what the Chamber of Commerce did in South Carolina but also how it built its successful case against the most seemingly harmless of regulations. The war on regulations is much bigger than the dimensions of a poster. Since 2004 the Chamber has brought the same set of technical arguments to court in at least nineteen lawsuits tearing down federal rules, in most cases successfully. Time and again its challenges to government actions have crippled the ability of federal agencies and boards to carry out basic functions of regulating American businesses—thwarting marching orders that had been clearly spelled out by Congress.

Even in cases that never made it to court, the Chamber has been able to make its influence known at a level available to few others—in part because it has the resources to sue if it doesn't get its way. When OSHA updated its rules for informing employees about workplace dangers, for example, Chamber lobbyists got an exclusive audience with fourteen representatives from four different federal agencies, including Cass Sunstein, chief of the White House Office of Information and Regulatory Affairs. The Chamber and affiliated industry groups had seven meetings with the White House on the matter in all; the AFL-CIO labor federation, one.

In that instance, all those billable hours were for naught. Obama's regulators rebuffed Chamber demands that included keeping workers in the dark about the threat of combustible dust—tiny airborne particles of anything from aluminum to sugar that can fuel rare but deadly factory explosions.

The modus operandi is not simply to weigh in on objectionable rules but, where possible, to get rid of them entirely. Nowhere has the Chamber's obstructionist power been as fully realized as in its campaign to eviscerate the Dodd-Frank Wall Street Reform and Consumer Protection Act. Dodd-Frank (named after its sponsors in Congress) was a monumental effort to shore up weaknesses in oversight of banking and investing that had led the financial system to the brink of collapse. In contrast to the ambiguity surrounding the labor board posters based on a 1935 act, this law instructing federal agencies to act was brand-new, its sponsors very much alive, and it proved quite specific about what it expected each government agency to do.

Based on Dodd-Frank, the SEC was to receive a long to-do list from Congress that mandated more democratic corporate board elections, rewards for whistleblowers who called out wrongdoing inside publicly traded companies, and disclosures of payments to foreign governments in exchange for natural resources like oil or gas. Another rule required similar information from manufacturers whose products included minerals from the Congo war zone.

The Commodity Futures Trading Commission (CFTC) would be tasked with keeping an eye on mutual fund investments once overseen only by the SEC, and it would rein in the Wild West trade in financial derivatives by setting limits and creating a trading clearinghouse.

The so-called Volcker rule would bar banks from investing from their own accounts, via hedge funds or other means. And a brand-new Consumer Financial Protection Bureau would spring from the

Federal Reserve, without much power of its own but still with authority to enforce existing laws and help consumers better understand financial products like mortgages.

DODD-FRANK AND OTHER POSTCRISIS financial reform proposals were not greeted warmly by the Chamber. In a feat of awkward sloganeering and worse timing, Tom Donohue declared war on what he called "the regulatory tsunami" in his State of American Business speech for 2011, not long before a massive earthquake inundated the eastern shore of Japan and sparked a nuclear catastrophe at a poorly regulated power plant.

Untimely hyperbolic metaphors aside, the whole idea that a cresting wave of government regulations was overwhelming American business was questionable. Donohue rightly acknowledged that Republican administrations have been as fond of writing rules as Democratic ones. The Bush administration pushed through more regulatory actions in 2003 than the Obama administration did in 2010, and almost as many in 2008, Bush's last chance to leave a mark on the inner workings of government.

But that was nothing compared to the flood of activity spawned by the Reagan and first Bush administrations, which were far more prolific in their rule writing than any administration to come. The tide slowed considerably after President Clinton signed a landmark 1993 executive order requiring federal agencies to consider costs and benefits—and results—before pushing through new regulations. President Obama added his own spin in 2011, asking agencies to review existing rules to make sure they were not unnecessarily burdensome, and to take action to rewrite or even repeal bad regulations. Dodd-Frank and the Affordable Care Act would require new regulations to take hold, but that hardly added up to a bureaucratic crisis.

While Donohue's rhetoric swelled, his deputies were working aggressively, investing a fortune in lobbying hours, to bend federal agencies' rules to members' needs. In 2010, driven largely by financial reform, the U.S. Chamber and its subsidiaries spent some $136 million solely on Washington lobbying—four times as much as it spent on swaying elections that record-breaking year. Chamber representatives had thirty-seven meetings with members of the CFTC alone, sometimes bringing along with them the commission's own former chair and chief of staff, who were now working as lobbyists for the industry they once regulated.

Donohue personally met with SEC chair Mary Schapiro to raise objections to the so-called proxy access rule, a part of Dodd-Frank that would require publicly traded companies to include, on ballots for shareholder elections, candidates who sought to challenge the board's nominees.

The idea behind the rule, which shareholders had sought for years, was to foster stronger management and accountability on corporate boards—no small thing in the wake of the financial crisis. If directors wanted to keep their posts, they would have to listen to shareholders or potentially face ouster come election time.

Not surprisingly, the measure scared executives at big companies. For one thing, open votes could lead to the ejection of board members who approved outsize pay packages or other measures that enriched top staff at shareholder or public expense. Not long before, Donohue had been accused of just that: as a board member of Qwest Communications, he had approved more than $9 million in compensation for the CEO for 2003 alone, and up to $12.5 million the following year. The supersize pay came on the heels of steep losses and restated earnings under its previous CEO.

Glass Lewis, a shareholder advisory group, raised "serious concerns about the objectivity and independence" of the Qwest board; most of its members had financial interests in the company or ties to founder Phil Anschutz. Tom Donohue was among them, since Qwest was a $100,000-level donor to the Chamber. Anschutz remained on the Qwest board of directors; through 2003, he also sat on the U.S. Chamber's.

Glass Lewis, whose clients included union pension funds, recommended that Donohue and another board member up for reelection be removed. Its head of research would later call Qwest "one of the worst boards in Corporate America when it comes to fulfilling their fiduciary responsibilities to investors."

Since Donohue had no challenger, the vote was symbolic; he won reelection. (He left the board in 2005.) Having outside board candidates on the ballot—as the SEC was proposing under Dodd-Frank—would have made such a feat more difficult.

Donohue also served on the board of Sunrise Senior Living, founded by a protégé, Paul Klaassen, who had been a driver and a speechwriter for Donohue in the Citizen's Choice days. Klaassen, like Anschutz, sat on the U.S. Chamber's board of directors. Another Sunrise board member, William Little, simultaneously chaired the National Chamber Foundation, the Chamber's nonprofit think tank.

Sunrise too faced embarrassing scrutiny: it had restated its income by some $173 million between 1996 and 2005. (Donohue served on the audit and compensation committees.) Union pension fund shareholders sued and reached a settlement, and the company was forced to adopt some of the very reforms that the Chamber of Commerce was fighting against nationally, including bringing on more independent directors. And once again shareholder advisory firms called for Donohue's ouster.

While he was continuing to serve at Sunrise, Donohue also sat on the board of Union Pacific, the rail giant, which since 2006 had given the Chamber nearly $1 million, including $100,000 for the 2006 elections. (Anschutz served on the Union Pacific board too.) Both firms counted him as an independent director.

Between his pay at the Chamber and the board service and stock, Donohue had become a wealthy man. In 2009 he received $3.9 million in compensation from the Chamber alone, and $4.7 million the following year, most of it in bonuses. On top of that, since taking the Chamber's helm, he has earned more than $9 million more from his board service and exercise of stock options.

Donohue suggests that his lucrative board service has helped him be a more effective advocate. "That I serve on corporate boards gives me a better understanding of what goes on in a boardroom," he explained as the SEC opened a probe into Sunrise. "The better you understand something, the better you can figure out how to deal with it."

Sunrise Living provided an apt learning experience. The SEC ultimately alleged accounting fraud against two executives who were seeking to make earnings targets and reap the resulting bonuses; the officials and the company accepted judgments from the court without admitting wrongdoing.

When the Chamber seeks to influence an industry regulator like the SEC, it does so with the understood threat of lawsuits hanging over the proceedings. Even before Dodd-Frank went into effect, the Chamber went to court to block an early version of the SEC's proxy access rule, which sought to promote competitive board of directors elections. Dodd-Frank included language that confirmed and amplified the SEC's power to act. The Chamber's hired law firm successfully claimed that the SEC had violated the Administrative Procedure Act—the same law the Chamber had used to thwart the labor board posters. And the anti–Dodd-Frank lawsuits kept coming, all of them claiming in some way that regulators had not considered every possible consequence of their rules.

One regulator at the CFTC called the Chamber's lawsuit and others that followed the "sword of Damocles" hanging over him and his colleagues as they moved to bring Dodd-Frank to life, a sword that has left them "virtually paralyzed by intimidation."

Technically, the SEC does not have to conduct a cost-benefit analysis of its own regulations. But it does have to act fairly and deliberately. As any parent knows, fairness is in the eye of the beholder. Here was a child who lashed back at parental authority and who could afford the best regulatory lawyers in the business.

Using the Administrative Procedure Act to kill shareholder insurgents was a repeat performance for the Chamber's hired attorney, Eugene Scalia of the law firm Gibson, Dunn and Crutcher. If the last name sounds familiar, that's because he's the son of Supreme Court justice Antonin Scalia. The junior Scalia had worked with the Chamber to set the stage in 2004, with a case clobbering a seemingly innocuous rule that asked mutual funds to maintain independent boards of directors, where the majority of members did not have intertwined business relationships with the funds.

In that mutual funds case, Scalia argued that companies would incur massive costs, and shareholders would suffer—prime evidence being a not exactly independent report commissioned by the mutual fund giant Fidelity. A federal judge was persuaded that the SEC hadn't really thought things through, and voilà—by showing that the rule was "arbitrary" and "capricious," the Chamber had bought a vital legal precedent it would cite in future cases. At the time, Donohue called the decision "a significant victory."

Seven years later, fighting shareholders seeking to shake up corporate boards post–Dodd-Frank, Scalia represented the Chamber as plaintiffs alongside the Business Roundtable, which came armed with its very own research bought from a subsidiary of the insurance firm Marsh & McLennan. The consultants compiled a treasure chest of arguments that allowing insurgents to challenge sitting board members would be costly and cumbersome. It didn't matter that the study was invalid by scientific standards and came from a plainly conflicted source, an elite group of business leaders who would be at the mercy of their shareholders were proxy access to advance. Under the Administrative Procedure Act, it was enough that someone had raised the issues and that the SEC had not dealt with them.

As Scalia and the Chamber had hoped, Judge Douglas Ginsburg of the D.C. Circuit Court of Appeals found that the SEC "had failed to respond to substantial problems raised by commenters"—specifically, to take an example cited by the court, the Business Roundtable's own study.

Ginsburg and colleagues accused the SEC of "ducking serious evaluation of the costs that could be imposed upon companies from use of the rule by shareholders representing special interests, particularly union and government pension funds." It didn't matter that the

SEC had spent, by Chair Mary Schapiro's calculation, 21,000 staff hours researching its rules—the court deemed that the SEC had not done sufficient analysis.

The swift obliteration of the board elections rule—which was not even part of Dodd-Frank, technically—had a chilling impact on the entire machinery of financial reform, at the SEC most of all. No agency could risk more accusations that it hadn't properly evaluated all potential costs and consequences of a piece of Dodd-Frank. If that happened, urgent chunks of financial reform would be tied up in court for years and might never see the light of day.

At the CFTC, which was charged with regulating sometimes risky swaps and other financial derivatives, the ruling and others that followed made an already difficult job of scripting rules close to impossible. Bart Chilton was until 2014 a member of the commission, a Democrat nominated by President George W. Bush after a career of advocating for farmers in Washington. He watched important pieces of Dodd-Frank stall in mile five of their marathon. "We get to the point where we're so concerned about potential litigation risk that we beat things to death internally, and that either slows or stops important financial regulation rules from going forward," Chilton explains. "They won. They beat the government."

Dennis Kelleher, whose advocacy group Better Markets serves as a lonely lobbying counterbalance to banks, compares the scenario to Lucy taunting Charlie Brown with her football. If the SEC has to regulate in a way that considers and minimizes every possible cost to business, there's no game to play. "No matter how many times Lucy puts up the football, she's going to pull it away right when Charlie Brown is about to kick," he laments.

The lawsuit slamming down open votes for corporate boards was just the first case of many to come. The cases eviscerating Dodd-Frank were filed either by the Chamber or by Scalia and relied on the precedents they had set together.

At the end of 2011, Scalia tilted at one of the most controversial elements of Dodd-Frank: its limits on the trade in financial derivatives. Although his clients this time were two securities industry groups, the brief was written from the same script he had crafted with the U.S. Chamber. While Scalia thundered in court, the Chamber stormed the other two branches of government, hounding Congress as well as regulators to relinquish other Dodd-Frank controls on derivatives.

Derivatives take many forms in the wild, most commonly as "swaps"—transactions in which buyers and sellers agree to exchange payments tied to changes in the price of commodities, interest rates, and other market fluctuations. Financial derivatives can help businesses and investors manage risks—balancing out one investment with another that is likely to move in the opposite direction. For more than a century, enterprises from farmers to fuel dealers have relied on a well-functioning marketplace in derivatives to make sure that a bad season or a price spike doesn't drag them out of business.

But as the financial crisis that unspooled in 2008 painfully demonstrated, untethered and overleveraged derivatives can be dangerous. Major financial institutions had built a wildly profitable trade in derivatives that were tied to the performance of home mortgages, most of them sold purely for speculative purposes. After banks recklessly loosened their standards for lending, more mortgages than expected began to fail, and the whole house of cards came crashing down, at monumental cost to taxpayers and the economy.

Out of the wreckage, with Dodd-Frank, Congress took on a charge that was both agonizingly complex and at its heart simple: to rein in financial derivatives so the trades happened in daylight, not in secret, and on a cushion of safety, not risk. A misguided 2000 law, the Commodity Futures Modernization Act, had barred the CFTC and SEC from regulating most swaps. Now it was Dodd-Frank's job to put some order back into the disastrously broken market.

Generally speaking, under the new law, swaps would have to be "cleared" through entities that guarantee the deals in case they go bad. No one trader could pile up mountains of high-risk holdings, as AIG and others had done to such costly effect. And at the very least parties in the swaps would have to put up extra (and refundable) money, known as margin, to back up the transactions.

Scalia attacked Dodd-Frank's limits on the volume of derivatives contracts that traders could hold, winning round one by questioning—in a technical argument that hinged on a single comma—whether Congress required regulators to act at all. Meanwhile a colleague at his law firm—Gibson, Dunn and Crutcher—who was also being paid by the U.S. Chamber, waged a relentless campaign among regulators to carve out spacious exemptions to Dodd-Frank's derivatives rules. Meetings and letters warned of the consequences for even the slightest slip-up: lawsuits to block the rules once passed.

Former Bush White House budget official Michael Bopp is the force behind the Coalition for Derivatives End-Users, a Chamber-coordinated group of major businesses that, as Dodd-Frank moved toward passage, stormed Congress, advocating to ensure that they could continue trading in swaps unimpeded.

The Business Roundtable and GE Capital, later joined by the Chamber of Commerce, paid Gibson, Dunn more than $4 million to sponsor Bopp's efforts. As one admiring industry lawyer observed of the campaign: "If people can put Main Street instead of Wall Street in front of the politicians and say, 'Hey, look, we're not Wall Street, we're just normal people using these instruments to help our business,' it's helpful."

Signing up members whose core business lay far beyond the financial-services industry—they included Coca-Cola, Caterpillar, Ford, IBM, Microsoft, Procter & Gamble, Duke Energy, and BP—the Coalition staged a fly-in one-day lobbying blitz hitting sensitive players on the Hill.

The show of force ensured that Dodd-Frank exempted businesses that used swaps to hedge their risks from having to put up extra cash—or even disclose their activities to investors.

This was no small matter. After all, we're talking about some of the biggest manufacturing and energy companies in the nation, many of them effectively operating like banks by extending credit to other businesses via swaps, or borrowing heavily from big banks; none of that activity is recognized by investors or regulators as debt. It's the same maneuver that allowed Greece, for many years, to borrow from Goldman Sachs without the European Union noticing that it was deep in the hole—and by then both the Greek and European economies were in big trouble.

Not incidentally, major financial institutions profited heavily from the corporate swap business. Derivatives-dealing giants Goldman Sachs and JPMorgan Chase were both members of the Business Roundtable, and Morgan was especially vocal in demanding that Congress and the regulators give their corporate customers a free pass to trade in derivatives. By the beginning of 2013, the two firms would hold half the value of all derivatives deals held by banks; add Citibank and Bank of America, and it was 93 percent, representing $216 trillion in notional value.

Blythe Masters, head of commodities trading for JPMorgan Chase and chair of a major investment-industry advocacy group, became another key figure in the battle to kill the derivatives regulation. She had as much at stake as any player in the battle over derivatives in Dodd-Frank, having played an instrumental role in positioning JPMorgan as a leader in the burgeoning 1990s derivatives trade. Starting with Exxon, Masters had built an entire business model around allowing companies to effectively borrow without having to put aside substantial capital reserves.

Masters—whose investment-industry group would later hire Eugene Scalia to sue over Dodd-Frank limits on derivatives trading—claimed to the Senate Agriculture Committee that running companies' swaps through clearinghouses would in many cases be prohibitively expensive for the firms, "preventing them from managing risk and inhibiting their growth." Clearly, the real problem was that limits on corporate derivatives would kill the business she had built.

But corporate borrowers didn't want to give up the pipe, either. With the banks safely hidden offstage in the wings, the Coalition for Derivatives End-Users took up the crusade for its Dodd-Frank exemption, using the same argument Masters had made—in a much more sympathetic package.

Dodd-Frank passed with the offending provisions removed, and it became law. But Bopp and his posse didn't stop—they went back to Congress demanding additional exemptions from the regulations for the booming corporate trade in derivatives.

JUST LIKE JUDGES, MEMBERS of Congress like to have authoritative reports to consult, in dimensions big enough to cover their rear ends. The Chamber obliged by providing them with a strange study commissioned from an economics consulting firm that claimed Nobel Prize–winning economist Joseph Stiglitz as an adviser—which was news to Stiglitz. The study, from Keybridge Research, analyzed responses by seventy-four Chamber of Commerce and Business Roundtable members to questions about their use of derivatives.

"Keybridge Research did not participate in the design, sampling, implementation, or gathering of responses for this survey," the firm felt compelled to note in the study. The Chamber's consultants nonetheless confidently estimated that a 3 percent cash cushion on derivatives trades would lead to a $100 billion decline in cash flow for the S&P 500 and reduce capital spending by about $6 billion, leading to the loss of up to 130,000 jobs.

When Stiglitz and other economists mocked its findings, Keybridge distanced itself from its own research. "It was a hypothetical study," its president explained sheepishly, written at the request of a client—the U.S. Chamber of Commerce.

It fell to a few lonely outside experts—a finance professor from the Massachusetts Institute of Technology, a former Goldman Sachs executive—to point out the fatal flaw in the study's premise. The math assumed that the alternative to a 3 percent margin is a free ride for the companies trading in swaps. But that's not how the derivatives market actually works. Companies have to pay, one way or another, for the risk of their deals—it's just that before Dodd-Frank, those costs were buried in the price of the swaps. A derivative gone bad, as

AIG and JPMorgan Chase know all too well, is the costliest kind of penalty—for the companies and sometimes for the entire economy.

But by that point, the fictional math had already taken root. The Chamber organized another fly-in of executives to lobby Congress and explain how they used derivatives to hedge risk in a boring and unprofitable way and would suffer mightily if they had to set aside funds to insure their own bets in the market.

"Our members are united in one respect: they use derivatives to manage risk, not create it," was a line Bopp used repeatedly to describe the companies he represented. And for some of them, that was true. But many manufacturing, energy, and agricultural companies that use derivatives to hedge legitimate risks also play the market for their own financial gain or have financial divisions that realize gains on such trades.

To take one example, Chesapeake Energy is a member of the Chamber and its Coalition for Derivatives End-Users. It uses derivatives to hedge, protecting itself from fluctuations in energy prices, and it told regulators emphatically: "We don't speculate." Yet as it happily tells its shareholders, it also seeks to profit on such deals. And why shouldn't it?

Then there's Cargill, another Coalition for Derivatives End-Users member, which had members of Congress salivating over visions of mom-and-pop home cooking. "We offer customized hedges to help bakeries manage price volatility of their flour so that their retail prices for baked goods can be as stable as possible for consumers and grocery stores," Cargill lobbyist Jon Hixson told a House committee early in Dodd-Frank's formulation. "We offer customized hedges to help a restaurant chain maintain stable prices on their chicken so that the company can offer consistent prices and value for their retail customers when selling chicken sandwiches."

Dennis Kelleher, of Better Markets, calls the end-user sales pitch "motherhood, apple pie, bunnies and rainbows." Now step back from the lunch counter to see the bigger picture. Cargill is a huge player in the derivatives markets, so big that following Dodd-Frank's passage, it became the first nonbank to register as a dealer, which all companies trading in more than $8 billion in swaps must do. As Hixson's testimony suggests, the company is more than an end user. Other coalition members, such as GE Capital, Shell, BP, and Constellation Energy, are themselves significant players in the derivatives markets. Because they are not buying derivatives in volumes greater than their sizable assets, they hold themselves out as merely hedging—but they very much operate as players in the swap markets, just not ones that have to register with the CFTC.

In short: many of the "end users" were not in fact humble businesses merely looking to keep the lights on. They were—in the view of MIT finance professor John Parsons, who has twice warned Congress against exempting them from Dodd-Frank–related derivatives regulations—ideologues determined to restore the orgiastic glory of the pre-2008 over-the-counter derivatives market.

"They've been captured by this fringe group of people who believe that no regulation is better regulation," Parsons laments of the U.S. Chamber. "The terrible tragedy at the moment is that at the very time when we could use a good business lobby to help create a more secure marketplace, we're stuck with these insane loonies who will just block anything."

Businesses clamoring for open trading drowned out Parsons's warnings. It wasn't enough that Dodd-Frank exempted businesses from having to move their trades through clearinghouses or put up margins on their derivatives. The coalition subsequently persuaded a massive majority of members of the House to vote, twice, to have banking regulators simply not count the derivatives risk on companies' books in deciding how much capital they had to have on hand to operate safely. The bill also removed from the CFTC, SEC, and other regulators the power to ever make end users put up collateral to back up their swaps.

The exemptions would effectively override Dodd-Frank, allowing many habitual users of risky financial instruments to hide their activities almost entirely from outside view. As Parsons points out, that's how the shadow market in over-the-counter derivatives emerged in the first place: traders exploited an existing loophole and then successfully pressured Congress and the commission for further deregulation of the derivatives trade, until it grew into a $600 trillion–plus speculative market.

Yet preposterously, the House claimed in advancing the bill that restrictions on derivatives trading would increase, not diminish, risks to the economy. The same unfounded talking points, straight from the Coalition's agenda and research, echoed in doomsday letters from members of Congress to regulators.

Bopp's lobbying army made sure to enlist the chairs of congressional banking and agricultural committees to warn regulators that companies that were merely looking to transact business would be crippled by Dodd-Frank. Those regulators, in turn, knew full well that Congress controlled their agencies' budgets.

"If end-user transactions are subject to margin requirements, costs for consumers could increase, and end-users may divert working capital from activities that promote economic growth and job creation," wrote Representatives Frank Lucas (R-OK) and Spencer Bachus (R-AL), and Senators Debbie Stabenow (D-MI) and Tim Johnson (D-SD), relying on little more than the companies' claims that this was so. At the time, U.S. companies were sitting on an estimated $2 trillion in cash—hardly a job-creating use of those resources.

In the case of the CFTC, such pressure secured nonfinancial companies the exemption from oversight they had been seeking. Its original rule required registration and clearing for companies dealing in at least $1.5 billion in swaps a year. In the final rule, that baseline went up to $8 billion.

For the CFTC commissioners, there wasn't much point in putting out tough rules—they would just get slammed down anyway. To reiterate the words of former commissioner Bart Chilton, speaking while still in office: "We get to the point where we're so concerned about potential litigation risk that we beat things to death internally, and that either slows or stops important financial regulation rules from going forward."

To take an example: the CFTC had already acknowledged that limits on financial derivatives would impose costs on companies that used them—for instance, on airlines trying to protect themselves from fluctuations in the price of fuel. According to Chilton, the Chamber and members fighting the rules didn't elaborate, when given the chance to comment in public (and in private, in meetings with commission staff), on what those costs would actually be or how the commission might go about calculating them.

And yet when Scalia's lawsuit on behalf of the derivatives industry inevitably crashed in, it hammered the commission for its failure to tally the costs. "I'm convinced that that was their strategy all along," says Chilton. "They didn't want to provide information because they didn't want it to be used against them."

Chilton calls the strategy the Quadrakill. As he put it in a speech a few weeks after the securities industry filed suit to block derivatives regulation:

> First, if you don't like a bill, amendment or provision thereof, you try to defeat it with a vote. Just say, then vote, no (or nay, or whatever). If that fails, go to stage two. You can try to defund it through the appropriations process. If that doesn't work, there is stage three. This is where you can try to stop it, change it or delay it through the regulatory rulemaking process. If all of those things fail, you can go to DEFCON four: litigation. That's the D.C. Quadrakill: 1. kill bill; 2. defund it; 3. regulate it; and, 4. litigate it.

With Scalia, the Chamber added step 4a to the Quadrakill: litigate it, and set a precedent that will not only defang the measure in question but also preempt other regulation in the future.

The Dodd-Frank lawsuits kept coming, continuing to stab at technicalities. An SEC rule requiring companies to disclose payments to foreign governments for oil and gas drilling rights also got the Scalia treatment—this for a rule that the securities commission estimated would cost about $10,000 annually for each publicly traded company. The Chamber's lawsuit countered that revealing payments would result in "crushing competitive losses." It won that one too.

The CFTC's lawyers had better results in fortifying their rules against the assault. In 2013, when a Scalia lawsuit sought to block the CFTC from regulating mutual funds that held derivatives, federal appeals judges roundly rejected it.

Three years after Dodd-Frank became law, the paranoid caution that Bart Chilton described in writing the rules was finally paying off at the CFTC. Its careful rule-writing survived the threat of lawsuits. The understaffed agency was also keeping pretty close to pace on putting Dodd-Frank into effect. The same could not be said of the besieged SEC, which had missed most of its deadlines and proposed scarcely more than one in three of the new rules required by the law.

THE U.S. CHAMBER OF Commerce's fights to restrict shareholder democracy and to defend the right of nonfinancial companies to speculate using derivatives were obscure, technical battles slung out between lawyers and lobbyists. In public, the Chamber practiced the art of distraction, mounting a wildly histrionic campaign against the newly created Consumer Financial Protection Bureau (CFPB), charged under Dodd-Frank with assisting those most victimized by the mortgage meltdown and financial crisis: American consumers.

The bureau was the brainchild of Harvard consumer law expert Elizabeth Warren, who in a landmark 2007 essay for the journal *Democracy* unleashed a commonsense plea for a financial product safety commission. "Consumers can enter the market to buy physical products confident that they won't be tricked into buying exploding toasters," she memorably noted. "Consumers entering the market to buy financial products should enjoy the same protection." Warren had no shortage of horrendous financial products and features to point to, starting with the then-legal secret kickbacks to mortgage brokers who sold high-interest loans to unsuspecting borrowers.

As manifested in Dodd-Frank, the CFPB (or CFPA, for Agency, in its first iteration) had no exorbitant powers. It would simply constitute, for the first time, a single agency where staff would put consumers' needs front and center—something that was not a priority for banking regulators, whose prime directive was institutional safety and soundness. On behalf of the Federal Reserve, the CFPB would enforce updated and strengthened versions of laws that had for years protected the public in financial transactions, and it would educate consumers in plain English (and Spanish) about rights they never knew they had. Dodd-Frank added crucial pieces to the puzzle, including professional standards for mortgage sales (and a ban on kickbacks) and measures to make sure borrowers can actually repay their mortgages.

You'd think that industry would appreciate having an agency around that would police bad actors and encourage consumers to trust the products on which they spend their hard-earned money. As Warren worked to nurture the bureau to life, she made the case in a speech at Chamber of Commerce headquarters: "A cop on the beat looking out for consumers does not reduce the freedom or effectiveness of markets; rather, it permits honest competition to flourish. If you are one of the guys who don't use steroids when you play ball, then you don't want to compete against those who are juicing."

That would assume that honest and fair competition was what Chamber members—identities, as always, anonymous—subject to the CFPB's oversight actually sought. The evidence screamed otherwise. The bureau, popular with the public, was hardly immune from the Chamber's efforts to meddle. This time it took to both the courts and Congress to block the agency's ability to function.

On its website and in a blitz of D.C.-targeted advertising, the Chamber flung out a wildly exaggerated threat: "The CFPA would make a bad economy even worse. Help stop big government before it's too late." A TV ad showed a sleepless small merchant tossing and turning in bed, worrying about the fate of his business. Like other Chamber attacks on the agency, the ad cited a study from University of Chicago and George Mason University economists that found that it would have a harmful impact on the availability of credit to businesses and consumers.

That study, funded by the American Bankers Association, had just one problem: by the time it was published, the most aggressive part of the section of Dodd-Frank that created the bureau—the provision that would have empowered it to create stripped-down "plain vanilla" standards for financial products like mortgages, giving less profitable transactions an edge in the marketplace—was out of the picture in the House version of the bill and off the Obama administration's agenda. That didn't stop economists from factoring it into their research, or the Chamber from using it.

The Chamber's lobbying budget allowed for the laser targeting of key members. It spent $85,000 in 2011 for the lobbying services of a firm called Cyber Security Research Consultants, whose principal is Geoffrey Gleason. Its lobbying, according to Gleason's disclosures to the Senate, had nothing to do with hackers and their threats. Instead, a focus that year was the appropriations bill for financial services, which provided funds to operate the CFTC. The White House had sought $308 million to fund the CFTC's mandate to regulate the massive and chaotic market in derivatives. The House came back with a pitiful $172 million instead.

The CFPB should have been safe. It had been a central part of the Dodd-Frank bill in 2010 and was symbolic of the government's move toward financial reform. Congressional Democrats, wary that opponents would use the appropriations process to cut—or cut off—funding for the bureau, created a mechanism through which it would be funded directly from the Federal Reserve, at an estimated $329 million.

But in the summer of 2011, a House appropriations subcommittee short-circuited Dodd-Frank. In its budget for financial services, it included a measure that limited transfers from the Fed to the bureau to $200 million—a cut destined to severely hamper the bureau's ability to fight financial institutions' abuse of consumers. With that business done, Gleason continued to lobby on the so-called Volcker rule, which prohibits banks from gambling on speculative instruments, months after *it* had passed as part of the Dodd-Frank financial reform measure. The Chamber paid him an additional $119,000 for that work.

Why would the Chamber hire a "cyber research" agency to help it kneecap the CFPB? Gleason has refused to respond to questions, but his participation may have helped secure direct access to an influential member of the committee in charge. Before he hung out a shingle as a Washington lobbyist, his job had been as the liaison to the House Appropriations Committee for Frank Wolf (R-VA), a high-ranking member of that committee.

Representative Wolf needed the personal attention. In the battles over trucking regulation between the Clinton administration and safety advocates, he had sided with safety—and had pressed for an investigation that eventually led to the departure of transportation official George Reagle, whom Tom Donohue had so carefully cultivated as an ally. This time around Wolf sided consistently with the Chamber and opposed stronger regulation.

The Chamber's point man for these efforts was Tom Quaadman, VP of its Center for Capital Markets Competitiveness, whose previous experience included a stint as chief of staff to Staten Island congressman (and previously, New York City Council member) Vito Fossella. Before entering politics, Fossella had worked for the accounting giant Deloitte Touche, and in one of his stints on the House Financial Services Committee, in 2007, he earned the eternal gratitude of the securities industry by sponsoring a successful bill lowering fees on trades—saving $700 million for mostly high-volume traders, at the expense of taxpayers and the budget of the SEC, the industry watchdog whose work was funded in part by those fees.

When the Bush White House sought to charge similar fees on

commodities trades to help fund the CFTC, Fossella once again sided with the securities industry to oppose the move, loyally defending its privilege of getting a free ride at government expense. He warned fellow members of Congress, without substantiation, that fees "would reduce liquidity" in futures exchanges. The proposed fees never materialized, leaving the derivatives regulator's budget completely at the mercy of Congress—and funded by taxpayers instead of traders.

In the roller-coaster months leading up to the late summer 2008 collapse of Lehman Brothers, Fossella, as chair of a congressional task force on capital markets, preposterously blamed "overregulation" for the chaos in the credit markets and unleashed a proposal to, as he described it, "modernize a system to allow the markets to work to provide adequate investor protection, knowing full well that you're never going to eliminate risk from the system, and enhance and promote individual responsibility and good business practices." In short: to allow the financial markets to regulate themselves come what may—with a boost of cheap borrowing from the Fed, of course.

Before Fossella could release a threatened bill, his career screeched to a halt when a drunken driving arrest forced him into an admission that he had fathered a child with a woman who was not his wife. His chief of staff, Tom Quaadman, jumped to the U.S. Chamber, bringing Fossella's determination to deregulate with him.

While the CFPB's budget was ostensibly independent of Congress, the nomination of its director was not, and the unabashedly partisan Elizabeth Warren was out of the running as unconfirmable. But the Obama administration had no appreciably better prospects with its ultimate nominee, former Ohio attorney general Richard Cordray. Senate Republicans successfully filibustered Cordray's confirmation, forcing President Obama to make a maneuver known as a recess appointment to sidestep the Senate blockade.

It wasn't the only appointment the president was forced to make behind a wall of congressional opposition, that same day as Cordray's tapping by the president for his post. A Washington State Pepsi bottler and U.S. Chamber member, Noel Canning, sued to block the appointments, and the Chamber ultimately took the reins of the case as the appeals made their way to the Supreme Court. As a result of the Chamber-backed Noel Canning suit, the fate not only of the CFPB's leadership but also that of the rules it had painstakingly crafted following Dodd-Frank ended up in the hands of the justices— a court that under Chief Justice John Roberts has ruled in favor of the Chamber's position in more than two out of three cases.

Thanks to the maneuvers of Senate Democrats, Cordray was confirmed in the summer of 2013 by conventional means, as were the two NLRB nominees to replace those whom Hill Republicans had deemed objectionable, rendering the lawsuit moot. But the threat of the lawsuit, with the possibility that the Supreme Court could invalidate a year and a half of costly work—including important rules protecting borrowers and the mortgage market—continued to hang over the Consumer Financial Protection Bureau. In 2014, the justices unanimously ruled the NLRB recess appointments invalid, giving CFPB foes ammunition to challenge any rules advanced in Cordray's first months in office as well.

"There will be lots of lawsuits, lots of uncertainty about what the rules of the road are, and lots of taxpayer money wasted on things that potentially turn out to be invalid," warned Andrew Pincus, a partner at the lobbying firm Mayer Brown who received $660,000 from the U.S. Chamber in 2011, largely for his and one colleague's work attacking the CFPB.

OF COURSE, ANY UNCERTAINTY about the rules of the road was 100 percent intentional, inflicted by companies seeking to undo the amply clear will of Congress, the White House, and the regulators. Into the void it had helped to create, the Chamber heaved proposed alternatives to the CFPB that Congress had already rejected: a bipartisan panel, a budget at the mercy of Congress. In short, the independent bureau was to become just like the CFTC, an easy target for industry to manipulate.

As the fate of her creation lay in the hands of the Supreme Court,

Elizabeth Warren, now serving in the U.S. Senate, observed the war against consumer protection with horror and awe and noted that the U.S. Chamber of Commerce was at the center of the maelstrom. She described the arc of the assault to a group of liberal legal advocates. Step one: "Because of *Citizens United,* powerful interests have undue influence over elections and therefore over what legislation gets passed."

Step two moved the battlefield from Congress to the courts: "The Affordable Care Act case dramatically rewrites Congress's authority to legislate"—because while the Supreme Court upheld Obamacare, it also said that Congress could not write laws compelling consumer actions by individual members of the public.

Friendly judges at lower courts have played their part too. "The D.C. Circuit's aggressive approach to reviewing agency decisions means that some laws passed by Congress will, in effect, be neutered by a hostile court"—prime examples being the slew of lawsuits brought by the Chamber of Commerce. "And even if laws get passed and agencies can make their regulations stick, decisions to restrict access to justice mean that individual citizens may never be able to get in the door to exercise their rights in court."

The U.S. Chamber of Commerce had played a pivotal role in each of these fronts. Now it was on the verge of destroying the most concrete, direct, and popular reform to come out of the financial crisis. All it took was nearly bottomless funds to spend on campaigns, on lobbying, and on legal briefs—really, to buy the system itself.

CHAPTER 9

Why American Jobs Come Last

Clients: Manpower, Walmart, Coca-Cola

Shrinking paychecks, lower job security, an uncertain future: it's the lament of the American worker, twenty-first-century edition, whose median wages have settled back right where they were in 1979. About 6.9 million of us work part-time simply because we cannot find full-time employment, nearly double the number before the 2008 recession. Combined with the unemployed, ghost workers make up one in seven in the American labor force.

The reasons for these sorry trends aren't much of a mystery. Millions of middle-class U.S. jobs have moved overseas, with the help of trade agreements that open access to workers who cost a fraction of what Americans do. The shift has utterly altered how Americans work and how much we can expect to earn and save—an equation that a flood of inexpensive imported products and swelling consumer debt have not changed.

Since 1999 major companies have cut 3 million U.S. jobs, while adding 2.5 million overseas, where labor costs are cheaper. No outside economy has driven that upheaval more than China's. An analysis by the Economic Policy Institute, a labor-union-backed group, attributes the loss of 2.7 million U.S. jobs between 2001 and 2011 (2.1 million of them in manufacturing) to the trade gap between China and the United States.

Today, for every dollar's worth of goods the United States ships to

China, China sends four dollars in stuff back—a gap that continues to grow. The gulf is widened further by the Chinese government's currency manipulation, which keeps Chinese imports artificially cheap and U.S. exports costly.

It's no secret that China is waging war on the American economy. U.S. companies doing business in China feel the pain every time a patent gets stolen—sometimes openly, in the name of "indigenous innovation" by the Chinese government—or when they're shut out of Chinese government contracts, as they were until very recently. The U.S. Chamber of Commerce has rightly called foul on such moves.

But when it comes to the ways China treats its massive labor force, the Chamber's China affiliates have jumped behind enemy lines, promoting conditions that are optimal for U.S. companies doing business in China but worse than ever for workers there. That hurts not only Chinese workers but also those in the United States, who are forced to compete on the same playing field. And right now, thanks to advocacy by the Chinese franchise of the Chamber of Commerce, China is building the workforce of the future: an army of temp workers. Their fate is yours.

EVERY WEEK IN CHINA 125,000 people go to work as "associates" for Manpower. In the English-speaking world, we would recognize them as temp workers—hired by the agency, then sent out on assignments for a few months. They labor on assembly lines for IBM, Intel, Tyco, Hewlett-Packard, and other U.S. companies that have located production lines in China. The elite corps run air-conditioning systems, procure raw materials, and design molds for electronics manufacturing. Others, by the tens of thousands, piece together electronics, fabricate plastics, and clean components. The labor is cheap by U.S. standards, but not by as much as you might think. The hourly minimum wage for Shenzhen workers in 2013 was 14.5 yuan, or $2.37 an hour.

Just two years earlier, Manpower's army of laborers barely numbered fifteen thousand. Now, the temp giant—the company that might have hired you or your mother for a stretch when the household bank account ran dry—has more workers on the job in China than it does in the United States. "It's a matter of *when* China becomes our largest market," says Manpower CEO Jeff Joerres.

Darryl Green, who runs Asia operations for Manpower, describes the objective more precisely. "I would say in five years from now, we would like to have not 125,000 associates; we'd like to get up to in the millions," he says from his office in Japan. "The magnitude of the opportunity is stunning. It's huge. For us it's a market that we really need to be in, that the government would like us to be in, and it is fulfilling an essential social need."

Manpower is a corporate member of China's satellite of the U.S. Chamber of Commerce, called the American Chamber of Commerce, or AmCham, one of more than one hundred global Chambers now twinkling in economies around the world. They are not legal affiliates of the Washington organization, but they are certified by Chamber of Commerce headquarters on H Street and frequently collaborate with Washington, exchanging delegations to share intelligence, business opportunities, and strategies.

AmCham has had a foothold in China since it opened a Shanghai outpost in 1915 to lubricate trade that at the time was led by lamp oil and cigarettes. Capitalism had no place in China at midcentury, but in 1987 AmCham China returned to widen a trickle of market experimentation by the Chinese government into a torrent of opportunities for U.S.-based companies. Today AmCham South China, AmCham Shanghai, and AmCham Beijing, as well as the American Chamber of Commerce in China, all smooth the way for U.S. enterprises to thrive in China's peculiar state-run capitalism, in which one difficult local official can doom a foreign investor.

More than half the businesses surveyed by AmCham Shanghai complain that Chinese officials unfairly favor Chinese companies. Making things worse, the U.S. Foreign Corrupt Practices Act strictly forbids companies seeking to do business to make the customary gifts to officials. That doesn't stop some from trying: Daimler AG and

Control Components are among the companies that the Department of Justice and the SEC have fined for bribing Chinese officials.

Instead of making direct bribes, AmCham breaks out the open bar and practices the art of political seduction for which the U.S. Chamber is world famous. "We're here for companies to network, to share information, to take advantage of business services that aren't available elsewhere, and in particular to access the Chinese and U.S. governments on issues of common concern," promised past AmCham China chairman Emory Williams.

"What can AmCham do for you?" the Shanghai chapter's pitch asks prospective members. "AmCham can help you . . . lobby the government! Use AmCham Shanghai to speak directly to [Chinese] government entities on business issues." A single ticket to AmCham Shanghai's 2011 annual "government appreciation dinner," held in a ballroom festooned with American flags, cost nearly as much as a month's wages for a factory worker. And that was just to influence the hundred or so local officials in attendance. Sponsors included Exxon, Dow, Coca-Cola, Honeywell, and Citi.

The AmChams are U.S. companies' vehicle for realigning national business climates in their interests—by opening up labor markets, by slashing tariffs and other trade barriers, and, when deemed necessary, by buying their way in. Whether they're called the Cámara de Comercio (Colombia) or Kaubanduskoda (Estonia), global branches of the Chamber have lubricated their influence with cocktail parties and charity golf tournaments. The State Department and other government agencies rely on the AmChams as what former commerce secretary and U.S. ambassador to China Gary Locke called "their eyes and ears on the ground."

In some cases corporations interested in building business in a particular country would team up with the U.S. Chamber of Commerce to explore starting an AmCham, as a Westinghouse executive did in 1976 as his company secured a $150 million government contract to provide telecommunications services in Nigeria via balloons suspended ten thousand feet in the air. Clearly, this was a place where

U.S. business ought to establish a beachhead. In preparation for his trip to Lagos and on "temporary detail for the United States Chamber of Commerce," Westinghouse wrote the U.S. embassy there seeking "views on feasibility and desirability of establishing an American chamber of commerce in Nigeria."

In a meeting with State Department officials earlier that year, the Chamber had listed Nigeria as one of the nations where it badly wanted to establish an AmCham but had not yet succeeded. Among the other countries on the list were Kenya, Panama, and Sweden.

Henry Kissinger's State Department pushed the partnerships too, asking its embassies around the world to share success stories "about any particularly fruitful relationships and cooperative efforts that might be helpful to other [diplomatic] posts seeking closer working relationships with chambers in their areas." The cable noted that the State Department needed answers quickly, because several State officials would be attending the Chamber of Commerce's convention that April.

The State Department took the lead on particularly delicate diplomacy in Egypt, where U.S. companies had flocked at the invitation of President Anwar Sadat and sought to form a local chamber of commerce to concentrate their political influence. To inoculate against the threat of nationalist backlash from Egyptians—one cable from Cairo referred to it as "political sensitivity to organizations of U.S. corporations"—U.S. diplomats worked with the Chamber to establish a joint U.S.-Egypt Chamber of Commerce, with both American and Egyptian members. That was something of a ruse: the embassy made clear that the ambassador still sought to meet with the U.S. businesses privately, to "permit a candid exchange of views without running the risk of being overheard by Egyptian hosts."

Egypt wasn't the only place where locals lashed out at what they saw as imperialist incursions by foreign business with backing from the U.S. government. "In previous times one sent gunboats. Today, diplomats and money," the head of West Germany's trade union federation railed against the American Chamber in 1974, in remarks that the U.S. embassy in Bonn made sure to share with colleagues across the region. Accusing the Chamber of conspiring with German officials to reduce labor's power, he spat back: "The federal republic is no banana republic and colonialism is dead in Europe."

With steady support from Secretary of State Kissinger, whose team pressed for closer relations between local chambers and embassies, the AmChams rebuffed such dissent and remained an integral part of the U.S. diplomatic fabric.

And so it remains decades later, as WikiLeaks cables vividly revealed. In Nicaragua, the AmCham president teamed up with the son-in-law of opposition leader Violeta Chamorro to create a coalition that could topple leftist president Daniel Ortega in the 2011 elections. (It didn't work.)

In Egypt, the chair of the American Chamber frequently advised the U.S. ambassador on how to navigate business and political interests, both during and after his term at AmCham. Before stepping up to head the Egyptian-U.S. Chamber in 2003, Taher Helmy helped write the law privatizing many state-owned companies, then handled more than $3 billion in such deals through his own law firm. While he helmed the Egyptian Chamber, he also chaired a USAID-funded economic think tank that he co-founded with the son of President Hosni Mubarak. USAID proceeded to also give $4.2 million to the U.S.-Egyptian Chamber to build its network of Egyptian businesses.

In China, the relationship between the American Chamber and politicians was more distant and fraught. Chinese law officially recognizes only the national AmCham, but meanwhile South China and Shanghai AmChams have become in many ways the voice of the United States in their regions. The WikiLeaks diplomatic cables show the State Department routinely deferring to AmCham positions and member surveys on sensitive diplomatic issues, in particular China's penchant to steal U.S. intellectual property for its own firms and policies favoring domestic companies.

In South China and Shanghai, the AmChams even offer a special fast-track visa for employees of American companies who seek to travel to the United States, who then get virtually guaranteed approval from the U.S. consulate. And when China sought to pave the way for the establishment of nonprofit organizations, it was AmCham that handed a copy of the draft law to the U.S. embassy—not the other way around—and it was AmCham members who were invited to advise the Chinese government on the matter.

When the U.S. Chamber targets actions of the Chinese government it doesn't like, the echo is heard around the globe. In 2009 the Chinese government issued new rules that required companies that teamed up with government-run enterprises to share proprietary technology and give preferential treatment to Chinese enterprises. The companies were being enlisted against their will in China's quest, under the banner of "indigenous innovation," to become a global high-tech leader—with the help of intellectual property purloined from foreign corporations. U.S. business revolted. The U.S. Chamber's report rallying to the defense of its member companies defined the debate in Washington, including later hearings on Capitol Hill, with the chair of one House foreign affairs subcommittee, Representative Ed Royce (R-CA), crediting the Chamber with "sounding the alarm."

The Republican-controlled House would loyally and consistently defend the Chamber-defined agenda to protect U.S. interests in hostile Chinese territory, with far-reaching consequences for the American economy.

The Chamber's voice wasn't the only one in the mix; the Business Roundtable and high-tech companies also made pleas and threats to the Chinese government. By the middle of 2011 one particularly loathed set of Chinese rules, which effectively shut foreign firms out of government contracts, was gone.

But no act of the Chinese government so distressed AmCham members as its 2006 push to strengthen the laws protecting the rights of the vast and increasingly aggrieved workforce that made the nation's economic miracle possible. The National People's Congress proposed standard contracts between workers and employers and insisted that most Chinese workers have them. Manpower, an AmCham member that had until then limited itself to recruiting IT experts, executives, and the like, advised the Chinese government as experts on the staffing business. Other U.S. companies, including General Electric, were privately consulted by the Chinese government when the new law was just an idea in formulation.

China still being nominally a people's state, workers would win some rights in the contract law that U.S. workers would envy. Workers are to be consulted about work and safety rules, even if they are not in a labor union (and unlike American workers, most are). And employees are entitled to open-ended contracts, under which they can be terminated only with documented cause, and they must receive severance pay. AmCham South China, for one, "acknowledges and supports worker rights in China, including the right of employees to organize, join and participate in trade unions as recognized by both Chinese law and International Labor Organization conventions."

Even more radical from the point of view of American business was the Chinese government's proposed treatment of temporary workers. Under the law as initially proposed, temporary workers were supposed to be used only for jobs that are, well, temporary, and unskilled. But if the job became long term, temps were to have the right, after a year of labor secured through an employment firm, to a permanent position. In just 101 Chinese characters, China promised a new right to permanent employment.

If that wasn't bad enough from the AmCham members' perspective, another provision explicitly stacked the deck in favor of workers and to employers' disadvantage. As one English translation put it: "If an employer and any employee have a different understanding of the existence of the labor relation between them, the employee's understanding shall prevail."

AmCham and many of its more than thirteen hundred member companies in China responded to the proposed law with alarm. Left unchanged, the labor contract law would have made it much more difficult for companies to shed workers or to win labor disputes.

Already labor organizers in China were hounding U.S. companies to stop taking advantage of temporary workers and finding some success. In Beijing, KFC announced in 2006 that it would stop hiring agency workers and would begin hiring employees directly, after complaints from "temps"—one said he had been at KFC for eleven years—that they lost hours and pay with no notice or explanation.

The possibility that the new law could crack down on how multinational companies dealt with their workforces sent some AmCham members into a frenzy. When Chinese legal scholar Liu Cheng convened an invitation-only meeting of labor lawyers and scholars merely to debate the new rules, a group speaking for AmCham Shanghai stormed the meeting and promised to pull their business out of China. "They very openly threatened, as we in the West would say, capital strike," recounted labor organizer Ellen David Friedman, who was not at the meeting but received a detailed account from Cheng. "It was, 'We came to China because of the good environment for investment,' which means cheap labor and liberal terms of employment, 'So if you make it harder for us we're going to have no choice but to pack up and go elsewhere.'"

AmCham Shanghai later disavowed the action. But Cheng was so appalled that he wrote to the U.S. ambassador to China demanding an apology and expressing outrage at what appeared to be an attempt—through economic blackmail, no less—to interfere in China's sovereign right to establish its own laws. An apology never came.

AmCham Shanghai "really hopes that the laws cannot be enforced so that its members can maintain low price policy," Cheng told an audience at Harvard Law School in 2007, during a North American lecture tour that Friedman organized. "Otherwise, without the sweatshops providing them low-price products, they cannot make so much money! Laws with low cost of violation are paper tigers, which encourages the behavior of violations! The real purpose of AmCham Shanghai is to let labor laws be paper tigers forever!"

But if the Chinese AmChams were counting on the laws not being enforced, they made a fierce effort to alter the proposal all the same.

The AmChams massed forces against the rule that would have required companies to hire workers directly after a year—converting them at that moment from a temp to a permanent worker, with social and health insurance coverage. Comments submitted to the National People's Congress from James Zimmerman, vice-chair of AmCham China, pleaded to keep temp workers—known in China as "dispatch" laborers—in the mix.

> The form of dispatched labor is a form of allocating human resources in a market economy. . . . Outsourcing non-core duties . . . is a mature and flexible employment model that can reduce costs. Because dispatched labor has such positive values, the government should not ban it but guide and regulate it as a normal form of employment through laws and regulations so that it can better serve the needs of the socialist market economy.

The AmCham letter warned gloomily that restrictions on the use of temp laborers would prove costly to the Chinese economy and to the workers themselves, who would have fewer employment opportunities to choose from. At the time AmCham China's government affairs committee was chaired by an executive from IBM.

AmCham Shanghai weighed in too, in more alarmist fashion. In an awkward translation from the Chinese, it warned that "once the Draft comes into effect, unemployment amounting to hundred thousands of persons will be produced deliberately while the same amount of employment opportunities will be destroyed." ("AmCham Shanghai has never, and is not, lobbying against the proposed legislation," it later clarified in a statement. "The goal of our comments was to contribute to the government's development of a fair and effective employment contract.")

These letters, and similar missives from the Chamber's European equivalent and the Business Roundtable, appear to have carried more weight than comments submitted to the National People's Congress website by more than one hundred thousand Chinese. A second draft of the law allowed for the use of permanent freelancers—and comments were submitted privately, by invitation only. AmCham China was among those invited to comment on the revised law.

And so the course of history shifted. Under the final law, as AmCham China and its members requested, Chinese could legally work as permalancers, under contract to temp agencies but never entitled to a permanent job.

They are workers like thirty-two-year-old Yuan Mi Ju, who hails from Hunan and earns the minimum wage for Shenzhen, which in 2011 was 1,100 yuan a month, or about $175. Like thousands of other workers at a Merry Electronics plant in Shenzhen, which assembles cell phone speakers, earphones, and other audio parts for Nokia, Sony Ericsson, and Motorola, she found her job via a notice posted outside the factory. But the address listed wasn't for the plant where she now shows up five days a week. Instead, the flyer sent her to Xing Cheng, a so-called labor dispatch firm. She signed a contract for three years—not with Merry Electronics, as she initially believed, but with the agency.

"We are all a little bit surprised," she says, looking around at three other women who have also been hired out to the Merry Electronics factory and could be pulled out at a moment's notice. "For me, if there were such an opportunity, I would prefer to be a permanent worker. I would take it for sure, the stability."

Temp status diminishes workers' leverage against their employers, who are not their employers at all. Deng Shi Ping has worked at the plant since 2008 and watched in amazement a year later as temps started replacing permanent workers like him; they quickly became the majority of workers at the Merry Electronics plant. He estimates that of the nearly eight thousand workers in his factory, three out of four are temps—paid the same wage as the much smaller number of permanent workers, which is unusual for Chinese temps, but without the health or other social insurance that permanent workers receive. And, of course, they have no job security.

In 2010 hundreds of temp workers at the Merry Electronics plant went on strike and thronged into the streets of Shenzhen in their white work coats. They won a 10 percent salary increase—but their jobs can still vanish in a moment.

"I would never sign a contract if it was from a dispatch company," Deng avers. But he understands why Merry Electronics has turned to temp labor: because it can. "The company saves money with dispatch workers," he notes. "When there is a low season, they can just let them go. They can also let them go without any reason in times of strike. And they don't have to pay for their insurance."

Even after the new law was in place, U.S. companies in China continued to complain of the burdens of paying for social benefits and the difficulty of firing Chinese employees: more than half of companies surveyed by AmCham China in 2008 said these factors had a negative impact on their businesses. They needed help.

The bad news for the workers presents a golden opportunity for Manpower. In 2011 Manpower took over REACH HR, a Chinese firm that supplies these workers to factories in Guangdong province, where Shenzhen is located, and began to help U.S. and European companies set up shop all over the mainland. It now trains workers on behalf of its clients, just as Manpower does in the States, and sends them to work.

"When the Labor Contract Law came into effect, now all of a sudden this looks like a market that may become more interesting for us," says Jeff Joerres. The Milwaukee temp labor giant is now on course to take the place of the Chinese government as the middleman between companies and their workers. In Deng Xiaoping's People's Republic of yore, regional labor councils sought to make sure that enough bodies were in place and prepared to carry out assigned tasks in factories and other places of work.

But in the heaving commerce that drives the new China, legions have come of age in a more dynamic but far less secure economy. As demand for workers mushroomed, so did an undergrowth of entrepreneurs: small and often shady local operations that charged workers for their services and often left them stranded without benefits. In many cases, according to trade unions, the temp firms were run by friends and family members of the government agencies in charge of overseeing employment and benefits. This is the scruffy native market Manpower seeks to conquer.

In Shenzhen's industrial zones, signs appear every few feet— printed or hand-painted, on the pavement, tacked to doors and the sides of buildings, propped up against streetlight poles—advertising labor opportunities. The signs promise to provide workers with jobs in nearby factories that will pay them from 5.5 to 7 yuan an hour, or roughly one dollar.

At Manpower, workers' two-year contracts bind them not to a particular factory, but to Manpower itself. Whenever they are not on assignment, they earn a minimum wage of about $200 a month. Manpower allows that more than two out of three of its temp workers would actually like to be in a permanent position. But employers are typically another story. They prefer to hire as demand surges and let workers go when the orders slow.

Until 2008 China's businesses hired temp workers at their own peril. Officially, hiring such employees was against the law. Now temp workers keep China's factories thrumming. Estimates range wildly depending on who is doing the counting, but one generous count cited by a government labor official puts it around 27 million, or about 8 percent of the workforce.

Andreas Lauffs is an attorney whose team at the firm Baker & McKenzie has advised Apple, Microsoft, Qualcomm, Kraft, and other large multinational companies on the intricacies of employing workers in China. (It's the same firm where Egypt's Taher Helmy is a partner.) He's from Germany and isn't surprised that U.S. companies have had the hardest time swallowing the 2008 labor law. What China did, in essence, was insist that companies doing business in China allow their workers rights that European companies have long granted to theirs.

"For Europeans, the Chinese law is not so unusual," says Lauffs.

"They're used to employee consultations, used to the statutes not allowing people to be fired just at will, the company having to produce certain statutory grounds [for terminating employees] and being stuck in some cases with a large workforce." They may not have appreciated having China yank away a major advantage to doing business in Asia, but nor was the setup wholly alien. By contrast, American companies, he says, "find it very difficult to do business in China."

Now temp labor gives them an out. U.S. companies with operations in Asia had surely noted developments in Japan, which in 2004 allowed manufacturers for the first time to hire temps from agencies as a way to work around strict laws protecting employees from dismissal. Four years later one in three of all workers in Japan were temps—and Sony, Toyota, Mitsubishi, and Mazda were among the companies that shed tens of thousands of those workers that year.

In China, big companies now will routinely bring all their workers to a dispatch company, have them sign contracts with the agency, and then continue to use them in the factory.

Coca-Cola won a 2009 award for corporate social responsibility from AmCham Shanghai, not long after the U.S. Chamber honored its China division for international community service for refurbishing a village. But according to news reports and student activists who went undercover as temp workers at Coca-Cola plants, the company was also a serial abuser of temp labor. Specifically, they charged, a Coke plant in southwestern China dismissed employees en masse from its distribution operation, then rehired them via a temp agency that Coca-Cola controlled, at a lower salary. Coca-Cola has not responded to the allegation.

Another company that has turned to temp labor is Foxconn—the manufacturing behemoth that produces and assembles components for Apple and other consumer tech companies. In Beijing a company called Beijing Xinbao Labor Dispatch advertises Foxconn as one of the employers it recruits for. For a 200-yuan service fee, workers are promised a two-year contract, a spot in a dorm, and up to 1,700 yuan a month.

Like Deng Shi Ping at Merry Electronics, corporate adviser Andreas Lauffs has watched as employers have turned over entire factories to temps hired from agencies. At that point, the employer's legal responsibility to the workers ends; so does its obligation to provide health and social insurance.

Lauffs's clients may not share his opinion, but he thinks employers have gone beyond the law's intentions in turning their factories over to the temp firms. "There's too much dispatch labor going on," comments Lauffs. "Too many workers don't have employment contracts or employment protection. Dispatch labor should be limited to certain exceptional situations." It's also supposed to be used only for unskilled jobs, but labor groups report that many of the temp workers are being hired for positions that require technical expertise. He says the law is pretty clear: all employees should be directly employed by the company to which they're providing service. The opposite is now happening, and Lauffs blames a fuzzy law. "Labor dispatch exploded," he says, "and now it's almost out of control."

Manpower, meanwhile, is charging ahead with its plans to become China's leading broker of human labor. Its business in China grew 80 percent in 2010. The following year, Manpower acquired one of the more reputable operations in Guangzhou, REACH HR, which hires out tens of thousands of temp factory laborers to assemble products for Chinese and American companies. The company has zeroed in on manufacturers' need for assembly-line workers. Says CEO Joerres: "We have a test that will assess the person's ability to do repetitive work for long periods of time and maintain quality. I've taken the test, and I'm a disaster."

REACH HR's head office is located in the Tianhe district of Guangzhou, surrounded by banks and bond and insurance companies. Its office on the second floor is dark and locked because the company had outgrown the space: its nearly five hundred employees now work in a large cubicle farm one floor up. Chinese pop blares from the PA system as lunchtime comes to an end—"cheerful music," says Nikki Gao, the commercial director of Manpower China, to wake and energize napping employees.

Temp work in China is in its infancy. Just one worker out of every hundred works for a company like Manpower; in the United States, the rate is nearly double that. But that already adds up to tens of millions of workers in China, and their ranks are growing each year, in a nation where workers not long ago ruled, at least theoretically. Now the government has put the needs of businesses first and turned the lives of Chinese workers into something unmistakably American: insecure and moldable to the needs of their employers.

IN PRINCIPLE, THE CHAMBER has stood up for investment in the American economy. In the depths of the recession spurred by the 2008 financial crisis, working with a president it didn't especially like, the usually anti-intervention, tax-unfriendly Chamber of Commerce became a vocal advocate for the $831 billion stimulus package. Said Donohue, in the face of jeers from some Republicans in Congress: "We're going to support this program because we need the money in that economy." Needless to say, members like earth-moving equipment company Caterpillar would do quite well too.

Still, the Chamber unsuccessfully fought key provisions in the bill, including fast-track environmental review for stimulus-funded projects. It also opposed a "Buy American" rule that required any public works projects on government buildings to use only iron, steel, and other manufactured materials made in the United States. Its hostile stance put the Chamber squarely in opposition to the U.S. steel industry—and to ensuring that the money spent on the stimulus spurred domestic manufacturing jobs.

The talk was tough. Chris Braddock, who ran procurement policy for the Chamber, told Agence France-Presse that Buy American was an economic death wish: "Since 95 percent of the world's consumers live outside the United States, American workers would be the first to suffer as 'Buy American' provisions trigger retaliation by other countries—that is, 'Buy German,' 'Buy Chinese,' and so on."

What Braddock and the Chamber didn't say as they loudly decried "Buy American" was that China actually *did* already have a Buy Chinese program, on a much larger scale than the Obama administration sought. Starting in 2006 China explicitly gave preferences to Chinese businesses in its government contracts—deals for buying goods, from airplanes to office furniture, estimated to be worth as much as $200 billion every year. Local Chinese governments had already released catalogs of products that government officials could purchase, and by the end of the year Beijing had announced it was creating a national list. Almost all the companies on the list were Chinese, and the products were a direct assault on some of the very goods U.S. businesses might hope to provide, including computer hardware and software, office equipment, communications technology, and energy devices.

So why not the same treatment for U.S.-made goods in America, insisting on home-grown supplies for government purchases under the stimulus program? Because breaking into China appeared to be more important to the Chamber than bolstering the manufacturing market at home.

U.S. COMPANIES HAD SOUGHT to enter into the business of providing goods and services to the Chinese government, sans any offensive obligation to hand over their intellectual property. The "Buy American" stimulus program directly threatened that diplomatically sensitive pursuit, among other privileges U.S. companies pursued in China. In 2011, an agreement between President Obama and Premier Hu Jintao broke through, paving the way for U.S. business to win Chinese government contracts.

U.S. companies' quest for expanded business opportunities in China also fueled the Chamber's vocal defense of China's mightiest form of U.S. job-killing protectionism: its deliberate devaluation of its currency, the yuan. The U.S. Chamber was among the business groups that killed prospects for a popular bill in Congress that would have allowed the imposition of tariffs on currency manipulators, including China, to help counter the effects. It argued, with good reason, that the likely result would be Chinese retaliation. But it can't be forgotten that a devalued yuan serves as a boon to U.S. companies manufacturing in China, which get to produce goods cheaply as a result.

The fact that China already had thrown a blanket of protectionism around its own economy didn't enter the conversation. Late in 2009, as the Democratic House considered a boost to stimulus spending, the Chamber backed the bill but again objected loudly to the Buy American provision.

"The question is, are we going to become more protectionist?" Donohue asked on Fox Business Network. "If you look in this stimulus bill, there's more Buy America. Well, that's great. What happens when all those other countries say buy home and don't buy America? We're the largest exporters in the world and this can really hurt us."

In the end, the Chamber's objections to Buy American and to environmental reviews weighed a whole lot less than the $100 billion that the stimulus would push into business opportunities for government contractors. The final stimulus bill proffered a double win for the Chamber: an enormous subsidy from the federal government for the companies that would supply the machinery for the big U.S. rebuild—with a Buy American provision so scaled down it posed little threat to members with interests in China.

Chamber chief lobbyist Bruce Josten wrote to members of the Senate urging them to back moving the stimulus bill to a vote, which required the support of sixty of its members.

But the White House wouldn't forget the Chamber's attempts to undermine the vital Buy American elements of the stimulus. During the 2010 elections, as the U.S. Chamber threw tens of millions of dollars into attack ads against Democrats, even President Obama was drawn to pose an incendiary question: could some of the dues payments from international chamber members be finding their way into the vicious campaigns to elect Republicans to Congress?

"One of the largest groups paying for these ads regularly takes in money from foreign corporations," the president said in the heat of election season. "Groups that receive foreign money are spending huge sums to influence American elections, and they won't tell you where the money for their ads comes from."

Obama's obvious reference to the U.S. Chamber's political spending was prompted by a report from the liberal think tank Center for American Progress that found that dues payments from AmCham members and other foreign companies involved with the Chamber made their way into the U.S. Chamber's general fund—the same fund from which it financed its record-breaking 2010 spending on attack ads and other political warfare against incumbent Democrats. Since foreign contributions to federal elections are verboten, here we had a U.S. president, on the eve of an election where the Chamber was poised to spend heavily to defeat his party in Congress—and therefore his ability to advance his legislative agenda—accusing the organization of an illegal conspiracy to sway a U.S. election.

The Chamber countered that it kept all international funds strictly segregated from political accounts—but Obama and the Center for American Progress did have a point. The nonprofit organization does not have to account for its own finances in any great detail, and any funds it takes in from foreign nations could, at least theoretically, free up other dollars for political warfare.

The Chamber told *Politico*'s Ben Smith simply that "we have a system in place" to prevent foreign funding for the Chamber's "political activities" in the United States.

NONETHELESS, MANY FOREIGN NATIONS have a stake in the Chamber's success. As CEO of the U.S. Chamber, Tom Donohue flies all over the world to crack open markets for U.S. businesses and urge on the AmChams as they do battle with the scourges of globe-trotting businesses seeking inexpensive labor—local corruption, bureaucracies, protectionism, and attempts by governments to expand the rights of workers. He's an unappointed ambassador who portrays himself as an honest broker above the political fray. "Unlike other voices in our country, we don't play politics with a commercial and strategic relationship of this importance," he told a Shanghai audience in 2011.

But the Chamber's approach to issues of corruption in the United States is another story. On Capitol Hill, the U.S. Chamber's Institute for Legal Reform has gone on an offensive to eviscerate the Foreign Corrupt Practices Act (FCPA), a law that prohibits U.S.-based companies from bribing foreign officials.

Like the campaign finance regulations that the Chamber has so aggressively worked to reverse, the FCPA grew out of a surge of post-Watergate investigative fervor on Capitol Hill. In the mid-1970s, the SEC and a congressional subcommittee unveiled disturbing and outright embarrassing examples of U.S. companies paying big bribes to foreign governments to win business opportunities. United Brands and Lockheed Martin were among the companies caught greasing their way into deals. Many had covered up their activities with bogus bookkeeping.

Back when the bill was under debate in 1977, the Chamber sent a staff associate to testify in opposition. Voluntary disclosure to the SEC, he assured Congress, already sufficed. Without heed to such objections, the Carter-era antibribery act became the bane of U.S. companies seeking to stretch their footprint in emerging markets, especially in Latin America, Asia, and the then Soviet Union, where corruption was one of the few things an adventurous businessman could count on.

Where the United States led, other forward-looking governments followed. In 1997 the Organisation for Economic Co-operation and Development (OECD), an international alliance of which the United States is a member, issued its Convention on Combating Bribery of Foreign Public Officials in International Business Transactions. Six years later the United Nations followed suit to combat "an insidious plague" with its own Convention Against Corruption, which requires signatories (the United States and China included) to make bribery of domestic and foreign government officials a prosecutable crime.

Under the Bush administration, the U.S. Department of Justice began ramping up its prosecutions of FCPA violators. Of those there was no shortage, and many U.S. companies appear to have been caught by surprise by the sudden rise of criminal cases against them.

There's a reason Mercedes SUVs are standard-issue government cars in countries all over the world: DaimlerChrysler set up kickback schemes to bribe officials in at least twenty-two nations to secure its place as an official vendor. In Mexico, Tyson Foods bribed government veterinarians to certify that meat was safe for export and executives put their wives on the company payroll. Kellogg Brown & Root and partners in a joint venture bribed the Nigerian government to secure natural gas facilities worth more than $6 billion. Kellogg agreed to pay a $402 million criminal fine.

All these cases and hundreds more have been prosecuted by the Justice Department under the FCPA in the past decade. The Chamber's Institute for Legal Reform resolved to put an end to that. In 2011, it hired former U.S. attorney general Michael Mukasey to lobby Congress to neuter the law. And it set out to create loopholes big enough that they could legitimize many transactions that would otherwise have been prosecuted.

The Chamber's wish list for the FCPA stood to undermine much that the OCED and UN had been working toward in their resolutions barring corruption of government officials. The OCED had made fighting corruption a priority after economists found ample evidence that it hurt the economic growth of the countries it sought to aid. The president of the World Bank called corruption a "cancer" on nascent economies that had to be eradicated. In 2000 Harvard economist Shang-Jin Wei estimated that if low-corruption Singapore ended up with the level of graft of high-corruption Mexico, it would be the equivalent of a 50 percent tax on Singapore.

Of course, that tax would be largely borne by the local economy and small businesses, for which graft represents a large share of earnings. When corruption gets entrenched enough, it's like goo in the gears of an economy, weighing it down. Left largely unsigned are global companies that can relocate at will, moving on to new territory when the waters are poisoned, and spending relatively small sums to secure their own market position.

To big U.S. corporations, bribery is no obstacle. Their problem is laws that penalize the practice—and that therefore give U.S. companies a disadvantage in international markets when they are competing with less ethical competitors writing checks. Those were fewer in recent years, what with the 140 nations now signed on to the UN convention. Nonetheless it was in the name of market competitiveness that in February 2012 the Chamber and its Institute for Legal Reform led a parade of trade organizations seeking to influence the State Department and the SEC's promised new guidance on the law—the Obama administration's guidelines for interpreting regulations.

Their letter to the two administration officials in charge of FCPA enforcement, Lanny Breuer at the Justice Department and Robert Khuzami at the SEC, stressed that the business groups were merely asking for "clarification" on what exactly they meant when they ordered firms not to bribe a "foreign official." Would payments to a sovereign wealth fund be okay? And did you, SEC and State Department, really want to hold parent companies liable for the actions of their overseas subsidiaries?

As the Institute for Legal Reform laid out in its blueprint, it sought to exempt from the FCPA any enterprise with less than 50 percent government ownership, and to only include entities that performed "governmental or quasi-governmental functions." That would open the door to exchanges of funds between U.S. companies and foreign officials that until now had been barred as verboten bribery. The Chamber further demanded that U.S. government regulators spell out every possible exception and enforce only violations that had been explicitly delineated.

Also on the Chamber's agenda was an exemption for international subsidiaries of U.S. companies, and protections of companies from liability where rogue employees broke the law. The exemptions it sought were far-reaching.

But for companies like Walmart, already knee-deep in scandal, nothing short of repealing the FCPA would have let them off the hook. Just weeks after the Chamber's bald plea to the Obama administration to open the door to global graft, a devastating *New York Times* investigation detailed Walmart's extensive bribery of Mexican officials to secure permits to open stores south of the U.S. border.

When the retailer's U.S. lawyers got wind of the Mexican subsidiary's payoffs, they dispatched investigators, who found that the Mexican company officials had sought to cover up the scheme. The lead investigator determined that the payoffs had likely violated both U.S. and Mexican laws. But instead of investigating further or notifying authorities in either country, Walmart headquarters in Benton, Arkansas, pulled the plug on the inquiry. The Department of Justice subsequently launched an investigation into possible FCPA violations.

The article put a public spotlight on the U.S. law that Walmart had clearly, badly broken—and on the U.S. Chamber's campaign to eviscerate it. Walmart had two members on the board of the Institute for Legal Reform, which had taken the lead on defanging the FCPA. (When two Democratic members of Congress wrote a letter to Tom Donohue seeking details about company officials' role in the Institute for Legal Reform project, Walmart responded: "Walmart has never lobbied on the FCPA.")

And Walmart wasn't alone. The staffs of Representative Henry Waxman (D-CA) and Representative Elijah Cummings (D-MD) combed the board memberships of the Institute for Legal Reform and found that eight out of its fifty-five board members were affiliated with companies that had settled with the U.S. government over allegations of FCPA violations. Another six had undergone investigations.

One prime example: Johnson & Johnson, which in 2011 had

agreed to pay a $21.4 million criminal penalty after subsidiaries in Greece, Poland, and Romania paid health care providers to induce them to buy their products. It separately acknowledged paying kickbacks to the government of Iraqi president Saddam Hussein under the UN Oil for Food Program, to secure contracts to provide humanitarian supplies.

Even while the Chamber and the Institute for Legal Reform sought to narrow the reach of the law, their own member companies committed violations that would have been permitted under the rewrite it sought. The CEO of Portland-based metal recycler Schnitzer Steel serves as vice-chair of the U.S. Chamber's board. The SEC alleged the company under the CEO's predecessor had paid its way into business with government-owned steel mills in China and South Korea, through cash payments to plant managers that it booked as "commissions," "gratuities," and such.

Under a settlement with the SEC and a deferred prosecution agreement with the Department of Justice, the company and its Korean subsidiary had to pay out $15 million in disgorgement, fines, and interest. If the Chamber had had its way, unless it was evident that the U.S. corporate parent was actively involved in the scheme, actions by foreign subsidiaries like Schnitzer's would have moved out of the corruption law's stunted reach.

Much like U.S. companies that moved operations overseas to find cheaper, more pliable labor, the Chamber of Commerce traveled abroad to open opportunities unavailable at home—to play by rules long ago deemed unacceptable by Congress and the American people, in places free of the increasing responsibilities U.S. businesses carried at home to their own citizens.

The nation that the Chamber sought to build in the United States—without constraints on greenhouse gas emissions, clean air enforcement, or obligations to provide health insurance to employees—was within reach. If it couldn't build such an employer's paradise in America, then friendlier nations, asking only for piddling graft payments as the price of entry, would readily do.

CHAPTER 10

With Enemies Like These: Why the Bad-for-Business Tea Party Is Good for the Chamber of Commerce

How do you solve a problem like Justin Amash? The congressman from western Michigan, elected in 2010, is steeped in the Tea Party, the purest of pure libertarians in Congress. Representative Amash has nothing good to say about the business lobbyists who grovel before him seeking favors. While bracing for a business-funded challenge in the 2014 Republican primary, he mocked the K Street business establishment to a South Carolina conservative club: "We want capitalism unless our friends are involved, in which case we don't want capitalism—we want corporate welfare."

Representative Amash wants to see massive cuts to defense spending. In a vote on the Keystone XL Pipeline, the tar-sands-oil conduit from Canada championed by the U.S. Chamber, he abstained because the bill exempted its operator from approvals other pipeline companies have to obtain—special treatment anathema to the libertarian credo. Amash is even against the back-to-basics Common Core curriculum beloved by the National Chamber Foundation, and for that matter any federal involvement in schools.

Oh, and he was a ringleader of the 2013 federal government shutdown and stonewall on the debt ceiling, a doomed quest by Republican radicals to repeal the Affordable Care Act. Party strategist Karl Rove has singled out Amash as the face of the enemy within the ranks—so committed to libertarian principle that, in Rove's words, "unless my side has something that's completely 100% perfect, I'm voting with the bad guys."

The clash of Republican civilizations came to a head with the ugly and embarrassing Washington shutdown, a moment when the Chamber of Commerce appeared to have been felled by a raging virus within the body of its GOP host. Renegade Republican members of Congress like Amash—unmanageable, angry, defiantly unreasonable, and always wildly ideological—had, over the Chamber's stern objections, brought governing to a halt and endangered the financial health of every business in the nation.

At the toxic root of the shutdown that began on October 1, 2013, was a nonsensical Republican-sponsored provision the House seeded into the federal budget, which would have defunded the Affordable Care Act. The Senate rightly refused to take up the poisonous measure as part of its $986 billion spending bill. The House in turn refused to remove it—and held out until Congress's legal authority to fund the government had expired.

The Chamber of Commerce—no fan of the Affordable Care Act, and leading patron of Republican Party leadership—understood and railed against the utter folly of the standoff. Not only did legions of federal workers and their families suffer the effects of unpaid furlough; removing government spending from the economy, even briefly, produced dramatic ripple effects in private-sector activity and profit. A looming debt default that could only be cured with an additional act by Congress to raise the nation's borrowing limit—action virulently opposed by Amash and his fellow radicals—only deepened the Chamber's gloom.

Still, while the Chamber's worry was obvious, its most fervent public expression came in the form of an anodyne letter to Congress warning, "It is not in the best interest of the employers, employees or the American people to risk a government shutdown that will be economically disruptive and create even more uncertainties for the U.S. economy."

With the stakes so high for its members, why didn't the Chamber of Commerce use its mojo to simply shut down the Tea Party circus? It was a question on the minds of many in Washington during the shutdown. "If Wall Street/Chamber so freaked out about the debt ceiling why aren't they carpet bombing tea party districts with issue ads?" tweet-wondered Glenn Thrush of *Politico*.

For one thing, because the Chamber is even more freaked out by the prospect of losing Republican control of the House of Representatives. It might find Tea Party antics dangerously maddening, but what was the alternative? Running primary challenges against incumbents like Amash runs the risk of handing formerly safe Republican seats to Democrats, if the incumbent survives the contest. Run ads in the primary against the eventual victor, and all you do is stockpile fuel for attacks against your party's nominee in the general election. The phenomenon became familiar to Republican political strategists during the messy 2012 presidential primaries, where Super PAC–funded attacks on Mitt Romney poisoned the minds of voters. A Democrat winning Amash's long-Republican seat, once held by Gerald Ford, was not out of the question: shortly after the government shutdown, a plurality of voters in that district told pollsters for MoveOn.org they would vote for a Democrat instead of Amash in 2014; the results of the survey were much the same for other Tea Party incumbents across the country. Such sentiment would fade as the shutdown receded into dim memory, and under the eye of more objective pollsters, but the risk of backlash remained.

The Chamber has shackled itself to the Republican Party—a party whose base of voters wants *more* defiance, more rebellion, more Tea Party. By a 54 to 40 percent majority, party voters told pollsters in the summer of 2013 that they want the GOP to move further to the right. And just about half of all voters in Republican primaries identify as Tea Party. The Chamber had long ago thrown in its lot with the Republican family, and it was going to have to make peace with its crazy younger brother.

In any case, the Chamber's own scorecards showed that the Tea Party faction was not doing much to damage the legislative agendas most important to top-shelf Chamber members. For 2011—the year sixty-six House Republicans refused to get behind the debt ceiling deal that John Boehner had hashed out with the Obama administration—the average GOP rating from the Chamber of Commerce stood at 95 percent out of a possible 100, higher than it had been in years. In 2012 the average was 92 percent. For every obstructionist vote on government spending, most Tea Party representatives could be counted on to deliver many more in favor of specialized business interests—for shale oil extraction in Alaska, for a ban on coal industry regulation, for repeal of a tax on medical devices, and on and on.

In 2012 as always, any candidate with a *How They Voted* score of 70 or higher got an automatic endorsement—a "Spirit of Enterprise" award—from the U.S. Chamber. Just 5 of the 240 or so GOP House members didn't make the cut. One was Texas libertarian granddaddy Ron Paul, on his way to retirement. Another was Todd "legitimate rape" Akin, who was so toxic, despite his 88 score on the Chamber's litmus test, that it refused to spend money to aid him in his Senate bid, even though his loss would keep a Democrat in a Missouri Senate seat that could have turned red.

By the Chamber's own standards, the vast majority of Republicans, including the Tea Party class of 2010, were reliable votes. That included wild man Justin Amash. In his first term, Amash's record with the Chamber was dinged by votes against funding transportation and the Export-Import Bank—those would be "corporate welfare," in the world according to Amash. The congressman also rejected as unlibertarian a bill requiring information sharing between business and government to ward off cyberthreats—and not least, a 2011 measure to raise the debt limit, a vote in which he and other Tea Partiers defied Republican leadership. Even so, Amash received his very own Spirit of Enterprise award from the Chamber of Commerce, with a passable 75 on his scorecard.

In the summer of 2013, Amash also got the best gift a politician could receive from the U.S. Chamber of Commerce: money, a generous $5,200 campaign donation from the Chamber's newly appointed chair, Steve Van Andel, the maximum allowed from an individual under federal law. The eldest son of former Chamber chairman Jay Van Andel, Steve Van Andel is also the chair of Amway, a powerful force in western Michigan business. Amway president Doug DeVos topped his business partner: in the multilevel marketing spirit, ten members of the DeVos clan made big donations to Amash, and DeVos wrote a letter soliciting contributions from his networks. Also on the DeVos/Van Andel gift list for 2014 was Michigan Tea Party congressman Bill Huizenga, who received an 80 on the Chamber's voter guide.

Like Van Andel and DeVos, the Chamber of Commerce has sought to cultivate mutually beneficial relationships with hard-line ideologues in its midst. "Tea Party—I'm not really sure what that is," mused Donohue at a Washington talk in 2013, just days after the government shutdown ended. "We think many of these issues that some of these folks have raised are really important issues: what are we spending, what is our revenue stream, what are we doing with health care, what's going on in this country. But we do believe to advance these issues that putting the country's whole financial system at risk is not a good idea." These were the conciliatory words of someone who differed on tactics, not on principles.

The real action in 2014 would come in the Senate. In 2013 Democratic Senate majority leader Harry Reid blunted the power of extremist-obstructionists like Senator Ted Cruz (R-TX) by unleashing the so-called nuclear option—allowing Senate measures to the floor with a simple majority instead of a three-fifths vote.

Now that majority controlled the U.S. Senate, a body only five seats away from Republican control—nothing that $50 million or so couldn't buy.

AMASH AND HIS TEA Party brethren make an important point—and maybe it's one that will now be heard: big business lobbyists pick winners and losers in the economy all the time. Most of all, they skew the game in favor of entrenched incumbents, at the expense of new players, technologies, and ways of doing business. When a constituent urged the congressman to bring down the cost of health care, he replied: "The people who come to me and ask for regulations the most are big corporations. They want to limit competition, want to drive out smaller competitors who have fewer employees, so they can monopolize the market and have fewer choices out there."

The U.S. Chamber is trapped in a gilded enclosure of its own making. For an organization dedicated to the promotion of free markets, its big-money-fueled political warfare, funded by industries with much at stake in the status quo, has a paradoxical effect: it crowds out efforts by business to evolve and find opportunity in healthier, more socially necessary practices.

The climate change showdown is just the most notorious example, but others abound, and the member defections sparked by the Chamber's atavistic opposition to greenhouse gas controls were not the last. In 2013 the Swedish construction giant Skanska quit the Chamber in protest of a Chamber-backed network, called the American High-Performance Buildings Coalition (AHPBC), "a unified voice of manufacturers and designers of green-building solutions" organized by the American Chemistry Council.

The AHPBC, a literal Astroturf operation, took root as the U.S. Green Building Council was embarking on an upgrade to LEED, the industry standard for environmentally sustainable construction widely used in North America. Under the proposed new green building scheme, structures would get points for (among much else) disclosing the chemical ingredients of construction materials and for maximizing the use of recycled products.

Nothing could have been less objectionable—except to chemical manufacturers. The AHPBC's members included trade groups for some of the dirtiest substances around, in particular those wedded to polyvinyl chloride, a widely used but also potentially carcinogenic substance.

The Chamber simultaneously pushed an amendment to an energy efficiency bill in Congress that would have applied a non-LEED—and chemical-industry-approved—standard for green-certifying federal government buildings. Its political leverage was considerable. The bill's cosponsor, Jeanne Shaheen (D-NH), in her 2008 election campaign, had been the target of $3 million in attack "education" from the Chamber. It spent more to attack Shaheen, a former governor, that year than on any other Senate race, taunting her with a playground chant: "Jeanne Shaheen—taxing machine," in a state without an income or sales tax. Nonetheless Shaheen won by a small margin on Barack Obama's coattails, but in 2014 she was steeling to face Republican Scott Brown—and yet another possible Chamber ad onslaught.

Lacking the ability to sway elections, construction firms like Skanska—companies that saw green building as a growth opportunity, not as an obstacle to profitability—had next to no chance of making government powers work in their favor. The head of Skanska's U.S. operations had little better option than to take to the *Washington Post*'s op-ed page and lament that "a few single-minded businesses are creating a false debate in Washington about LEED and attempting to slow down the green building boom." Environmentalists' outcry stalled not just the amendment but the entire package—leaving no one the victor but the chemical manufacturers.

While one can admire its effective exercise of influence, one doesn't envy the U.S. Chamber's impossible balancing act. It exists to maintain the credibility and might of business as a political force. Yet its own business model prompts it to consistently ally with odious causes, ones that politically—even commercially—could never stand on their own and whose agents will pay dearly for a cloak of secrecy. The Chamber has had great success in selling its power as a political lightning rod—but then ends up zapping much else that it touches.

Chamber representatives have said, over and over again, that the organization represents the agendas not of its big donors but rather of business in general, and that each position is carefully vetted by member committees. As a result, "the U.S. Chamber reflects the grassroots views of the entire business community," explains the official booklet describing how the staff and the board develop stances. "Everyone involved in the process must help develop positions that benefit the entire business community, rather than any given narrow interest." The Chamber declined to provide details on its process of developing policy positions.

But it's hard to see how smaller interests can play on a level field when even members don't know who is really paying the bills. Based on the weak signals that have escaped from the black hole so far, and the wave of defections, outside evidence that some of the Chamber's significant positions have been taken democratically, without favor to its biggest donors, has been scant.

The Chamber's fund-raising formula has profited its leadership and funded an enviable machine of Washington power, but at a cost to democracy. Even the editorial board of *Bloomberg View*—whose chair Michael Bloomberg was, before he became mayor of New York City, a Chamber board member—has called for an end to the deceptive game. As *Bloomberg View* put it: "If corporations want to play in the political arena, they should have the fortitude to do so openly and be held accountable for it."

Looking back through history, one sees a very different Chamber in its formative years—ideological, but also operating with an evident understanding that its interests were intertwined with those of working Americans. The success of its member businesses depended on the prosperity of the American middle class, which matured in the same era as the Chamber of Commerce itself.

Both thrived as U.S. industry grew into a world-dominating force, most famously in Henry Ford's credo that he had to pay his workers enough to afford a Model T. While the Chamber bitterly fought New Deal programs, financial regulations, and laws giving unions the right to organize, it also devoted considerable energies to building a broad-based prosperity that gave businesses a skilled and strong workforce, created a nation of consumers, and cultivated prosperous and hospitable places in which to do business.

In 1947 the Chamber held a conference on the future of American cities, the first of several conferences. "The city is a place where people live," a Chamber executive told his members. "We believe it is not only good sociology, but good business, for those people to live as comfortably, as happily, and as richly as possible." In the 1960s, as the scourge of mass poverty became a national scandal exposed by the likes of socialist author Michael Harrington, the Chamber organized a task force to identify business-friendly solutions. Its top recommendation: "Poverty in America is a problem that must not be underestimated. Its alleviation should be a prime social and national goal."

In the activist climate of the 1960s, the organization was compelled to show that it took the need for reform seriously and to inject business-friendly ideas into the national conversation. In 1966 it even held a National Symposium on Guaranteed Income, and while it did not take a position on the concept, most of its speakers, including conservative economist Milton Friedman, made a case in support, arguing that properly designed it would replace welfare with incentives to work.

But something changed in the last generation to break the social contract between American business and the American people, a pact that the U.S. Chamber of Commerce has played a role in dissolving. Now the Chamber has less of a stake in how well Americans do, because its most influential members are less interested in them, relatively speaking, as either workers or consumers. If nothing else, that's a matter of math. As the Chamber continually reminds decision makers, international markets are home to "80% of the world's purchasing power, 92% of its economic growth, and 95% of its consumers."

The U.S. Chamber's global ambitions have split local affiliates—the local chambers of commerce and business associations that contribute significant numbers of members, many of whom join the U.S. Chamber as well as the local one when they pay their membership dues. "They're sort of the backbone of the organization, they have been historically, because of their outreach," says Lawrence Kraus, a high-level U.S. Chamber staff member for decades through the 1990s. "Every local chamber has members of its own, so when you activate a local chamber, you're in essence getting access to all of their members."

State chambers of commerce and most of the local groups have remained stalwart allies. But some once-loyal members of the U.S. Chamber have made a public show of breaking their ties.

In 2009 Tony Sheridan decided it was time for his group, the Chamber of Commerce of Eastern Connecticut, to stop sending dues. "Frankly, it was very easy for us to make the break," Sheridan, the organization's president, recounts with a tinge of a native Irish brogue lingering on his tongue. The U.S. Chamber did little to help his local member group, he says, but could be counted on to solicit support for its own political agendas. Members were starting to quit in protest, especially over health care reform, which was a popular cause among many New England businesses. After all, companies in Connecticut just had to look over the Massachusetts border to see that their counterparts on the other side benefited from assistance in insuring their workers.

Sheridan and others also still resented the narrow defeat of three-term Connecticut Republican congressman Rob Simmons in 2006. The U.S. Chamber Vote for Business Bandwagon bus rolled into the state to tout its friend Simmons—and Sheridan suspects the move backfired. "They kind of brought their national politics to the state," says Sheridan—essentially using his organization's name, no less— "and people just don't appreciate that."

The final straw came as a Democratic president entered the White House. "It had to do with the way they were treating Obama after he got elected," says Sheridan, who describes himself as a conservative Democrat. "We have enough problems in this country without having that kind of destructive behavior." Not long after the resignation, Sheridan heard Tom Donohue on an NPR call-in show and could not resist airing his dissent; he told Donohue, and countless listeners, that the U.S. Chamber did not represent the way business operated in eastern Connecticut.

. . .

THINK ABOUT IT: A local chamber's job, if it's doing it right, is to cultivate the success of a place to do business—not just one company but a community of companies, their workers, and the quality of life in the place where they live. Joining the national group gets their own members some nice goodies—a discount on FedEx!—but not a whole lot else, unless they're fired up by the radical antiregulatory program and seek to do their part.

As the U.S. Chamber has entered the political fray as a proxy for the Republican Party, and taken sharply ideological positions on climate change, health care, Wall Street reform, and more—claiming hollowly that to do otherwise would be fatal to business—many local affiliates decided they had had enough.

Among the handful that have resigned are the Seattle Chamber, which broke away eight years after the Institute for Legal Reform's sneak attack on Washington attorney general candidate Deborah Senn, in pursuit of a pro–climate action business agenda. In Colorado, the board of the Aspen Chamber Resort Association—climate change very much on its mind—voted eleven to one to break from the national organization. In Kansas City, Missouri, the local chamber dropped its national membership after the U.S. Chamber viciously attacked popular Senator Claire McCaskill. "The Greater Kansas City Chamber isn't affiliated with the U.S. Chamber," the Missouri group's chief executive assured a correspondent. "Our focus is on civic progress for our two-state region. We do sincerely thank you for your concern—but it's not us."

That handful of defections has gained national attention, but protest is the easy part. Meanwhile, across the country, local chambers of commerce have been doing important work on building strong towns, cities, and regions, promoting the growth of economies from within. Take the Salt Lake Chamber of Commerce, a member of the national organization, which led the campaign—and raised more than $850,000—for a 2006 ballot measure to increase sales taxes by a quarter cent in order to fund the construction of new light-rail lines as well as highways. It also helped found and run a planning organization, Envision Utah, to steer regional development into the future.

"We had national experts come in and study our region and tell us what our region would look like if we didn't invest in both highways and transit," explains Salt Lake Chamber official Natalie Gochnour. "Our business leaders concluded we could pay now or pay later." The Utah ballot initiative passed by a two-thirds margin, with no organized opposition.

Yet even where local chambers invest their political capital in building better places to do business, the soil is not always fertile enough for new plants to take root. In Georgia, traffic tie-ups choke the Atlanta-area economy; local chambers all over the state have rallied in support of a proposed temporary tax for transit—backed by the state's Republican leadership. In 2012 a referendum was to be held. The Metro Atlanta Chamber of Commerce, a U.S. Chamber affiliate, openly kept tabs on which way state legislators were leaning and sent the list around to local business leaders, ostensibly to fact-check the list but also carrying an unmistakable political message. "During this fund-raising season, I hope that you will utilize this information when making decisions regarding your political contributions," the missive implored, according to a local blogger opposed to the tax.

The referendum lost in nine out of the state's dozen regions, including Atlanta, and it wasn't hard to see why. As one *Atlanta Journal-Constitution* reader put it, "Republicans have gained power by being anti-government anti-tax. How are you going to change those perceptions when you have a tax you and the business community (who contributes to your party) favors?" Building power around uncompromising ideology doesn't do much good when it gets in the way of progress.

IF YOU HAPPEN TO think government is supposed to spread power and opportunity widely—democratically, even—then the U.S. Chamber's success in rewriting the script of public service may feel dispiriting, if not alarming. But it shouldn't. In fact, the rise of the business political machine offers powerful testimony to decades of progressive activists' inroads in making Washington work in the public interest, from the Clean Air Act to the often intimate relationship between labor unions and the Democratic Party. Laws that seek to redress or prevent harm caused by companies have piled on very real costs for businesses, and Congress is perpetually poised, recent history to the contrary, to intervene on behalf of constituents when their ability to remain in office falls into jeopardy. We should be struck not by the fact that business organized to fight back, but that it didn't happen sooner.

The recent rise of business as an effectively organized force copied many pages from the labor, trial lawyer, and environmentalist playbooks—and emerged directly as a result of the success of activism in those realms. A basic principle of political physics is that every action has a reaction. It would be a sad statement indeed about American business if it just sat there helpless in the face of assault.

Still, in the wake of *Citizens United,* corporate secrecy, and the buying of Congress, those who think government should have a constituency broader than business naturally feel a sense of defeat. But that sense is also the wrong one. The modern U.S. Chamber of Commerce became what it is because it had a story to tell and a product to sell. So do many organizations—less well funded, usually, but no less legitimate—with a sharply different perspective on the ways business and government work together.

As a business owner, Terry Gardiner constantly dealt with the kind of regulatory headaches that the U.S. Chamber of Commerce would have us believe are killing American industry. His Alaskan seafood company, NorQuest, got slammed with an EPA fine for letting bloody fish waste wash into the sea at two of its processing plants. Gardiner had to fight to renew a Department of Energy license for a hydroelectric plant at a wooden dam on its cannery property, and he had to go through rigorous environmental assessments under the Endangered Species Act and Clean Water Act to make sure the plant wasn't harming salmon hatcheries or the Steller's eider, a rare species of waterfowl. To continue to operate its tiny renewable power source, Gardiner's company had to provide years' worth of data on water flows to the U.S. Fish and Wildlife Service, the National Oceanic and Atmospheric Administration, and other government agencies, and undergo an endless bureaucratic review.

The U.S. Chamber of Commerce has built its influence on business owners' resentments of such demands by the regulatory state. But Gardiner has always had a different way of looking at businesses' responsibility to the greater good. Before he founded the seafood company, he was speaker of the Alaska House of Representatives and helped broker the constitutional amendment that continues to give all Alaska residents a share of the state's oil revenues. When he sold NorQuest in 2004—by then, it was doing more than $100 million in annual sales—he resolved to take on a new mission: to make health care affordable for businesses and their workers.

His new organization, Small Business Majority, had all of $65,000 to spend on lobbying for health care reform as proposals swirled through Congress, versus nearly $9 million for the trade group for health insurance companies—and that doesn't count the insurers' political ad buys through the U.S. Chamber. In 2010 Gardiner's group spent just $10,000 on Washington lobbying, and after that, none. Before it will be able to take on Congress, Small Business Majority must first organize small businesses to see their interests, not as the Chamber would like them to, but as benefiting from health care reform, clean energy, and other innovations that the Chamber is doing everything it can to bury.

Right now the top priority for Small Business Majority is to make sure the new health care exchanges set up by the Affordable Care Act actually can succeed in minimizing the cost of health care premiums. One thing Gardiner and his colleagues found is that most small-business owners had no idea that Obamacare offered a tax credit to help them pay for employee health insurance. Small Business Majority let employers know how to take advantage of the tax credit, and it created an online calculator to help them figure out how much it would be worth.

While Obamacare was brewing in Congress, Small Business Majority participated in discussions on the Hill about how to reduce costs to employers. Its leaders were glad to see some big companies, including Walmart and Intel, in the discussions as well. But the U.S. Chamber, funded by insurance companies defending against threats to their bottom lines, was absent.

As Gardiner sees it, government helping business pay for health care is a matter of international competitiveness for U.S. companies, since they have to shoulder costs that their counterparts in other first-world economies don't. "American companies have to compete with Japanese companies, German companies, Canadian companies, French, in the global marketplace, on an import and export basis," he observes. "An adversarial relationship [between government and business], where can it go?" Gardiner posits. "You invest all this energy in fighting instead of trying to figure out how to make things work or how to solve problems."

Gardiner isn't alone in trying to rethink the relationship between business and government from a pro-business point of view. Frank Knapp, co-chair of the American Sustainable Business Council, is also president and CEO of the South Carolina Small Business Chamber of Commerce. He runs an advertising and public relations firm, and his clients have hardly been hippie idealists. In fact, his group grew out of battles like one he helped wage on behalf of restaurants and convenience stores to keep video gambling legal in their establishments—a cause opposed by the South Carolina Chamber of Commerce and influential Christian leaders in the state. On behalf of a video gaming company, Knapp's agency produced ads for the "Protect Freedom Committee," warning voters that their civil rights were being threatened by the heavy hand of government.

Before the issue could come to a voter referendum, a court banned gambling, but Knapp had made his point: small enterprises could and should organize to achieve good outcomes for businesses, without interference from narrow interests or ideology. Today, for instance, the Sustainable Business Council has been lobbying to *strengthen* required disclosure of the composition of chemical substances, because businesses that buy them are stuck wondering and worrying about what exactly they're getting. That may not be great for some chemical companies, but it's extremely helpful for everyone else.

In late 2011 the American Sustainable Business Council teamed up with Small Business Majority and a third group, the Main Street Alliance, and hired a pollster to ask five hundred randomly selected small-business owners about the threats they faced. By a huge margin of 34 percentage points, those polled said weak customer demand was their number-one problem, and the cost of health coverage was second. "Government regulation" trailed behind in third place, with just 14 percent of businesses saying it was their biggest burden.

In the survey business owners were also asked to choose from a menu the action that would do the most to create jobs in the United States. The most popular answer? "Eliminating incentives for employers to move jobs overseas." Cutting taxes came in second. Just 10 percent advised that reducing regulation was the best answer to what ailed them.

Small Business Majority regularly performs such random polls of company owners, with results typically dominated by those who identify as Republicans. It found, for instance, that a majority supported raising taxes on the top 2 percent of earners. (Not incidentally, only 5 percent reported a family income of more than $250,000 a year.) Most saw a role for government in helping small businesses thrive.

The constituency for investment in domestic prosperity is there, and so are the reasons to act. Just as big business over many years once became complacent and politically overpowered, unable to overcome its internal conflicts and competition to organize effectively, the rest of the nation now lives in that strange country—exiles from political power in their own land.

Small-business groups can't fight the Chamber's money, because they don't have it. In the wake of *Citizens United,* the American Sustainable Business Council has taken a strong stand on principle against *any* campaign spending by companies, calling it "inconsistent with long-standing democratic principles and practice." It's even pushing for a constitutional amendment to overturn the Supreme Court's decision—a worthy if far-fetched cause.

"You're not going to be able to compete in the media with the U.S. Chamber as far as paid advertising," Knapp observes. "Even communicating with the press is difficult. It costs money to have these organizations, and that is the thing small businesses don't have a lot of." Ironically, one of the greatest successes the Sustainable Business Council has had so far has been to help get Congress to legalize crowdfunding—a piece of a larger bill, strongly supported by the U.S. Chamber, that also rolled back disclosure and oversight for many publicly traded companies.

Luckily small businesses aren't on their own. Corporate money in politics has been around for as long as the corporate form itself, and the best way to fight back is to, well, fight back. All the Chamber of Commerce did was organize business around common goals and principles, just as groups on the left had done before.

While the Chamber has wooed and bundled big business under threat into a coherent political force in Washington, emerging industries and public interest groups remain balkanized and playing defense—much as corporate America did not so long ago. The Chamber built its base of power alongside the Republican Party; then by doing an end run around the party apparatus to the edges of the law—and when necessary, moving the goalposts—it was able to achieve ends for its constituents that Republicans could not or would not have done on their own. From the outside, its leverage was great.

The Democratic Party could use its own version of the Chamber of Commerce—an outside intervention to force dynamic change, and unite its own activists behind a common agenda and strategy that encompasses workers, consumers, and companies that care about their welfare. The Sustainable Business Council isn't willing to wage a war in which money is the ammunition, but someone else will have to, and the world of dynamic new business powers is not impoverished. The combatants may end up being companies like Skanska and Apple that left the U.S. Chamber, disillusioned; perhaps Google will finally heed the ceaseless calls to drop its Chamber membership and find fresh avenues for influence. The same technologies that foster crowdfunding for emerging businesses à la Kickstarter also harbor tremendous potential to pull together funding for political action from a constellation of fragmented companies, empowering them to form their own lobbying and campaign-cash forces to disrupt legacy industries' deep-pocketed lock on power.

As the Republican Party increasingly operates outside the realm of reason, it's the Democrats' turn to answer a call to duty, and to build a bridge for business to political power based on prosperity and social advancement.

We know the strategy works. After all, it's been done before.

Acknowledgments

Many people made this book possible, none more than Hillary Brenhouse, my research assistant. With persistence, grace, and keen intelligence she conducted many of the interviews for this book, including those with contract workers in China.

Great thanks are also due to the many past and present associates of the Chamber of Commerce who shared their recollections and insights.

With gratitude I rest this work on the shoulders of some excellent journalists who chronicled the U.S. Chamber's journey as it progressed. You'll see many of their names in the endnotes, but special honors go to Peter H. Stone, who has spent decades at the *National Journal* and then the Center for Public Integrity and *Huffington Post* probing Washington influence.

The staff at Public Citizen, Dennis Kelleher at Better Markets, Lisa Donner and Marcus Stanley at Americans for Financial Reform, Christie Setzer and Dennis Yedwab of Chamberwatch all generously shared research and observations.

Then I had to write. Thank you to Liena Zagare for encouragement and the beautiful Ditmas Workspace. Amy Cortese, Joe Conason, Esther Kaplan, Ben Smith, Dean Starkman, Sasha Abramsky, Mike Hudson, Mark Smith, Matt Ryan, and Audrey Korelstein were generous with advice, feedback, and Wi-Fi along the way.

My colleagues at the Columbia University Graduate School of Journalism deserve deepest thanks, especially Bill Grueskin, Mike Sullivan, Jonah Nigh, and the staff of The New York World. I was also blessed to have the assistance of Columbia's extraordinary librarians.

My agent, Larry Weissman, had the foresight to see that the Chamber of Commerce story needed to be told as a whole. Just as important, he put this book in the hands of editor Christopher Jackson, the much better for it.

And to my family, which now has me back: Thank you. Again.

Notes

xv   **"creates an environment where meaningful** John McCain, press release, October 6, 2000. Accessed via http://1.usa.gov/1GmSJi1.

xvi   **But unlike the U.S. Chamber** Freedom Partners, IRS filing, 2012. Accessed via http://bit.ly/1wr9uoY.

xvi   **Organizations like Americans for Prosperity** Koch Industries spent $16.4 million in lobbying in 2013. U.S. Senate Lobbying Disclosure Act database, accessed via http://1.usa.gov/1yPZI1Z search for client Koch Companies and filing year 2013.

CHAPTER 1: ONE HOUR

4   **Trucking is the circulatory system** American Trucking Associations, *American Trucking Trends 2011* (Washington, DC: American Trucking Associations, 2011).

4   **take action to deal with truck driver fatigue** Section 408 of ICC Termination Act, Pub. L. No. 104-88, 109 Stat. 803 (1995).

4   **From 1992 to 1999, the annual number** U.S. Department of Transportation, Office of Inspector General, *Motor Carrier Safety Program, Federal Highway Administration,* Report No. TR-1999-091, April 26, 1999, p. 17; Federal Motor Carrier Safety Administration, Large Truck and Bus Crash Facts, p. 4.

5   **It wouldn't take a great feat** U.S. Department of Transportation, Federal Motor Carrier Safety Administration, Docket No. FMCSA-97-2350, *Federal Register* 65, no. 85, May 2, 2000.

5   **Data on truck crashes show** U.S. Department of Transportation, Federal Motor Carrier Safety Administration. "2010-2011 Hours of Service (HOS) Proposed Rule Regulatory Impact Analysis," RIN 2126-AB26, http://1.usa .gov/10f7inK.

5   **Clinton administration regulators estimated** As referenced in U.S. Government Accountability Office, "Commercial Motor Vehicles: Effectiveness of Actions Being Taken to Improve Motor Carrier Safety Is Unknown," July 17, 2000, http://1.usa.gov/1xFSlpz.

5   **And government studies found fatigue** National Transportation Safety Board,

"Safety Study: Fatigue, Alcohol, Other Drugs, and Medical Factors in Fatal-to-the-Driver Heavy Truck Crashes," NTSB No. SS-90/01, February 5, 1990.

5 **"Even with this change, drivers could be** *The U.S. Department of Transportation's Proposed Hours of Service Regulations for Motor Carriers: Hearings Before the Subcommittee on Ground Transportation, Committee on Transportation and Infrastructure, U.S. House of Representatives,* 106th Cong. (June 22, 2000), testimony of Clyde J. Hart Jr., acting deputy administrator, Federal Motor Carrier Safety Administration, U.S. Department of Transportation.

5 **Drivers frequently hit the road exhausted** Merrill M. Mitler et al., "The Sleep of Long-Haul Truck Drivers," *New England Journal of Medicine* 337 (September 11, 1997): 760.

5 **"paternalistic" government rules** Michael Fix and George C. Eads, "The Prospects for Regulatory Reform: The Legacy of Reagan's First Term," *Yale Journal on Regulation* 2, no. 293 (1985).

6 **The Chamber's board of directors had unanimously voted** U.S. Chamber of Commerce, "Hours of Service of Drivers, Driver Rest and Sleep for Safe Operations," December 15, 2000, comment to U.S. Department of Transportation, Federal Motor Carrier Safety Administration, Docket No. FMCSA-97-2350.

6 **the organization had successfully lobbied for a clause** Ibid.

6 **The number of trucks on the road** Randel Johnson and Peter Eide (U.S. Chamber of Commerce), comment to U.S. Department of Transportation, December 15, 2000, accessed via http://1.usa.gov/133cLis.

6 **"Our members, as well as the entire American business** *Hearing on Short Line Rail Infrastructure Before the Subcommittee on Ground Transportation, Transportation and Infrastructure Committee, U.S. House of Representatives,* 106th Cong. (July 24, 2000), statement of Thomas Donohue.

7 **An overwhelmingly pro-regulation Congress** In 1983, in a defeat for the Chamber, Congress rejected a measure that would have allowed lawmakers to veto federal regulations they didn't like. One of the opponents, James Florio (D-NJ), warned that the amendment was "a great opportunity for all the special interests to stop regulations from taking effect." See Howard Kurtz, "House Votes to Reject New Type of Legislative Veto," *Washington Post,* November 5, 1983. In the meantime, as the 1984 elections approached, the White House shut down its regulatory task force.

7 **many trucking companies secured scarce** Carole Shifrin, "The Byzantine World of Trucking Industry," *Washington Post,* March 2, 1980.

8 **The 1970s push to deregulate** Bradley Behrman, "Civil Aeronautics Board," in James Q. Wilson, ed., *The Politics of Regulation* (New York: Basic Books, 1980), p. 76.

11 **It amped up the limit** Federal Motor Carrier Safety Administration, "Hours of Service of Drivers," December 29, 2010, http://www.fmcsa.dot.gov/regulations/hours-of-service.

12 **In a single week, truck drivers could** Joan Claybrook (Public Citizen) to Federal Motor Carrier Safety Administration, "Comments on Notice of Proposed Rulemaking, Hours of Service of Drivers," Docket No. FMCSA-2004-19608, http://bit.ly/1wUZ3d8.

12 **"I understand markets.** Ed Slattery, interview by author.

12 pressed to reduce driving time from eleven *Federal Register,* December 29, 2010.

13 Of the nearly $12 trillion in goods U.S. Department of Transportation, Bureau of Transportation Statistics, *2007 Commodity Flow Survey* (April 2010), table 1a, "Shipment Characteristics by Mode of Transportation for the United States: 2007."

13 The Obama administration ultimately opted In yet another twist, the 2014 congressional budget deal included a provision that suspended the Obama administration weekly driving limits to allow for study of their effects. "Truckers Get Relief on Rest Rules, in U.S. Budget Deal," Jeff Plungis, *Bloomberg News,* December 10, 2014.

14 the Institute for Legal Reform U.S. Chamber of Commerce, Institute for Legal Reform, IRS Form 990, 2010, accessed via http://bit.ly/1IPsov6.

15 Between 1998 and 2012 the Chamber invested "Top Spenders," OpenSecrets .org, http://www.opensecrets.org/lobby/top.php?indexType=s.

15 a dozen appeals fighting regulations in the D.C. court Review of filings via Public Access to Court Electronic Records (PACER), U.S. Department of Justice.

16 Some of its most aggressive assaults The U.S. Chamber Litigation Center has compiled an exhaustive and useful library of files related to cases in which the Chamber was a plaintiff or filed friend-of-the-court briefs, accessible at http://www.chamberlitigation.com.

16 upheld a half-million-dollar cap *DRD Pool Service Inc. v. Freed,* 186 Md. App. (2009).

16 strict financial caps on noneconomic damages Rachel M. Janutis, "The Struggle Over Tort Reform and the Overlooked Legacy of the Progressives," *Akron Law Review* 39, no. 4 (2006): 943–74; Baker & Hostetler LLP, "Ohio Tort Reform," http://bit.ly/1A07I1J.

16 "Ohio Chamber members are urged to contact Ohio Chamber of Commerce, "Legislative Wrap-Up," *Ohio Matters,* December 2003.

17 "distribute information about Ohio's economic climate Citizens for a Strong Ohio, IRS Form 990, 2004, accessed via http://bit.ly/1yNEGMv.

18 a record-setting $7 million-plus advertising Deborah Goldberg, "The New Politics of Judicial Elections," Brennan Center for Justice, New York University, December 31, 2004.

18 all three of its candidates won Jim Provance, "Heavy Fund-Raising Advantage Fuels GOP Sweep of Ohio High Court Seats," *Toledo Blade,* November 4, 2004.

20 Taken together, unions spend Tom McGinty and Brody Mullins, "Political Spending by Unions Far Exceeds Direct Donations," *Wall Street Journal,* July 10, 2012.

21 "stop whining" Rachel Konrad, "U.S. Chamber of Commerce Chief Endorses Offshoring," Associated Press, July 1, 2004.

23 Hundreds of local chambers remain members "Accreditation Statistics, June 2013," and accompanying questionnaire, U.S. Chamber of Commerce, "Accreditation," http://www.uschamber.com/chambers/accreditation.

23 In 2011–12 Chevron gave the Chamber $1.5 million Company website disclosures.

24 *Bloomberg News* figured out Drew Armstrong, "Insurers Gave U.S. Chamber

$86 Million Used to Oppose Obama's Health Law," *Bloomberg News,* December 17, 2010; AHIP, IRS Form 990, 2009.

24   **AHIP gave another $16.2 million to the Chamber** Chris Frates, "AHIP Gave More than $100 Million to Chamber's Efforts to Derail Health Care Reform," *National Journal,* June 13, 2012.

CHAPTER 2: THE BASTARD CHILD

27   **first convention in Washington** "Seek World Trade," *Washington Post,* January 19, 1913.

28   **a clause in a tariff law that exempted it** Tariff Act, ch.16, §II(G)(a), 38 Stat. 72 (1913). As IRS staff note in their guide to tax exemptions for trade associations: "There is no legislative comment on the statute. It is generally assumed, however, that its passage was the result of a U.S. Chamber of Commerce request for an exemption for nonprofit 'civic' and 'commercial' organizations—a request that resulted in the enactment of what is now IRC 501(c)(4) (for nonprofit 'civic' organizations) and IRC 501(c)(6) (for nonprofit 'commercially-oriented' organizations)." John Francis Reilly, Carter C. Hull, and Barbara A. Braig Allen, "IRC 501(c)(6) Organizations: Exempt Organizations-Technical Instruction Program for FY 2003," http://www.irs.gov/pub/irs-tege /eotopici03.pdf.

28   **"American business must become militant,"** "The Responsibility of the Business Man to His Government," p. 11, quoted in Harwood Lawrence Childs, *Labor and Capital in National Politics* (Columbus: Ohio State University Press, 1930), p. 70.

28   **It had to stop looking to government** "Concern over Skilled Labor Demand," *Crockery and Glass Journal,* November 10, 1927.

29   **"the inherent strength of our** "Congress Is Urged to Leave Trade Alone," *New York Times,* January 1, 1931; "Trade Horizon Brightens," *Los Angeles Times,* January 1, 1931.

29   **"We have left the period of extreme individualism** Quoted in International Industrial Relations Institute, Mary Van Kleeck and Mary L. Fleddérus, eds., *On Economic Planning: Papers Delivered at the Regional Study Conference of the International Industrial Relations Institute (IRI), New York, November 23–27, 1934* (New York: Covici, Friede, 1935).

30   **If trade associations could not agree** Arthur M. Schlesinger Jr., *The Age of Roosevelt,* vol. 2, *The Coming of the New Deal, 1933–1935* (New York: Sentry Books, 1958), pp. 98–99.

30   **When the administration sought to renew** *Social Security Act of 1935, Hearings Before the Committee on Finance, U.S. Senate,* 74th Cong. (April 1935), testimony of Henry Harriman.

31   **the number of strikes more than doubled** *National Labor Relations Act and Proposed Amendments, Hearings Before the Committee on Education and Labor, U.S. House of Representatives,* 76th Cong. (June 19 and 20, 1939).

31   **"to investigate, record, control, and prosecute** I. F. Stone, "U.S. Chamber Recommended This Kind of 'Exposure' in 1935," *I.F. Stone's Weekly,* November 9, 1959.

31   **"subversive doctrines"** *Investigation of Nazi Propaganda Activities and Investigation of Certain Other Propaganda Activities, Before the Special Commit-*

tee on Un-American Activities, U.S. House of Representatives, 73rd Cong. (December 17 and 18, 1934).

32   **"duty to show both in theory** U.S. Chamber of Commerce, Committee on Socialism and Communism, *Communist Infiltration in the United States: Its Nature and How to Combat It* (Washington, DC: U.S. Chamber of Commerce, 1947), p. 115.

33   **"If our free, competitive institutions are** Archie Gray, in *Oil and Gas Journal,* September 15, 1958, quoted in Theodore Levitt, "Business Should Stay Out of Politics," *Business Horizons* 3, no. 4 (1960).

33   **Political Participation Program** Arthur H. Motley, "Business in Politics," *Business Horizons* 3, no. 4 (1960).

33   **Monsanto used the program** "Training Pays Off," *Nation's Business* 49, no. 11 (November 1961): 62–63.

34   **"The usual plums for politicking** Levitt, "Business Should Stay Out of Politics."

35   **some 120 regulatory measures emerged from Congress** Cass R. Sunstein, *After the Rights Revolution: Reconceiving the Regulatory State* (Cambridge, MA: Harvard University Press, 1993).

35   **The Toxic Substances Control Act** Toxic Substances Control Act, Pub. L. 94-469, 90 Stat. 2003 (1975).

35   **the Occupational Safety and Health Administration** Steven Kelman, "The Occupational Safety and Health Administration," in Wilson, p. 239.

35   **The Chamber supported Nixon's carefully calibrated** Ibid., p. 241.

36   **Nixon created the EPA** Sunstein, *After the Rights Revolution,* p. 28.

36   **"Our national government today** Richard Nixon, "Special Message to the Congress About Reorganization Plans to Establish the Environmental Protection Agency and the National Oceanic and Atmospheric Administration," July 9, 1970, http://bit.ly/1FQrHA4.

36   **"We can no longer afford to consider air** Richard Nixon, "Annual Message to the Congress on the State of the Union," January 22, 1970, http://bit.ly/1DTpkuG.

38   **"One of the bewildering paradoxes of our time,"** "The Powell Memo," August 23, 1971, http://reclaimdemocracy.org/powell_memo_lewis/.

39   **"create a business environment** "Changing of the Business Guard," *Nation's Business* 85, no. 8 (August 1997): 68–69.

CHAPTER 3: THE ASTROTURF ASSAULT

40   **Donohue came from a humble household** U.S. Census, 1940.

40   **worked as a fund-raiser for nonprofits** Departments of Labor and Health, Education and Welfare and Related Agencies Appropriations Bill, U.S. Senate report, 89th Congress, 1966.

41   **Fairfield University was the target** Joseph Richard Preville, "Fairfield University: The Emergence of a Modern Catholic Institution," Ph.D. diss., Boston College, 1985, p. 195.

41   **As *Tilton v. Richardson* made its way** Ibid., p. 171.

42   **At least nine other Klassen associates** Jack Anderson, "Klassen Helps Run Up Postal Costs," *Washington Post,* September 29, 1973.

42   **"You will be surprised how much time** *Status of U.S. Postal Service in the*

Western Region, Hearings Before the Subcommittee on Postal Facilities, Mail, and Labor Management, Committee on Post Office and Civil Service, U.S. House of Representatives, 93rd Cong. (August 1973), memorandum from Thomas J. Donohue, Assistant Regional Postmaster, General Customer Services, January 12, 1973.

43 **more than $40,000 a year** Hearings before a subcommittee of the Committee on Appropriations on Treasury, Postal Service, and General Government Appropriations for Fiscal Year 1976: U.S. Senate, 94th Congress (1975), p. 1489.

43 **a drink in a stairwell** James Toedtman, "Full-Court Press for Business," *Newsday,* January 4, 1998.

44 **"This communication should not be deemed** *Toxic Substances Control Act (1975), Hearings on S.776 Before the Subcommittee on the Environment of the Committee on Commerce,* 94th Cong. (March 3, 5, 10, and April 15, 1975).

44 **would have given $50 million in urban planning grants** *Land Use and Resource Conservation Act (1975), Hearings on H.R. 3510 and Related Bills Before the Subcommittee on Energy and Environment and Committee on Interior and Insular Affairs,* 94th Cong. (March–April 1975).

45 **"merely the first step on the road toward more** Ibid., Statement of the Chamber of Commerce of the United States by James R. Graham.

45 **"I never heard from the Chamber** Mark Green and Andrew Buchsbaum, "How the Chamber's Computers Con the Congress," *Washington Monthly,* May 1980.

46 **"Lobbying that counts is done through** *Public Disclosure of Lobbying Activity (1979), Hearings on H.R. 81 Before the Committee on Administrative Law and Governmental Relations of the Committee on the Judiciary,* 96th Cong. (February–March 1979), statement of Hon. Tom Railsback.

46 **perhaps a half-dozen registered lobbyists** Ibid., testimony of Frederick K. Krebs.

46 **His success against the Udall bill** "Citizen's Choice: A New Way to Be Heard in Washington," editorial, *Nation's Business* 64, no. 11 (November 1976): 76.

46 **"fight the unnecessary growth of the federal** Thomas J. Donohue, statement to White House Conference on Balanced National Growth & Economic Development, 1978.

46 **Members would pay fifteen dollars a month** "A Voice That Makes Washington Sit Up and Listen," *Nation's Business,* May 1978.

47 **a massive direct mail campaign** Thomas B. Mechling, "Patriotism, Capitalism and Positive Thinking," *Commonweal* 107, no. 15 (August 1980).

47 **"Our members are housewives, teachers, professionals** *Program Evaluation Act of 1977 and Federal Spending Control Act of 1977, Hearings Before the Committee on Rules and Administration, U.S. Senate,* 95th Cong. (September 28, 1977; April 19 and June 8, 1978), testimony of Thomas Donohue.

47 **Amway itself was a crucial recruiting** Wilbur Martin, "Amway Founder: A Salesman for Free Enterprise," *Nation's Business* 67, no. 5 (May 1979), 83–85.

47 **its board was hardly representative** William H. Jones, "Marriott Asks Support for New Lobby Unit," *Washington Post,* March 8, 1978.

47 **Fifteen of the sixteen members, the exception being** "Citizen's Choice Board of Directors and Officers," 1979, Collection of Senator H. John Heinz III, Legislative Assistants' Files—1970–1991, Carnegie Mellon University, http://bit.ly/1sBZapp.

47   it claimed to have 75,000 members *Taxpayer Safeguards, Hearing Before the Subcommittee on Oversight of the Committee on Ways and Means, U.S. House of Representatives,* 97th Cong. (April 26, 1982), testimony of Thomas Bell.

48   **"arbitrary regulation"** Robert Walters, "Anybody but Kennedy," Newspaper Enterprise Association syndicated column, July 24, 1979, http://bit.ly/1vO MmMq.

48   **"a blind man searching for a black cat** Allan J. Cigler and Burdett A. Loomis, eds., *Interest Group Politics* (Washington, DC: Congressional Quarterly, 1991), p. 184.

48   **Nader-inspired consumer protection agency** Charles Mohr, "Business Using Grass-Roots Lobby," *New York Times,* April 17, 1978.

48   **"whose budgets most need to be cut."** Results reported in "Washington Letter," *Nation's Business* 67, no. 3 (March 1979), 7–8.

49   **"According to a Citizen's Choice poll** "Summary of Conversation with American Enterprise Institute (Marvin Kosters)," October 31, 1978, Collection of H. John Heinz III, Legislative Subject Files—1975–1991, Carnegie Mellon University, http://bit.ly/1uItI9y.

49   **"Citizen's Choice believes that EXCESSIVE** "Citizen's Choice Day, October 31, 1979," Collection of H. John Heinz III, Legislative Assistants' Files—1970–1991 (1977–1991), http://bit.ly/133RNA5.

49   **"Citizen's Choice members feel strongly that** *A Bill to Amend the Federal Election Campaign Act of 1971 to Provide for Financing of General Election Campaigns for the House of Representatives, Hearings on H.R. 1 and Related Legislation,* 96th Cong. (March 1979), testimony of Thomas J. Donohue.

50   **In industries like power generation** Paul L. Joskow, "Inflation and Environmental Concern: Structural Change in the Process of Public Utility Price Regulation," *Journal of Law and Economics* 17, no. 2 (1974): 291–327.

50   **no relationship between the volume of nonmilitary** Song Han and Casey B. Mulligan, "Inflation and the Size of Government," *Federal Reserve Bank of St. Louis Review* 90, no. 3 (2008): 245–67, http://bit.ly/1wXtcaR.

51   **"The American taxpayer has established** "The Commission and Nationwide Taxpayer Hearings," Citizen's Choice, Collection of H. John Heinz III, Legislative Assistants' Files—1970–1991 (1977–1991), http://bit.ly/13nrPsr.

52   **Walker, meanwhile, headed Reagan's transition team** David Vogel, *Fluctuating Fortunes: The Political Power of Business in America* (New York: Basic Books, 1979), p. 243.

53   **"Such a tax package would increase** *The 1981 Economic Report of the President, Hearings Before the Joint Economic Committee,* 97th Cong. (January 1981), testimony of Richard Rahn.

53   **Rahn and the Chamber won the massive tax cut** A decade later Rahn would characterize the Kemp-Roth deal as just a down payment on the downsizing of the corporate tax burden. "We have won this battle," he told a tenth-anniversary panel at the Heritage Foundation, "but we have certainly not won the war." "A Tenth Anniversary Celebration of the Kemp-Roth Tax Cuts: The Importance of America's Victory Over Washington," Heritage Foundation, August 13, 1991, http://herit.ag/12TyPN1.

53   **an arcane change to depreciation schedules** *The Economic Recovery Tax Act (1981), Hearings Before the Committee on Finance, U.S. Senate,* 97th Cong.

(May 13, 14, and 18, 1981), statement of Robert McIntyre, Citizens for Tax Justice: "Costing over a half trillion dollars over this decade, the program would reduce the corporate tax burden by 40% in five years and would eventually eliminate the corporate income tax entirely."

54   The Chamber held out for months "$100 Billion Tax Bill Agonizing to House Republicans," *Washington Post,* August 8, 1982.

54   the powerful defense contractor Paul Thayer Ann M. Reilly, "Business and Reagan: More Blowups Ahead?" *Dun's Business Month,* December 1982, pp. 40–41.

54   pressed for cuts to welfare programs "Chamber's Ponderous Decision Making Leaves It Sitting on the Sidelines," *National Journal,* July 24, 1982, p. 1298.

55   "If H.R. 4961 is passed in these troublesome Lesher quoted in Jonathan Chait, "Republicans, Taxes and the 1982 Mistake," *New Republic,* June 24, 2011.

55   Citizen's Choice published a lengthy interview with Bartlett "Exploring 'Reaganomics' with Bruce Bartlett," *Citizen's Voice,* December–January 1982, p. 6.

55   But as Bartlett noted years later Bruce Bartlett, "Will Higher Taxes Tank the Economy?" *Fiscal Times,* June 24, 2011.

55   "the man who is to federal tax rates Ronald Reagan, "Remarks to the U.S. Chamber of Commerce on the Economy and Deficit Reduction," November 19, 1987, http://bit.ly/1tQkKdg.

55   "Unless something is done immediately *Taxpayer Safeguards, Hearing Before the Subcommittee on Oversight of the Committee on Ways and Means, U.S. House of Representatives,* 97th Cong. (April 26, 1982), testimony of Thomas Donohue.

56   In 1976 the Chamber had 49,350 firms Burdett A. Loomis, "A New Era: Groups and the Grass Roots," in Allan J. Cigler and Burdett A. Loomis, eds., *Interest Group Politics* (Washington, DC: Congressional Quarterly, 1983). The Chamber's own annual report shows 52,000 in 1975, 227,000 in 1983.

56   For some, the tax showdown Robert D. Hershey Jr., "Chamber of Commerce Is Budgeting," *New York Times,* October 1, 1983.

57   "For the last six and a half years "Hello, Have We Got a Deal for You," *National Journal,* October 17, 1987.

57   extreme care not to alienate Mark A. Smith, *American Business and Political Power: Public Opinion, Elections, and Democracy* (Chicago: University of Chicago Press, 2000), p. 55.

57   "If we haven't got a strong consensus "Chamber's Ponderous Decision Making."

57   "positions on national issues" U.S. Chamber of Commerce, Report of the Ad Hoc National Business Council on Injury Compensation, *Compensation for Injury from Exposure to Hazards* (Washington, DC: U.S. Chamber of Commerce Resources Policy Department, 1985), preface.

57   "A basic ethic in American society Ibid.

57   "human capital investment initiative" U.S. Small Business Administration in cooperation with the U.S. Chamber of Commerce's Center for Workforce Preparation and Quality Education, *Today's Small Business for Tomorrow: A Skilled Work Force* (Washington, DC: U.S. Chamber of Commerce, 1993).

58   "This isn't Mr. Dukakis coming in," Quoted in Rich Thomas, "Doing Business with Business," *Newsweek,* November 29, 1992.

58   what it called a national health care strategy Walter J. McClure, *An Analysis*

of Health Care System Performance Under a Proposed NHI Administrative Mechanism (St. Paul, MN: InterStudy, 1977).

59 **requiring employers to pay for 50 percent** John Judis, "Abandoned Surgery: Business and the Failure of Health Care Reform," *American Prospect*, Spring 1995.

59 **"If there is one group that will benefit from health-care reform** Quoted in Roger Thompson, "Small Firms' Stake in Health Reform," *Nation's Business* 81, no. 11 (November 1993): 18.

60 **Rising health care costs were hurting** Graham K. Wilson, "Interest Groups in the Health Care Debate," in Henry J. Aaron, ed., *The Problem That Won't Go Away: Reforming U.S. Health Care Financing* (Washington, DC: Brookings Institution Press, 1996).

60 **supported employer mandates to provide health insurance** Cathie Jo Martin, "Mandating Social Change: The Business Struggle Over National Health Care Reform," *Governance: An International Journal of Policy and Administration* 10, no. 4 (October 1997): 397–428.

60 **The committee secured a couple of meetings** Robert Patricelli, interview by author.

60 **"The Chamber's current posture is disturbing,"** Quoted in Jack Nelson, "Conservatives Strain GOP, Chamber of Commerce Ties," *Los Angeles Times*, April 9, 1993; John Mintz, "GOP Right, Chamber in Bitter Feud," *Washington Post*, April 2, 1993.

61 **"The far right considers the Chamber** Archey quoted in Wilson, "Interest Groups," p. 117.

61 **"Where do they get the right to tell us** Archey quoted in John Cunniff, "Chamber of Commerce Is Accused of Kowtowing to Clinton," Associated Press, May 19, 1993.

61 **"unified in their interest in creating and preserving** Gorr quoted in, among other sources, Daniel Wattenberg, "Clinton's Echo Chamber," *American Spectator*, June 1993.

61 **"We accept the proposition that all employers** Patricelli quoted in Judis, "Abandoned Surgery."

62 **"We think a compromise is possible** *Health Security Act (1993), Hearings on S.1757 Before the Committee on Labor and Human Resources, U.S. Senate*, 103rd Cong. (October 15, 1993), testimony of Robert Patricelli.

62 **a chorus of angry conservative commentators** Judis, "Abandoned Surgery."

63 **"A few individuals within the Chamber** Richard Rahn, "The Most Destructive Disease," *Washington Times*, July 22, 2009, http://www.cato.org /publications/commentary/most-destructive-disease.

CHAPTER 4: BUSINESS TAKES CHARGE OF CONGRESS

64 **"I was taken by Jimmy Stewart,"** Thomas Donohue, *Newspaper Roundtable*, C-SPAN, July 3, 1997.

65 **the wealthiest 1 percent of the population** Thomas Piketty and Emmanuel Saez, "Income Inequality in the United States, 1913–1998," *Quarterly Journal of Economics* 128, no. 1 (February 2003).

66 **'Don't do that until you check** Donohue quoted in W. John Moore, "As Bad as He Wants to Be," *National Journal*, October 4, 1997.

66 **While the truck drivers who ultimately paid** Melinda Henneberger, "Master Persuader Will Run the Leading Business Lobby," *New York Times,* June 24, 1997.

66 **(At the time, just 250 of the Fortune 1000** Thomas J. Donohue to Roy E. Marden, January 3, 1998, Legacy Tobacco Documents Library, Bates No. 2076396942, University of California, San Francisco. As part of a historic 1998 settlement with state attorneys general, the five major U.S. tobacco companies agreed to publish their internal documents.

67 **public debut in front of the Washington media corps** "Political Agenda of the Business Community," C-SPAN2 broadcast from National Press Club, October 1, 1997, accessed via http://www.c-span.org/video/?92285-1/us-business.

68 **a survey and database of workplace injury reports** *American Trucking Associations, Inc., v. Reich,* U.S. District Court for the District of Columbia, Civil Action No. 96-552.

68 **"there was a great need for leadership at the Chamber** Thomas Donohue, "American Business: Engine of the Opportunity Society," speech to the Heritage Foundation, July 10, 1988.

69 **As recently as the 1960s** See U.S. Chamber of Commerce, *The American Competitive Enterprise System* (Washington, DC: U.S. Chamber of Commerce, 1947); U.S. Chamber of Commerce, *Citizens Course in Freedom vs. Communism: The Economics of Survival,* 8 booklets (Washington, DC: U.S. Chamber of Commerce, 1962).

70 **He doubled the size of the lobbying staff** Dawn Kopecki, "New President Sweeps Out U.S. Chamber's Dusty Corners," *Washington Times,* January 26, 1998; Nancy E. Roman, "Chamber of Commerce Doubles Hill Team; New Lobbyists to Counter Union Efforts," *Washington Times,* December 27, 1997.

70 **And he went on a whirlwind tour** Jan Norman, "New U.S. Chamber Chief Brings His Bid to Revive Group to O.C.," *Orange County Register,* February 5, 1998.

70 **The Chamber was so eager** Louis Jacobson, "Grade Grubbing at the U.S. Chamber," *National Journal,* October 3, 1998.

70 **"It's almost impossible to go too far** Luntz quoted in Joshua Green, "John Edwards, Esq.," *Washington Monthly,* October 2001.

70 **game plan laid out by longtime Chamber lawyer** U.S. Chamber Institute for Legal Reform, "1999 Agenda and Activities," Tobacco Documents Library, Bates No. TI16521028.

71 **R. Bruce Josten, a proud free marketeer** "As Bad as He Wants to Be."

72 **"The Chamber has been kind of a weak sister** Roy Marden to Tom Collamore (Philip Morris), November 22, 1994, Tobacco Documents Library, Bates No. 2047905357.

72 **"Is it fair to get a couple of million dollars** Saundra Torry, "Tort and Retort," *Washington Post,* March 6, 1995.

72 **"We are writing to you at the request** Coalition for a Balanced Budget to Samuel D. Chilcote Jr. (Tobacco Institute), July 24, 1995, Tobacco Documents Library, Bates No. TI10932095.

73 **blitz dozens of newly elected Republicans** Lane Gay and Grover G. Norquist, "Big Labor Buys Some Time," *American Spectator,* August 1998.

74 **"Our effort will be purely educational,"** Fund-raising memo from the Coalition, subject: "YOUR HELP URGENTLY NEEDED TO STOP UNION

POWER GRAB," accessed via Tobacco Documents Library, Bates No. TI1092291.

74 **"We've got this puppy** Josten quoted in Steve Pearlstein and Frank Swoboda, "Labor vs. Business: Mixed Election Results and More Modest Goals," *Washington Post,* November 10, 1996.

74 **By Donohuean standards, the amount of money** Jim VandeHei and Juliet Eilperin, "Rift over Issue Advertising Strategy Develops Among GOP Supporters," *Roll Call,* September 1, 1997.

74 **Big Labor's one-way conversation** *The Mary Matalin Show,* July 16, 1996. Matalin played audio clip of the Coalition pro-Nethercutt ad.

75 **The accusation of a lie was itself a lie** Kevin Sack, "Organized Labor Fires Back on Medicare," *New York Times,* August 30, 1996.

75 **a victory his campaign consultant credited** Larry McCarthy to Alan Kranowitz, Bruce Josten, and Elaine Graham, "Next Steps for the Coalition," November 7, 1996, attachment to Sandstrom Statement of Reasons.

75 **twelve thousand runs of four Coalition ads** "The Coalition: Americans Working for Real Change, Report on Accomplishments," memo circulated to contributors, December 19, 1996, included in *In the Matter of the Coalition et al.,* MUR No. 4624, Federal Election Commission, Statement of Reasons by FEC governor Karl J. Sandstrom, September 6, 2001, accessed via http://1.usa .gov/1vP1edx.

75 **"In short: mission accomplished!"** "The Coalition: Americans Working for Real Change, Report on Accomplishments."

75 **seven sets of videotapes of the ads** *In the Matter of the Coalition et al.,* MUR No. 4624, Federal Election Commission, General Counsel's Report, April 20, 2001.

76 **For $500, the RNC even sent the Coalition** Republican National Committee invoice, July 23, 1996, attachment to Sandstrom Statement of Reasons.

76 **The FEC subpoenaed Boehner** Kevin Galvin, "FEC Investigating Labor's Issues Ads Campaign," Associated Press, July 3, 1998.

76 **Josten himself pressed "play"** Bruce Josten, response, February 29, 2000; included in MUR No. 4624, Sandstrom Statement of Reasons.

76 **"It is highly probable that the discussion** MUR No. 4624, General Counsel's Report.

77 **"The facts obtained thus far provide** Ibid.

78 **In the smoke of leftist revolution** Wallace Whitworth, "Capital Gains: A Conversation with Bruce Josten '69," *Mercersburg,* Spring 2009.

78 **"My goal is simple** Tom Donohue to Roy Marden (Philip Morris companies), January 5, 1998, Tobacco Documents Library, Bates No. 2076396939.

78 **The cigarette giant had nonetheless** "1995 Public Policy Grants," Tobacco Documents Library, Bates No. 2047243272.

78 **It was telling the public** Bruce Josten to Tom Donohue, Jim Robinson, and Frank Coleman, "Tobacco Settlement—Press Inquiries," April 13, 1998, Tobacco Documents Library, Bates No. 83666021.

78 **the Chamber spent $100,000 on television ads** Raja Mishra, "Ads and Star Power Join Tobacco Fight," *Philadelphia Inquirer,* May 21, 1998.

79 **$100,000 in 1998 for the Chamber's "revitalization project"** "Chamber of Commerce of the United States of America," internal Philip Morris Memo, Tobacco Documents Library, Bates No. 2076396935.

79   **"Who is next?" asked Josten rhetorically.** Josten quoted in "Ads and Star Power."

79   **"One can only imagine** "Dear Senator" letter from Donohue addressed to Senator Spencer Abraham, April 28, 1998, Tobacco Documents Library, Bates No. 207639994.

79   **also had a $100,000 check in hand** Letter from Tom Donohue to Tommy Payne, R.J. Reynolds, March 3, 1998; invoice from Agnes Warfield, U.S. Chamber, for $100,000 to Payne, December 18, 1998, for "revitalization investment." Tobacco Documents Library, Bates No. 522495827. Letter, Tom Donohue to Tommy Payne, January 15, 1999, Bates No. 522495823: "Dear Tommy: Your check has arrived!"

79   **would subsequently request $500,000** Untitled Philip Morris memo, filed with 1999 papers, Tobacco Documents Library, Bates No. 2077084915.

79   **R.J. Reynolds had been a member** "Charles B. Wade, Tobacco Executive" (obituary), *Washington Post,* July 19, 1994.

80   **Brown & Williamson was a dues-paying** Memorandum, "Contributions Budget and Corporate Memberships for 1979," October 9, 1978, Tobacco Documents Library, Bates No. 682172997.

80   **Tobacco Institute had bought an annual** Paul Emrick from Dennis Dyer, "T.I. Participation in the Government Affairs Eastern Roundtable—U.S. Chamber of Commerce," September 22, 1998, Tobacco Documents Library, Bates No. TI24110011–TI24110019.

80   **an innocuous guide** *A National Health Care Strategy: How Business Can Promote Good Health for Employees and Their Families* (Washington, DC: National Chamber Foundation, 1977).

80   **link between smoking and worker absenteeism** See, for example, James Athanasou, "Sickness Absence and Smoking Behavior and Its Consequences," *Journal of Occupational Medicine* 17, no. 7 (July 1975). Much of the evidence cited in the Chamber Foundation's booklet came from U.S. companies' assessments of their own employees' health issues.

80   **"The relationship between the Chamber and The Tobacco Institute** Letter from Samuel D. Chilcote Jr. to Richard L. Lesher, February 22, 1983, Tobacco Documents Library, Bates No. 690135737.

80   **"I am certain that future revisions** Tom Donohue to Kinsley Van R. Dey, Liggett & Myers, March 31, 1983.

80   **Tobacco Institute inked an agreement** Invoice request, January 1, 1985, National Chamber Foundation to Tobacco Institute; references October 1984 agreement for the Tobacco Institute to provide $4,000 a month in financial support to the National Chamber Foundation. Tobacco Documents Library, Bates No. TI51400303.

81   **"Assuming no one knows TI funded,"** Memorandum to Martin Gleason from Carol Hrycaj, re: NCF Tax Study Proposal, February 15, 1990, Tobacco Documents Library, Bates No. TI52150868. For more on project see Memorandum to Martin Gleason from Carol Hrycaj, re: Social Cost Council, January 18, 1990, Tobacco Documents Library, Bates No. TI5210901.

81   **"membership investment."** Philip Morris voucher, "Membership Investment for 1994," requested by Roy Marden, Tobacco Documents Library, Bates No. 2041159384.

81   **"Cld. we get more out of our membership** Handwritten note by Hamish Max-

well on letter from Richard Lesher to Maxwell, December 1, 1987, Tobacco Documents Library, Bates No. 2024266112.

81 **aimed to prove that no connection** David Zelkowitz to Roy Marden, "Subject: U.S. Chamber addendum," December 18, 1987, Tobacco Documents Library, Bates No. 2024266110. "Using major corporations as the sample, the study will attempt to show that absenteeism is not statistically related to smoking, but rather to other control variables, e.g., nature of job, ethnicity, etc." Tobacco Documents Library, Bates No. 2024266110.

81 **no statistically significant connection between** Carlos E. Bonilla, *Determinants of Employee Absenteeism: A Study* (Washington, DC: National Chamber Foundation, 1989).

81 **(Not incidentally, the ACLU** Morton Mintz, "The ACLU and the Tobacco Companies," *Nieman Reports* 52, no. 1 (Spring 1998).

81 **And nowhere in the report** Bonilla, *Determinants of Employee Absenteeism.*

81 **took money from tobacco companies** See, for example, "Excise Tax Falls Heaviest on Working Class, Minorities, Study Finds," Bureau of National Affairs, *Taxation, Budget and Accounting* newsletter, October 26, 1990. Accessed via Tobacco Documents Library, Bates No. TI52151049. The Tobacco Institute was a sponsor of the study, as noted in correspondence between Robert Ragland, chief tax counsel of the National Chamber Foundation, and issue analyst Carol Hrycaj of the Tobacco Institute, October 6, 1990. Tobacco Documents Library, Bates No. TI52151051.

81 **It reduced the dues it gave to the Chamber** Roy Marden to Tom Collamore, "Subject: RE Tort Reform," November 22, 1994, Tobacco Documents Library, Bates No. 2047905357.

82 **"It's been a wild four months, Roy!"** Thomas J. Donohue to Roy E. Marden, January 5, 1998, Tobacco Documents Library, Bates No. 2076396939.

82 **The Chamber urged Senator Spencer Abraham** Tom Donohue to Senator Spencer Abraham, April 28, 1998, Tobacco Documents Library, Bates No. 2076396994.

82 **to Senate majority leader Trent Lott** Tom Donohue to Senator Trent Lott, June 12, 1998, Tobacco Documents Library, Bates No. TI5961826.

82 **met privately with House Speaker Newt Gingrich** "Congressional Activities to Date on Senator McCain's Tobacco Legislation," memo from the files of Roy Marden (Philip Morris), May 21, 1998, Tobacco Documents Library, Bates No. 2076396992.

82 **"Your help is needed IMMEDIATELY** Grassroots Action Information Network, "Senate May Vote on Biggest Tax and Spend Bill Ever in Tobacco Industry Overhaul," May 19, 1998, Tobacco Documents Library, Bates No. 2076396991.

83 **"a beltway buy targeted to opinion elites,"** BMSG Worldwide, to John Scruggs, Philip Morris, April 18, 1999, Tobacco Documents Library, Bates No. 2077084948.

83 **"Chamber is the client** David Sylvia (Philip Morris) to David Nicoli and John Scruggs (Philip Morris), "Subject: Chamber Update," June 7, 1999, Tobacco Documents Library, Bates No. 2078706520.

84 **"Tom C can you work out contribution** John Scruggs to David Sylvia, David Nicoli, and Tom Collamore, "Subject: RE: Chamber Update," June 7, 1999, Tobacco Documents Library, Bates No. 2078706521.

84 "Chamber is doing good work," Beverly McKittrick to Tom Collamore and John Scruggs, "Subject: RE: Tom Donohue/US Chamber," June 4, 1999, Tobacco Documents Library, Bates No. 2078706528.

84 "Research has identified several salient messages David Sylvia (Philip Morris) and Jon Richter (KRC Research) to John Scruggs and David Nicoli (Philip Morris), "Re: Chamber of Commerce Poll: Proposal to Develop Survey Instrument," May 18, 1999, Tobacco Documents Library, Bates No. 2073333230.

84 "This technique is a step toward totalitarianism U.S. Chamber of Commerce Media Relations, press release, July 21, 1999, Tobacco Documents Library, Bates No. 2071710725.

85 Like a political consulting firm See, for example, Bruce Josten to Roy Marden, "Subject: FYI," July 20, 1998, cover sheet, Tobacco Documents Library, Bates No. 2076397030.

85 In 2000 it filed a brief urging the Supreme Court *Philip Morris v. Engle, Howard, et al.*, No. 99-1277, March 1, 2000.

86 Defense contractors—biggest among them General Accounting Office, Report to Senator Paul Simon, *Worker Protection: Federal Contractors and Violations of Labor Law,* October 1995.

87 General Electric had to be forced Ken Silverstein, "Unjust Rewards," *Mother Jones,* May–June 2002.

87 Already, the Chamber and the Trucking Associations *U.S. Chamber of Commerce v. Reich*, U.S. Court of Appeals for the D.C. Circuit, No. 95-5242.

87 OSHA predicted that the rules would prevent Richard Wolffe, "U.S. Plans Ergonomic Standards for Workplace," *Financial Times,* November 23, 1999.

87 "Too many American workers," Memorandum for the heads of executive departments and agencies, President William J. Clinton, May 24, 1999.

87 All these acts drew lightning bolts See, for example, the complaint in *LPA v. Herman* (*LPA, Inc., v. Chao*, 211 F.Supp.2d 160 [2002]), which claimed regarding one of the plaintiffs, a Massachusetts medical equipment leasing company, "If any of its full-time technicians were to take extended leave due to the birth or adoption of a child, CounterPulsation would not immediately be able to find a qualified temporary replacement for that employee, would lose revenues and profits during the period of the employee's leave as a result, and might be unable to continue its operations."

88 "We've got a pocket full of cash Donohue quoted in Mary Lynn F. Jones, "U.S. Chamber Unveils $5 Million Pro-Business Election Campaign," *Hill,* October 27, 1999.

89 promising to raise $30 million for 2002 David Nicklaus, "U.S. Chamber Happy with Its Political Gifts," *St. Louis Post-Dispatch,* July 21, 2001.

89 still employed only ten full-time lobbyists Mark Smith, *American Business and Political Power: Public Opinion, Elections, and Democracy* (Chicago: University of Chicago Press, 2000).

89 a high rate of fatal failures Cindy Skrzycki, "The Regulators: High-Speed Legislation; Auto-Safety Bill Reflects Industry's Interests," *Washington Post,* October 24, 2000.

89 did not take on industry-specific causes Burdett A. Loomis, "A New Era: Groups and the Grass Roots," in Allan J. Cigler and Burdett A. Loomis, eds., *Interest Group Politics* (Washington, DC: Congressional Quarterly, 1983).

90   the Chamber routinely took funds from companies James VandeHei, "Political Cover: Major Business Lobby Wins Back Its Clout by Dispensing Favors," *Wall Street Journal*, September 11, 2001.

90   "inure to the benefit of any private shareholder John Francis Reilly, Carter C. Hull, and Barbara A. Braig Allen, "IRC 501(c)(6) Organizations: Exempt Organizations-Technical Instruction Program for FY 2003," http://www.irs.gov/pub/irs-tege/eotopici03.pdf.

91   "It takes $2.5 million a week Donohue quoted in Louis Jacobson, "Wheeling and Dealing for New Income," *National Journal*, November 10, 2001.

91   "We're only about a third of the way Donohue quoted in VandeHei, "Political Cover."

91   By decade's end U.S. Chamber of Commerce, IRS Form 990, 2010, accessible via http://bit.ly/12Rhm7L.

CHAPTER 5: WHY SCIENCE ISN'T SACRED

95   Actually, you may already be taking it GeoSyntec Consultants for the Strategic Environmental Research and Development Program, *Alternative Causes of Widespread, Low Concentration Perchlorate Impacts to Groundwater* (Arlington, VA: U.S. Department of Defense, 2005).

95   Generated in the production of rocket fuel C. A. Sanchez et al., "Perchlorate and Nitrate in Leafy Vegetables of North America," *Environmental Science and Technology* 39, no. 25 (2005).

95   the EPA sought to regulate Drinking Water Perchlorate Supplemental Request for Comments, EPA HQ-OW-2009-0297, *Federal Register* 74 FR 41883, August 19, 2009.

96   a legal precedent for finding agency actions illegal William L. Kovacs to Environmental Protection Agency, "Re: Request for Reconsideration of Information Quality Act Request for Correction Regarding 'Drinking Water: Regulatory Determination on Perchlorate' (RFC 12004)," May 28, 2013, http://uscham.com/1vhiAQG.

96   seeped into greenhouse-grown fruits "Statement as regards the presence of perchlorate in food, agreed by the Standing Committee of the Food Chain and Animal Health, July 16, 2013," European Commission, Health and Consumers Directorate-General. Accessed via http://bit.ly/1DAXOFw.

96   "precautionary principle" "In cases where the scientific basis is lacking, or uncertainty exists, the precautionary principle will guide the Commission in the decision-making process." Emma Bonino, European Commissioner for Consumer Policy and Health Protection, intervention at the Joint European Parliament and Commission Conference on Food Law and Food Policy, Brussels, November 4, 1997, http://europa.eu/rapid/press-release_SPEECH-97-233_en.htm.

97   pioneered the use of White House reviews to alter James Tozzi, interview for National Archives, March 2009, http://thecre.com/video/National_Archive.html.

97   One pending rule William L. Kovacs to Environmental Protection Agency, "Re: Proposed Expansion of EPA Power to Regulate Coal Ash, Docket ID No. EPA-HQ-RCRA-2009-0640," November 19, 2010, http://uscham.com/1DxbSKS.

98 proposed rules on indoor air quality Occupational Safety and Health Admin-
    istration, "Indoor Air Quality," RIN 1218-AB37, http://1.usa.gov/100zFGf.

98 Tozzi and Philip Morris Letter from John Tozzi (Philip Morris) to Elizabeth
    Fontham (Louisiana State University Medical Center), March 25, 1997, Leg-
    acy Tobacco Documents Library, Bates No. 2505153381, University of Cali-
    fornia, San Francisco. "Our operating activities are funded with a grant from
    Philip Morris, Inc."

98 hounded the study's lead researcher Richard Carchman (Philip Morris) to
    Elizabeth Fontham, November 12, 1996; Elizabeth Fontham et al. to Richard
    Carchman, March 11, 1997. Fontham and her fellow investigators indicated
    that they were seeking independent reanalysis of the study data. The study in
    question was Fontham et al., "Lung Cancer in Nonsmoking Women: A Mul-
    ticenter Case-Control Study," Cancer Epidemiology, Biomarkers and Preven-
    tion 1, no. 1 (1991).

98 a one-sentence amendment inserted into Technically, the appropriations provi-
    sion provided guidance to advance rules under the already passed Paperwork
    Reduction Act of 1980. Tozzi, interview by author.

98 Chamber's lobbyists quarterbacked the amendment Tozzi memorandum to
    Data Access Working Group, April 28, 1999, Tobacco Documents Library,
    Bates No. 2077162259.

98 research data did not count as a government record Forsham v. Harris, 445
    U.S. 169 (1980).

99 thousands of comments flooding into OMB Jim Tozzi to Data Access Working
    Group, April 16, 1999, Tobacco Documents Library, Bates No. 2077162248.

99 "will allow the public, for the first time, William Kovacs to Chamber policy
    committees, March 5, 1999, Tobacco Documents Library, Bates No.
    2077162135.

99 forces of free inquiry Office of Management and Budget, "Request for Com-
    ments on Clarifying Changes to Proposed Revision on Public Access to Re-
    search Data," http://www.whitehouse.gov/omb/fedreg_2ndnotice-a110.

100 55 percent of the comments submitted supported the data release Eric A.
    Fischer, "Public Access to Data from Federally Funded Research," Congres-
    sional Research Service, March 1, 2013.

100 a peer-reviewed Harvard study Douglas W. Dockery et al., "An Association
    Between Air Pollution and Mortality in Six U.S. Cities," New England Journal
    of Medicine 329 (1993): 1753–59.

101 to block the EPA from imposing rules on ozone and soot Business Counsel,
    National Chamber Litigation Center, vol. 21, no. 1, Spring 1999.

101 to open that research to challenge by outsiders Alexander Nathan Hecht, "Ad-
    ministrative Process in an Information Age: The Transformation of Agency
    Action Under the Data Quality Act," Journal of Legislation 31 (2004–5): 233.

101 A required EPA cost-benefit analysis "Conversation with Douglas Dockery
    ScD," http://defendingscience.org/conversation-douglas-dockery-scd%20/.

101 Kovacs demanded it anyway. Aaron Zitner, "Health Study Data Demanded by
    U.S. Chamber," Boston Globe, December 10, 1999.

101 The dean of Harvard's public health school Health Effects Institute, "Reanaly-
    sis of the Harvard Six Cities Study and the American Cancer Society Study of
    Particulate Air Pollution and Mortality," July 2000, http://pubs.healtheffects
    .org/view.php?id=6.

101 **delayed their going into effect** Donald T. Hornstein, "Accounting for Science: The Independence of Public Research in the New, Subterranean Administrative Law," *Law and Contemporary Problems* 66, no. 4 (Autumn 2003).

102 **called the Data Quality Act** Hecht, "Administrative Processes," 233–74.

102 **Kovacs and Tozzi met and talked** Tozzi, interview by author.

102 **a close-to-impossible task** One huge positive consequence of the Data Quality Act is that it gives researchers, journalists, and other members of the public access to the data and metadata underlying government-sponsored research.

103 **"I believe policymakers need to take a precautionary** Christine Todd Whitman, "Effective Policy Making: The Role of Good Science," address to the National Academy of Sciences, October 13, 2000, http://gos.sbc.edu/w /whitman2.html.

103 **energy task force** "National Energy Policy," report of the National Energy Policy Development Group, May 2001.

103 **perhaps even Iraq** Energy task force documents obtained by the organization Judicial Watch included a map of an Iraqi oil field and lists of international energy firms that might participate in their exploration. Accessed via http:// www.judicialwatch.org/maps-and-charts-of-iraqi-oil-fields/.

104 **spent mightily to help him keep his Senate seat** Joan Claybrook (Public Citizen) to Mark Everson (IRS), October 31, 2006, http://www.citizen.org /documents/acf1f3e.pdf.

104 **Donohue visited Abraham** Accessed via U.S. Department of Energy, National Energy Policy Development Group file release, accessed via http://1.usa .gov/1wCpvHF.

104 **The oil giant Chevron** Letter, Margot Anderson (U.S. Department of Energy) to David J. O'Reilly (Chevron Corporation), March 8, 2001. Accessed via U.S. Department of Energy, National Energy Policy Development Group file release.

104 **"We must be very careful** Letter from President George W. Bush to Senators Chuck Hagel, Jesse Helms, Larry Craig, and Pat Roberts, March 13, 2001.

105 **"Spence, we thank you for your participation,"** Thomas J. Donohue to Spencer Abraham, April 9, 2001. Accessed via U.S. Department of Energy, National Energy Policy Development Group file release.

105 **"a potential energy supply shortage of significant dimensions"** Letter from Senators James Inhofe and John Breaux to Energy Secretary Spencer Abraham, March 23, 2001. Accessed via U.S. Department of Energy, National Energy Policy Development Group file release.

106 **Clinton administration and eight northeastern states** "U.S. Expands Clean Air Act Lawsuits Against Electric Utilities," news release, U.S. Environmental Protection Agency, March 1, 2000. Accessed via http://1.usa.gov/1yU3hPF.

106 **American Electric Power** "U.S. Announces Single Largest Environmental Settlement in History," news release, U.S. Environmental Protection Agency, October 9, 2007, accessed via http://1.usa.gov/13seorl.

106 **Utilities would pay a high price** "Clean Air Act Issues in the 107th Congress," Congressional Research Service, January 2, 2001; EPA news release, American Electric Power Service Corporation, October 9, 2007.

106 **Cheney's task force asked the EPA** "National Energy Policy."

107 **to bulletproof the administration's actions** Jo Becker and Barton Gellman, "Leaving No Tracks," *Washington Post,* June 27, 2007.

107   **had made profit in erecting new plants less certain** NSR 90-Day Review Background Paper," U.S. Environmental Protection Agency, June 22, 2001, p. 23; citing National Coal Council, "Increasing Electricity from Coal-Fired Generation in the Near Term," May 2001, cited in U.S. Environmental Protection Agency, "NSR 90-Day Review Background Paper," June 22, 2001, p. 23, http://www.epa.gov/nsr/documents/nsr-review.pdf.

107   **new coal-burning plants with the technology required** National Coal Council, "Increasing Electricity from Coal-Fired Generation in the Near Term."

107   **Cheney demanded to know why** Becker and Gellman, "Leaving No Tracks."

107   **"National energy policy, indeed national security,"** Tom Donohue to Vice President Richard Cheney, "The U.S. Chamber Concludes That Immediate NSR Administrative Reform Is Needed," November 7, 2001.

107   **She was cc'ed on the letter** Becker and Gellman, "Leaving No Tracks."

108   **the EPA's June 2002 report** "New Source Review: Report to the President," U.S. Environmental Protection Agency, June 2002.

108   **"EPA relied primarily on anecdotal** "Clean Air Act: EPA Should Use Available Data to Monitor the Effects of Its Revisions to the New Source Review Program," General Accounting Office, GAO-03-947, August 22, 2003.

108   **In mid-2003 Whitman resigned.** Becker and Gellman, "Leaving No Tracks."

108   **"fall on our sword issues"** Work Plan for the Environment & Regulatory Affairs Division, U.S. Chamber of Commerce, PowerPoint presentation from William L. Kovacs, accessed via Tobacco Documents Library, Bates No. 2076396957.

109   **largely rested on a 2001 study** Frank M. Sachs et al., "Effects on Blood Pressure of Reduced Dietary Sodium and the Dietary Approaches to Stop Hypertension (DASH) Diet, *New England Journal of Medicine* 344 (2001): 3–10.

109   **bankrolled by $1.3 million** Salt Institute, IRS Form 990, 2004, accessed via http://bit.ly/1wAjTPg.

109   **fired off a petition** Request for correction under Information Quality Act from William L. Kovacs (U.S. Chamber of Commerce) and Richard L. Hanneman (Salt Institute) to National Heart, Lung, and Blood Institute Office of Communications, May 14, 2003. Accessed via http://1.usa.gov/1yWthyN.

110   **"claim that all persons should limit salt intake** Salt Institute and U.S. Chamber of Virginia, Case No. 04-CV-359, 2004, complaint.

111   **the UN Intergovernmental Panel on Climate Change** DRI/McGraw-Hill (for U.S. Department of Commerce), *Economic Effects of Using Carbon Taxes to Reduce Carbon Dioxide Emissions in Major OECD Countries,* January 1992.

111   **environmental, economic, and social upheaval** "IPCC Second Assessment: Climate Change 1995," Intergovernmental Panel on Climate Change.

111   **Burson-Marsteller public relations** Eric Pooley, *The Climate War* (New York: Hyperion, 2010), pp. 86–87.

112   **membership of the Climate Action Partnership** "Joint Statement of the United States Climate Action Partnership," January 19, 2007. Accessed at http://www.us-cap.org/media/release_USCAPStatement011907.pdf.

112   **"limiting global atmospheric GHG concentrations** "A Call for Action," U.S. Climate Action Partnership, January 2007.

113   **climate activists on the board** Ann Mulkern, "'Hot Button' Climate Issue Spotlights How U.S. Chamber Sets Policy," *Greenwire,* October 6, 2009.

113   **one-third of its $140 million in contributions** IRS Form 990, Schedule B,

2008, cited in Tom Hamburger, "U.S. Chamber of Commerce Grows into a Political Force," *Los Angeles Times,* March 8, 2010.

113 **three in four said that to counter global warming** John M. Broder and Marjorie Connelly, "Public Remains Split on Response to Warming," *New York Times,* April 27, 2007.

113 **United States could feasibly reduce greenhouse gases** McKinsey & Company, "Reducing U.S. Greenhouse Gas Emissions: How Much at What Cost?" December 2007.

114 **Union Pacific gave $600,000 to the Chamber's** Union Pacific Corporation, proxy statement, 2009, http://1.usa.gov/1E2O17U; proxy statement, 2012, http://1.usa.gov/1DxmMQN.

115 **cap-and-trade would inflict much milder hits** Bryan Buckley and Sergey Mityakov, "The Cost of Climate Regulation for American Households," George Marshall Institute, 2009, http://heartland.org/sites/default/files/636.pdf.

115 **The National Association of Manufacturers study** "Analysis of the Waxman-Markey Bill, 'The American Clean Energy and Security Act of 2009,' " Science Applications International Corporation, report for the American Council on Capital Formation and National Association of Manufacturers, accessed at http://accf.org/wp-content/uploads/2009/10/accf-nam_study.pdf.

115 **Even the hyperideological Heritage Foundation** William M. Beach, David W. Kreutzer, Ben Lieberman, and Nicolas D. Loris, "The Economic Costs of the Lieberman-Warner Climate Change Legislation," Heritage Foundation, May 2008.

116 **"You're always better off if you can get** Josten quoted in Geoff Kaus, "All Sides Gird for Cap-and-Trade Fight," *Roll Call,* March 31, 2008.

117 **"to advance human progress through an economic** IRS Form 990, accessed via guidestar.org.

118 **a three-hour private pseudodebate** U.S. Chamber of Commerce, Environment, Technology & Regulatory Affairs Division, Annual Report 2009.

118 **"doing God's work"** "Fred Palmer interview," Leo Hickman, *The Guardian,* March 8, 2011, http://www.theguardian.com/environment/blog/2011/mar/08/fred-palmer-peabody-coal-interview.

118 **"quite a spirited discussion,"** Kovacs testimony on American Clean Energy Security Act of 2009, U.S. House Subcommittee on Energy and Environment, April 24, 2009.

118 **"we would appreciate it if statements made** C. E. Holland (Johnson & Johnson) to Thomas J. Donohue, April 19, 2009, accessed via http://switchboard.nrdc.org/blogs/paltman/media/Tom%20Donohue%20Climate%20Letter.doc.

119 **"core principles" and a "transparent democratic process."** *American Clean Energy and Security Act of 2009, Hearings on H.R. 2454 Before the Committee on Energy and Commerce and Subcommittee on Energy and Environment* (April 24, 2009), testimony of William L. Kovacs.

119 **"hugely controverted"** U.S. Chamber of Commerce, "Petition of the Chamber of Commerce of the United States of America for EPA to Conduct Its Endangerment Finding Proceeding on the Record Using Administrative Procedure Act 556 and 557," June 22, 2009, http://uscham.com/1rSShPR.

119 **"there's no link between greenhouse gases** Market Call, CNNfn, July 16, 2001.

120 **Crops would grow faster and stronger** Ibid.

120 "It would be evolution versus creationism," Kovacs quoted in Jim Tankersley, "U.S. Chamber of Commerce Seeks Trial on Global Warming," *Los Angeles Times*, August 25, 2009.

121 "extreme rhetoric and obstructionist tactics" Peter A. Darbee to Thomas J. Donohue, September 18, 2009.

122 Nike also resigned from the Chamber's board Ann Mulkern, " 'Hot Button' Climate Issue Spotlights How U.S. Chamber Sets Policy," *Greenwire*, October 6, 2009.

123 meet with Senate leaders to craft R. Bruce Josten to Senators Barbara Boxer and James Inhofe, November 3, 2009. Accessed via https://www.uschamber .com/letter/letter-united-states-senate-climate-change.

123 "the Saudi Arabia of clean coal," Senators John Kerry and Lindsey Graham, "Yes We Can (Pass Climate Change Legislation)," *New York Times*, October 10, 2009.

123 "We'll start working with you Donohue quoted in Ryan Lizza, "As the World Burns," *New Yorker*, October 11, 2010.

124 not a single Republican could be persuaded Matthew Daly, "Climate Bill: Senate Democrats Abandon Comprehensive Energy Bill," Associated Press, July 22, 2010.

124 The EPA had officially determined *U.S. Chamber of Commerce et al. v. Environmental Protection Agency*, U.S. Supreme Court, No. 12-1272.

124 "the most aggressive voter-education Dan Eggen, "U.S. Chamber of Commerce Sets Sights on Democrats Ahead of Midterm Elections," *Washington Post*, March 16, 2010.

124 "This is how science works," *Coalition for Responsible Regulation v. EPA*, U.S. Court of Appeals for the D.C. Circuit, No. 09-1322, June 26, 2012, *per curiam* opinion.

125 "commercial identity theft masquerading as social *Chamber of Commerce of the United States v. Jacques Servin et al.*, U.S. District Court for the District of Columbia, Case No. 09-cv-02014-RWR, complaint.

126 "This case has not affected us at all," Andy Bichlbaum, interview by author.

CHAPTER 6: HOW CONSUMERS LOST IN THE COURTS

128 Bausch & Lomb had to make Deborah R. Hensler, Nicholas Pace, et al., *Class Action Dilemmas: Pursuing Public Goals for Private Gain* (Santa Monica, CA: RAND Corporation, 2001), p. 9.

128 Shell had to, yes, shell Ibid., p. 14. The initial settlement for $838 million grew into a larger fund.

128 American Home Products Linda Lloyd, "Drug Company to Change Its Name to American Home Products," *Philadelphia Inquirer*, January 25, 2002.

128 $2.1 billion Toshiba Andrew Pollack, "Toshiba Faces $1 Billion Bill over a Lawsuit," *New York Times*, October 30, 1999. $1 billion was the company's estimate of actual payouts under a $2.1 billion settlement.

129 In theory, such accountability incentivizes businesses Ibid., pp. 18–23.

129 the Class Action Fairness Act Provisions in law at 28 U.S.C. § 1332(d), 28 U.S.C. § 1453, and 28 U.S.C. §§ 1711–1715.

129 "A plot to murder a pregnant woman *Gordon Maag v. Chicagoland Chamber*

of Commerce, U.S. District Court for the Southern District of Illinois, 3:05-CV-00711, Exhibit from plaintiff, attached to first amended complaint.

129 **Chamber had given the state GOP** "Hidden Rivers: How Trade Associations Conceal Corporate Political Spending, Its Threat to Companies, and What Shareholders Can Do," Center for Political Accountability, 2006.

130 **won 12 of the 13 state high court races** Deborah Goldberg, "The New Politics of Judicial Elections," Brennan Center for Justice, New York University, December 31, 2004.

130 **had succeeded twenty-one times** Robert Lenzer and Matthew Miller, "Buying Justice," *Forbes,* July 21, 2003.

130 **They included oddball cases** Peter Hartlaub, "Teen Hit by Own Vehicle in Hot-Fry Incident Sues," *Daily News of Los Angeles,* September 10, 1998.

130 **Alabama jury awarded $225,000** Joann Muller, "Crass Actions: Chrysler Bites Back at Trial Lawyers," *Forbes,* March 31, 2003.

130 **died in the crash of a Dodge Neon** "Chrysler Group Sues Lawyers, Alleging Fraudulent Case," Associated Press, July 9, 2003.

131 **a record-setting $4.9 billion jury verdict** Andrew Pollack, "$4.9 Billion Jury Verdict in GM Fuel Tank Case," *New York Times,* July 10, 1999.

131 **additional funding from Koch Industries** John J. Fialka, "How Koch Industries Tries to Influence Judicial System," *Wall Street Journal,* August 9, 1999.

131 **Marcus teamed up with New York Stock Exchange chief Dick Grasso** Letter from Marcus to Geoffrey Bible (Philip Morris), May 18, 1998. Legacy Tobacco Documents Library, Bates No. 207276155, University of California, San Francisco.

131 **that would have drastically limited punitive damages** Jim Bennet, "Business Groups Hope Ads in Pivotal Electoral States Sway Clinton on Product Liability Bill," *New York Times,* April 30, 1996.

131 **Its focus and message were clouded by tobacco companies** Steve Parrish (Philip Morris) to Paul Beckner (Citizens for a Sound Economy), March 25, 1996, Tobacco Documents Library, Bates No. 2046982596. Lorillard was also a supporter.

132 **"was suggesting to the Chamber that they look at state tort** Steven Hantler, interview by author.

132 **more former U.S. attorneys general** Bernard Marcus to Geoffrey Bible, May 18, 1998, Tobacco Documents Library, Bates No. 2072706155.

132 **$46 million-a-year organization** IRS Form 990, U.S. Chamber Institute for Legal Reform, 2002.

133 **"You could sort of show the corporate leadership** Jim Wootton, interview by author.

133 **GM, Toyota, and Ford from the auto industry** James VandeHei, "Political Cover: Major Business Lobby Wins Back Its Clout by Dispensing Favors," *Wall Street Journal,* September 11, 2001.

134 **"We're the reinsurance industry** James Verini, "Show Him the Money," *Washington Monthly,* July–August 2010.

134 **Complaints from business about the burdens** Nathan Weber, *Product Liability: The Corporate Response* (New York: Conference Board, 1987).

134 **Insurance costs for U.S. businesses declined** Tillinghast-Towers Perrin and the Risk & Insurance Management Society, *Cost of Risk Survey,* January 1998.

134   consumer plaintiffs accounted for only Hensler, Pace, et al., *Class Action Dilemmas.*

134   their products were better made Weber, *Product Liability*, p. 2; Hensler, Pace, et al., *Class Action Dilemmas*, p. 9.

135   "brushing aside a mandate of this court State ex rel. *Ohio Academy of Trial Lawyers v. Sheward*, 86 Ohio St. 3d 451, 715 N.E.2d 1062 (1999).

135   rated each justice based on their history Ohio Chamber of Commerce, "The 2000 Business Evaluation of the Ohio Supreme Court," February 2000. As described in "Ohio Chamber Evaluation Highlights Significant Tilt on Ohio Supreme Court," PR Newswire, February 10, 2000.

135   "The Ohio Supreme Court is a significant threat "Ohio Chamber Evaluation."

136    $4.2 million into a campaign attacking Resnick "Panel Upholds Anti-Resnick Ad," *Columbus Dispatch*, October 20, 2000.

136   Alice Resnick—voting with her contributors *Judicial Elections: Past, Present, Future*, panel 1: *Reflections of a Survivor of State Judicial Election Warfare*, Manhattan Institute Conference Series no. 6, April 21, 2001, http://www .manhattan-institute.org/html/mics_6.htm.000.

136   "The particularly tough ad *Judicial Elections: Past, Present, Future.*

137   insurance industry was the biggest backer Funders to Citizens for a Strong Ohio—Calendar Year 2000, submitted in *King Lincoln Bronzeville Neighborhood Association et al. v. Brunner*, U.S. District Court for the Southern District of Ohio, Case No. 2:06-cv-00745. The list was also published in Jon Craig, "Business Group Releases Donors' List from 2000 Ad Campaign," *Columbus Dispatch*, January 28, 2005.

137   it endorsed fifteen candidates for judge *Judicial Elections: Past, Present, Future.*

137   the Chamber spent between $6 million and $7 million "Chamber's Ad Efforts Failed in Ohio, Worked in Other States," Associated Press, November 9, 2000.

137   an estimated $4.2 million to dislodge Resnick James Sample et al., *The New Politics of Judicial Elections: A Decade of Change 2000–2009* (New York: Brennan Center for Justice, 2010).

137   Justice Resnick survived the attacks In 2005 Resnick attempted to flee a DUI stop after refusing a sobriety test; she declined to run in 2006.

137   "concern for the integrity of both "Chief Justice Asks U.S. Chamber of Commerce to Stop Running TV Ads," *Memphis Commercial-Appeal*, November 4, 2000.

138   an order from Supreme Court justice Antonin Scalia U.S. Chamber of Commerce, "U.S. Chamber Wins Free Speech Case: Supreme Court Protects Issue Ads," press release, November 6, 2000.

138   "A fair and independent voice for Mississippi" *Chamber of Commerce v. Moore*, 288 F.3d 187, U.S. Court of Appeals, Fifth Circuit, April 5, 2002.

138   "emasculated" their ability Brief of amici curiae states, *Moore v. Mississippi*, on petition for a writ of certiorari, No. 02-305, U.S. Supreme Court.

138   "don't think it affected anyone's behavior Wootton, interview by author.

139   Donohue opened 2002 vowing to spend Brian Tumulty, "U.S. Chamber to Spend $40 Million on '02 Elections," Gannett News Service, January 15, 2002.

139 **$2.6 million to the American Taxpayers Alliance** "The New Stealth PACs," Public Citizen, September 2004, citing American Taxpayers Alliance IRS Form 990 for 2002, http://www.stealthpacs.org/funder.cfm?Org_ID=106.

139 **Mississippi had the most hostile legal environment** "U.S. Chamber of Commerce State Liability Systems Ranking Study," Harris Poll, January 11, 2002, http://courts.delaware.gov/superior/pdf/harris_2010.pdf.

139 **calling for a boycott of Mississippi businesses** "Mississippi Spurning," *Wall Street Journal,* May 13, 2002.

139 **the Law Enforcement Alliance of America** Peter L. DeCoursey, "Group Told to Stop Ad Campaign," *Harrisburg Patriot-News,* October 24, 2001.

139 **But more seriously, he's a former trial lawyer** For more on McRae, see Stephanie Mencimer, *Blocking the Courthouse Door: How the Republican Party and Its Corporate Allies Are Taking Away Your Right to Sue* (New York: Free Press, 2006).

140 **paying a staggering $246 billion to forty-six states** Mark Curriden, "Up in Smoke," *ABA Journal* 93 (March 2007).

140 **"Mississippi should erect billboards** *Horton v. American Tobacco Co.,* 667 So.2d 1289 (1995), No. 91-CA-00006-SCT, opinion.

140 **"We felt an obligation with tobacco to stand** Jonathan Salant, "Lawsuits Against Gun Industry Brings in Business Group, NRA," Associated Press, January 16, 1999.

141 **the Chamber put up more than $1 million** Robert Lenzer and Matthew Miller, "Buying Justice," *Forbes,* July 21, 2003.

141 **"Chuck McRae? He was the only judge** Mencimer, *Blocking the Courthouse Door,* p. 67.

141 **"the trial lawyer agenda."** Peter Overby, "Mississippi Judgeship Becomes Electoral Battleground," *All Things Considered,* NPR, November 4, 2002.

141 **"I would have to see the facts."** Chuck McCrae, interview by author.

141 **"made millions suing doctors, hospitals** Quoted in Laylan Copelin, "Mystery Election Lawyers Targeted," *Austin American-Statesman,* September 28, 2004.

141 **aggressively fought the court order to reveal its funders** *In re: Law Enforcement Alliance of America,* Supreme Court of Texas, No. 11-1012; Memorandum Opinion, Chief Justice J. Woodfin Jones, Texas Court of Appeals, Third District, No. 03-11-00634-CV. Reports that the Law Enforcement Alliance served as a conduit for Chamber judge-attack funds first surfaced in Pennsylvania the previous year. See, for example, Peter L. DeCoursey, "Issue Ads: Judge Refuses to Halt Ban; Attorneys to Decide Whether They'll Appeal," *Harrisburg Patriot-News,* October 27, 2001.

142 **spending $12.5 million on "contributions" in 2002** U.S. Chamber Institute for Legal Reform, IRS Form 990, 2003. Accessed via publiccitizen.org.

142 **declined to hear Mississippi's case seeking** *Moore, Attorney General of Mississippi, v. U.S. Chamber of Commerce,* 02-305, U.S. Supreme Court, November 12, 2002, certiorari denied.

142 **They decided which were vulnerable** *Avery et al. v. State Farm Mutual Automobile Insurance* Co., Supreme Court of Illinois No. 91494, deposition by Rob Engstrom (Institute for Legal Reform).

143 **a $1.05 billion judgment against State Farm Mutual** *Avery et al. v. State Farm Mutual Automobile Insurance Co.,* no. 5-99-0830, Illinois Appellate Court, 5th district, unpublished portion of opinion.

144   "You've passed all the tryouts *Avery et al. v. State Farm Mutual Automobile Insurance Co.,* Supreme Court of Illinois No. 91494, affidavit by Douglas B. Wojcieszak in support of petition to recall mandate and vacate judgment, September 8, 2011.

144   U.S. Chamber spent more money "Hidden Rivers."

144   Board members weighed in on the selection *State of Washington v. Voters Education Committee,* Superior Court of Washington for King County, No. 04-2-23551-1, deposition by Rob Engstrom, January 11, 2005.

145   "He has been described in some quarters "Nader Is a Good Guy, Says U.S. Chamber of Commerce Chief," *Wall Street Journal,* September 19, 1973.

145   in full freak-out mode "Chief's Opinion of Nader Is His Alone, Chamber Says," *Wall Street Journal,* September 20, 1973.

146   "This is wise counsel," "Ralph Nader, Capitalist," *Wall Street Journal,* September 21, 1973.

146   even invited Nader Robert Cole, "Unorthodox Insurer: State Farm President Voices His Own Views," *New York Times,* October 28, 1973.

146   "systematic destruction of documents" *Campbell v. State Farm Mutual Automobile Insurance Co.,* No. 890905231, slip op. at 53, Third Judicial District, Salt Lake City, UT, August 3, 1998, opinion of Judge William Bohling.

146   "The insured's medical records were not examined McKee quoted in Edward Walsh, "Auto Insurers Facing Legal Challenge," *Washington Post,* July 4, 1999.

146   One of the judges who had backed the verdict Dan Popkey, "Contributors Could Benefit from Eismann's Role," *Idaho Statesman,* March 8, 2001.

147   "That's obscene for a judicial race. Karmeier quoted in Ryan Keith, "Spending for Supreme Court Seat Renews Cry for Finance Reform," Associated Press, November 3, 2004.

147   Karmeier then cast the deciding vote State Farm went to court to make the case to keep Karmeier on the panel: *Avery v. State Farm,* Supreme Court of Illinois, No. 91494, opposition of defendant-appellant State Farm Mutual Automobile Insurance Company to plaintiffs-appellees' conditional motion for nonparticipation, January 21, 2005.

147   Engstrom and his colleagues delivered $1.5 million *Voters Education Committee v. Washington State Public Disclosure Commission and Deborah Senn,* Superior Court of Washington for King County, No. 04-2-23351-1, deposition of Stanton Anderson.

147   failed to register with the state Staff memo to State of Washington Public Disclosure Commission, September 9, 2004.

147   backed up the campaign with polling Alex Bellone (Public Opinion Strategies) to Rob Engstrom (Institute for Legal Reform), September 13, 2004. Certification and Complaint to the Washington State Public Disclosure Commission, Justice Robert Utter, Joaquin Avila, and Public Citizen, October 11, 2005, Exhibit 11.

148   she pushed to change the law on emergency care Deborah Senn, speech to Octagon conference, April 13, 2012.

148   she demanded that four insurers Tyrone Beason, "Senn Battles Insurers on ER Coverage," *Seattle Times,* March 2, 1999.

148   She also hit the company with $1.3 million "Washington State Insurance Commissioner Senn Announces Prudential Will Pay Full $700,000 Fine, Plus

Consumer Protection Costs," press release, Office of the Washington State insurance commissioner, March 12, 1997.

148 **Ten days before the primary** Deborah Senn, interview by author.

149 **a state commission concluded that the ads were not** Special meeting of the State of Washington Public Disclosure Commission, September 9, 2004, minutes.

149 **Having won the primary, Senn faced even more vicious ads** IRS report on Republican State Leadership Committee. The national group sent nearly $1.3 million to its Washington State PAC that year.

149 **Republican State Leadership Committee** OpenSecrets.org database, search for contributions to "Republican State Leadership Committee" for 2004.

150 **"Continuing our good working relationship** Greater Seattle Chamber, Association of Washington Business, Spokane Regional Chamber, Kelso Longview Chamber, Bellevue Chamber, and Tacoma–Pierce County Chamber to Tom Donohue (U.S. Chamber of Commerce), September 16, 2004. Certification and Complaint to the Washington State Public Disclosure Commission, Justice Robert Utter, Joaquin Avila, and Public Citizen, October 11, 2005, Exhibit 15.

150 **Punitive damages? Make them uninsurable** "Litigation Costs on Trial," *Chief Executive,* January–February 1995.

150 **"The industry will do what it always does** "Insurers Plot New Strategy for Superfund Reform Drive," *Business Insurance,* December 19, 1994.

151 **Normally, Starr trafficked** Starr Foundation, IRS filings 990-PF, schedules B and C, accessed via guidestar.org.

151 **Greenberg's foundation doled out more than $24 million** Rick Cohen, "Starr Crossed: Foundation Dollars Used to Further Corporate Interests," *The Cohen Report,* newsletter of Nonprofit Quarterly, January 31, 2008.

151 **it had $18.8 million in outstanding loans** National Chamber Foundation, Form IRS 990, 2010, accessed via guidestar.org.

151 **designated for a capital campaign** Eric Lichtblau, "Chamber of Commerce Accused of Tax Fraud," *New York Times,* September 10, 2010.

151 **"Irrational jury awards and liability inflation,"** "AIG to Add to General Insurance Loss Reserves," news release, February 3, 2003.

152 **six of the nine justices decided that the punishment was excessive** *State Farm Mutual Insurance Co. v. Campbell et al.,* U.S. Supreme Court, No. 01-1289, decided April 7, 2003.

152 **had put 475 lobbyists on the case** Public Citizen, *Unfairness Incorporated: The Corporate Campaign Against Consumer Class Actions* (Washington, DC: Public Citizen, June 2003).

152 **class action cases have increasingly shifted away from state** See, for example, Howard M. Erichson, "CAFA's Impact on Class Action Lawyers," *University of Pennsylvania Law Review* 156, no. 6 (June 2008).

152 **block any chance that a Kerry-Edwards White House** Greg Pierce, "Inside Politics," *Washington Times,* October 11, 2004.

153 **"We believed that the prospect of having a trial lawyer** Tom Donohue to U.S. Chamber Board of Directors, "President's Update," December 6, 2004.

153 **the November Fund had improperly failed to register** *In the Matter of the November Fund,* Federal Election Commission, MUR no. 5541, certification, March 9, 2005.

153 **The IRS never responded** Joan Claybrook, interview by author.

CHAPTER 7: HOW BUSINESS BOUGHT CONGRESS

155   the Chamber's $33 million in spending Lindsay Young, "Outside Spenders' Return on Investment," Sunlight Foundation, December 17, 2002, http://bit.ly/1wWhu2x.

155   resembled that of the 1962 Mets Jonathan Salant, "Chamber of Commerce $33 Million Lost Most Races," *Bloomberg News,* December 4, 2012.

156   The Chamber poured in $36 million Federal Election Commission independent expenditures database, 2014 election.

156   He systematically assessed funds Michael E. McGerr, *The Decline of Popular Politics* (Oxford: Oxford University Press, 1986).

156   Standard Oil—where the Rockefellers had made their fortune *Hearing on Campaign Contributions, U.S. Senate, Committee on Privileges and Elections (the Clapp Committee)* (October 18, 1912).

156   A railroad handed over Charles Gates Dawes, *A Journal of the McKinley Years* (Chicago: Lakeside Press, 1950), p. 97.

156   Hanna's camp estimated the total take William T. Horner, *Ohio's Kingmaker: Mark Hanna, Man and Myth* (Athens: Ohio University Press, 2010), p. 196.

157   While McKinley held court Ibid., p. 201.

157   Speakers and literature flooded Quentin R. Skrabec, *William McKinley, Apostle of Protectionism* (New York: Algora Publishing, 2007), pp. 140, 157.

157   "the foundation of American development "Our Home Defenders," Library of Congress, http://www.loc.gov/pictures/resource/pga.03756/.

157   The cash infusion bought McKinley James Ford Rhodes, *McKinley and Roosevelt Administrations 1897–1909* (New York: Macmillan Company, 1922), pp. 140–43.

157   But the president also was deeply implicated *Hearing on Campaign Contributions, U.S. Senate, Committee on Privileges and Elections (the Clapp Committee)* (1912–13), testimony.

158   It took six decades and a lawsuit Joel L. Fleischman and Carol S. Greenwald, "Public Interest Litigation and Political Finance Reform," *Annals of the American Academy of Political and Social Science* 425 (May 1976).

158   In 1976 the Supreme Court ruled *Buckley v. Valeo,* 424 U.S. 1 (1976), and subsequent FEC regulations.

159   "Look, I realize you went after me Kelly D. Patterson, "When Redistricting Means Never Having to Say You're Sorry: Utah's Second District," in David Magleby and J. Quin Monson, eds., *The Last Hurrah?: Soft Money and Issue Advocacy in the 2002 Congressional Elections* (Washington, DC: Brookings Institution Press, 2004).

159   "This is a country founded on free speech," U.S. Chamber of Commerce, "U.S. Chamber Vows Legal Fight Against Campaign Law," media release, March 2002.

160   "a patent fiction." *Federal Election Commission v. Wisconsin Right to Life,* 551 U.S. 449 (2007), Justice David Souter, dissenting opinion.

160   "We'll start having political shops Cole quoted in Peter H. Stone, "New Channels for Campaign Cash," *National Journal,* February 23, 2002.

160   "This law will not remove Senator Mitch McConnell, statement, December 10, 2003.

161   "If we had the ability to replace one with the other Miller quoted in David

Krantz, "Chamber of Commerce Backs Thune," *Sioux Falls Argus Leader,* February 3, 2004.

161 **Actually, Daschle voted 75 percent** "Daschle Voted with Bush 75% of Time in '02?!?!" *National Journal,* June 23, 2003.

161 **In 2002, at the local chamber's request** Steve Erpenbach (Daschle 2004 campaign state director), interview by author.

162 **"mayor's race,"** Mark Wegner, "Business Groups Look to Influence Tight Senate Races," *Congress Daily,* October 26, 2004.

162 **"doctors driven out of rural America** Script for "Daschle's Record" TV spot, as published by *National Journal,* August 30, 2004.

162 **even Hutterite colonies that had never allowed** Anonymous e-mail to South Dakota political blogger John Lauck: "Another factor that I feel was significant in the Daschle defeat was the Hutterite vote. I helped to register the people from our colony (most of whom had never voted before), and I know they voted for Bush/Thune/Diedrich. I also heard that there were several other colonies who allowed their people to vote for the first time." http://bit.ly/16rbS5Q.

162 **With help from another $3.2 million** National Republican Senatorial Committee, "Independent Expenditures and Coordinated Expenses, 2003–2004," Tom Daschle and John Thune, http://bit.ly/1FZcfSh.

162 **"Let me be clear that we tried very hard** Thomas Donohue to U.S. Chamber board of directors, "President's Update," December 6, 2004.

163 **It hadn't been wall-to-wall** Ibid.

163 **Miller reported the total as $25 million** Miller quoted in Nicole Duran, "Chamber Playing Defense," *Roll Call,* November 16, 2005.

163 **The Chamber's filings to the IRS** Chamber of Commerce of the USA, IRS form 990, 2004, line 81a.

163 **a pitiful one-tenth of the amount** This wasn't the first or the last time leaders floated big numbers that were disconnected from reality, presumably to pull in more money and spook opponents. In 2002 it promised "up to $30 million" but then fell short: a study of twenty-one contentious congressional races that year could tally only $222,000 in Chamber purchases of television ads. A field coordinator in Arizona dryly chalked the shortfall up to an "inability to reach fundraising expectations." David B. Magleby and Jonathan W. Tanner, "Interest-Group Electioneering in the 2002 Congressional Elections," in Magleby and Monson, *Last Hurrah?* That year it reported zero campaign spending to the IRS, only accounting for lobbying.

163 **The show of money in 2006** U.S. Chamber and Institute for Legal Reform, IRS Form 990. Accessed via National Center for Charitable Statistics, http://bit.ly/1uX0x2G and http://bit.ly/1z1iJP2.

163 **members of Congress who had voted for the Medicare** David Espo, "Medicare Ads Paid by Drug Industry," Associated Press, August 25, 2006. Donohue wrote to his board in early August: "The Chamber will run ads throughout the August recess and into the fall, starting with ads that focus on lawmakers' support for providing seniors with the new prescription drug benefit under Medicare." Tom Donohue to U.S. Chamber board of directors, July 2006.

164 **to dislodge a pillar of McCain-Feingold** *Federal Election Commission v. Wisconsin Right to Life,* 551 U.S. 449 (2007).

164 **"for the purpose of furthering electioneering** 11 CFR §104.20, "Reporting

Electioneering Communications," Federal Election Commission, issued December 26, 2007.

164 **all-time record holder for lobbying** "Lobbying: Top Spenders," Center for Responsive Politics, http://bit.ly/1o8vT8S.

164 **The Chamber spent $145 million** OpenSecrets.org, Lobbying Expenditures for U.S. Chamber of Commerce and subsidiaries, 2007 and 2008.

164 **Labor leaders thought it less than coincidental** Steve Rosenthal, interview by author.

165 **"From the business community's perspective** Miller quoted in Peter H. Stone, "Business Nervously Eyes the Senate," *National Journal,* July 26, 2008.

165 **Stewarded by Chuck Schumer (D-NY)** OpenSecrets.org, report for Democratic Senatorial Campaign Committee, 2008.

166 **The Chamber rallied to the Citizens United cause** *Citizens United v. Federal Election Commission,* 558 U.S. 310 (2010), No. 08-205, amicus brief, U.S. Chamber of Commerce.

167 **"Today's ruling protects the First Amendment** "Reactions to the Supreme Court Reversing Limits on Corporate Spending in Political Campaigns," *Washington Post,* January 21, 2010.

167 **"if, after a reasonable period of time, the private effort** U.S. Chamber of Commerce, *Social Security in the United States: Chamber Policies and Report of Committee on Social Security* (Washington, DC: U.S. Chamber of Commerce, 1944).

168 **the Chamber proper had just fifteen hundred** U.S. Chamber of Commerce, IRS Form 990, 2009, Schedule B. Accessed via "Truth in Testimony" form to the U.S. Congress Committee on Natural Resources, Christopher Guith, U.S. Chamber Institute for 21st Century Energy, http://1.usa.gov/1wf7fp8.

168 **The donor, as word on the Hill had it** America's Health Insurance Plans, IRS Form 990, 2009. Accessed via guidestar.org.

168 **Its members were insurers** Peter H. Stone, "Health Insurers Funded Chamber Attack Ads," *National Journal,* January 13, 2010.

169 **"They've been immoral all along** Glenn Thrush, "Pelosi Slams Insurers as 'Immoral' Villains," *Politico,* July 30, 2009.

169 **Many insurers and AHIP itself** See, for example, Aetna's earnings conference call on fourth-quarter 2009 earnings, in which Aetna CEO and chairman Ron Williams stated: "The fundamental trends and underlying issues driving the need for meaningful healthcare reform continue, and it is our hope that we return to a bipartisan approach to address the accessibility and affordability of health care in America."

169 **"You have our commitment to play** Ignagni quoted in Mike Madden, "Harry and Louise, Meet Thelma and Louise," *Salon,* March 6, 2009.

169 **"If private insurers say that the marketplace** Obama quoted in Ricardo Alonso-Zaldivar and Erica Werner, "Obama Takes on Insurers over Gov't Plan," Associated Press, June 23, 2009.

170 **One of the most painful items** In the first year after reform took effect, insurers were forced to refund $1.3 billion nationally to employers and individuals. Those employers were certainly saving money on premiums. So were all those who didn't receive rebates because their insurers were following the law: they kept their administrative costs in check, savings that then were passed along to

consumers. "Insurer Rebates Under the Medical Loss Ratio," Kaiser Family Foundation, April 2012.

171 spurned even mild scenarios John E. McDonough, *Inside National Health Reform* (Berkeley and Los Angeles: University of California Press, 2011), p. 36.

171 Of the nearly $124 million U.S. Chamber of Commerce, IRS Form 990, 2009.

172 John Kerry sought an amendment Jerry Geisel, "Senators Reshaping Reform Bill," *Business Insurance,* September 28, 2009.

173 Massachusetts had had a government-enhanced "Romneycare Facts and Falsehoods," Factcheck.org, March 25, 2011, http://bit.ly/1yPwdKq.

174 "the January surprise." James Gelfand, "Health Care Reform: Did Congress Cure Our System's Ailments?" PowerPoint presentation, available at http://www.slideshare.net/DEStateChamber/katie-hays.

175 Law helped beat it back "On behalf of Philip Morris, I want to express my sincere gratitude for your leadership and energy on tobacco related issues in the 103rd Congress." William I. Campbell (Philip Morris) to Steven Law (administrative assistant to the Hon. Mitch McConnell), October 12, 1994, Legacy Tobacco Documents Library, Bates No. 2046953677, University of California, San Francisco.

175 he did not believe nicotine was addictive *Hearing on Oversight of Tobacco Products Before the Subcommittee on Health and the Environment, Committee on Energy and Commerce, U.S. House of Representatives,* 103rd Cong. (April 14, 1994).

175 "I look forward to an increasingly close Steven Law to Howard Liebengood et al. (Philip Morris), January 9, 1996, Tobacco Documents Library, Bates No. 2046952808.

175 siphon funds from its national PAC E-mail exchanges among Philip Morris staff, Tobacco Documents Library, Bates Nos. 2062538605 through 2062538610.

175 "I had no idea Steven Law to Ralph Vinovich, December 21, 1994, and July 14, 1995, Tobacco Documents Library, Bates Nos. TI 36331697 and TI 36331698.

176 While American Crossroads could finance Kim Barker, "Karl Rove's Dark Money Group Promised IRS It Would Spend 'Limited' Money on Elections," *ProPublica,* December 14, 2012.

176 "How do I say no to a K Street lobbyist Craig Holman (Public Citizen), interview by author.

177 But if their scores were low Heidi Przybyla, "Chamber Democratic Attack Ads Outpacing Political Parties," *Bloomberg News,* June 14, 2012.

177 The Chamber would spend $133 million U.S. Senate lobbying disclosure database, available at http://soprweb.senate.gov/index.cfm?event=selectfields.

177 a war chest as big as $75 million "Release the Chamber: Biz Group Goes on the Air in Key Senate Races," *Talking Points Memo,* September 21, 2010.

177 "its hard-hitting $75 million ad campaign Jeanne Cummings, "Angry Member Groups Shun U.S. Chamber of Commerce," *Politico,* December 7, 2010.

177 Meeting at Karl Rove's house in Virginia Peter H. Stone, "Inside the Shadow GOP," Center for Public Integrity, October 27, 2010.

178 The other $29 million financed Campaign spending data from FEC Indepen-

dent Expenditure database for 2010, http://www.fec.gov/data/Independent Expenditure.do, and OpenSecrets.org.

178   **just 42 percent agreed—and 47 percent** Lydia Saad, "By Slim Margin, Americans Support Healthcare Bill's Passage," Gallup *Politics,* March 22, 2010.

178   **an astounding 27,500 TV ad spots** "Vast Majority of Chamber's 27,000 Ads This Year Focus on Health Care Reform," Media Matters, October 12, 2010, http://politicalcorrection.org/blog/201010120001.

179   **they usually don't work** Richard R. Lau, Lee Sigelman, and Ivy Brown Rovner, "The Effects of Negative Political Campaigns: A Meta-Analytic Reassessment," *Journal of Politics* 69, no. 4 (November 2007): 1176–209.

179   **Chamber lavished $400,000** Christopher Carney, interview by author.

179   **Kilroy sought to require disclosure** See, "Introduction of the Proxy Voting Transparency Act of 2009," *Congressional Record* 155, no. 114 (July 27, 2009).

180   **"The seniors defected from voting Democratic** Mary Jo Kilroy, interview by author.

180   **("Money—it's a five-letter word,"** Paul Hodes, interview by author.

180   **In the Ohio race for Senate** Lee Fisher, interview by author.

181   **"The Chamber will include Senate votes on this** R. Bruce Josten (U.S. Chamber) to senators, "Key Vote Letter Opposing the Motion to Reconsider the Vote on the Motion to Proceed and Any Vote Relating to Passage of S. 3628, the 'Democracy Is Strengthened by Casting Light on Spending in Elections Act (DISCLOSE Act),' " September 22, 2010, http://uscham.com/1zj9jOG.

181   **"The fact that this assault to the First** U.S. Chamber of Commerce, "Senate Should Focus on Jobs, Not Partisan Games," press release, July 26, 2010.

182   **$2 million in attacks on GOP-turned-independent** See the ad "Flip Flopper," produced by Revolution Agency.

182   **his compensation totaled $4.7 million** U.S. Chamber of Commerce, IRS Form 990, 2010, accessed via guidestar.org.

183   **a nonprofit organization run by Senator Lamar Alexander** David Morris, "Alexander Used Non-Profit Network to Raise Money, Hone Issues," Associated Press, June 21, 1995.

183   **sued the FEC, looking to close that little** *Van Hollen v. Federal Election Commission,* U.S. District Court for the District of Columbia, No. 11-0766.

184   **$32.6 million in spots that specifically** Federal Election Commission filings, U.S. Chamber of Commerce, for 2012 election.

CHAPTER 8: WHY BANKERS AND BOARDS GET RICHER

185   **in 2010 the federal regulator called for employers** National Labor Relations Board, "Proposed Rules Governing Notification of Employee Rights Under the National Labor Relations Act," *Federal Register* 75, no. 245 (December 22, 2010), http://1.usa.gov/1DPDCu9.

186   **the rate of union membership in the United States** U.S. Department of Labor, Bureau of Labor Statistics, "Union Members—2012," http://1.usa.gov/1x RnNRG.

186   **With its South Carolina affiliate** *Chamber of Commerce of the United States and South Carolina Chamber of Commerce v. National Labor Relations Board,* U.S. District Court for the District of South Carolina, No. 2:11-cv-

02516. The National Association of Manufacturers also filed suit, in the District of Columbia federal court, No. 1:11-cv-01629.

188 **Their congressional members' legal brief** *NLRB v. U.S. Chamber of Commerce*, U.S. Court of Appeals for the Fourth Circuit, No. 12-1757, amici brief of Hon. John Kline et al.

188 **When OSHA updated its rules** Office of Information and Regulatory Affairs, meeting record November 15, 2011.

189 **Obama's regulators rebuffed** Hazard Communication Final Rule, U.S. Department of Labor, Occupational Safety and Health Administration, *Federal Register*, 77, no. 58, March 26, 2012.

190 **In a feat of awkward sloganeering** Thomas J. Donohue, "State of American Business" speech, January 2011; South Shore Chamber annual lunch, March 10, 2011; Charles D. Ferguson and Mark Jansson, *Regulating Japanese Nuclear Power in the Wake of the Fukushima Daiichi Accident* (Washington, DC: Federation of American Scientists, May 2013).

190 **Donohue rightly acknowledged** As Donohue put it in his 2011 "State of American Business" speech: "We cannot allow this nation to move from a government of the people to a government of the regulators. That's where it has been headed under Republicans and Democrats alike."

190 **The Bush administration pushed through** Office of Management and Budget, "Completed EO 12866 Regulatory Reviews by Calendar Year, 1981–2011," http://1.usa.gov/16rqJgs.

190 **The tide slowed considerably** Executive Order 12866, "Regulatory Planning and Review," September 30, 1993, *Federal Register* 58, no. 190 (October 4, 1993).

190 **President Obama added his own spin** Executive Order 13563, "Improving Regulation and Regulatory Review," January 18, 2011, *Federal Register* 76, no. 14 (January 21, 2011).

190 **spent some $136 million** OpenSecrets.org lobbying database, U.S. Chamber of Commerce and subsidiaries, 2012, http://bit.ly/13wcvd0.

191 **thirty-seven meetings with members** Rulemaking records, External Meetings, Commodity Futures Trading Commission, Position Limits for Futures and Swaps (76 FR 71626) and Commodity Pool Operators and Commodity Trading Advisors (77 FR 17328).

191 **Donohue personally met with SEC chair** Mary Schapiro, calendar and staff memorandum, February 19, 2010. Donohue also met with Schapiro on February 10, 2009.

191 **approved more than $9 million** Qwest Communications proxy statements, 2004 and 2005; Edward Iwata and Barbara Hansen, "Some CEOs Get Stratospheric Pay for Mediocre Work," *USA Today*, May 2, 2004; "So, Apropos, Qwest Ready to Steal Show," Al Lewis, *Denver Post*, May 24, 2005.

191 **Glass Lewis, a shareholder advisory group** Carrie Busch (Glass Lewis), shareholder advisory report, November 2003.

191 **Anschutz remained on the Qwest board** Anschutz is reported as being a member of the U.S. Chamber board on its IRS Form 990 in 2003 but not in the 2004 filing.

192 **"one of the worst boards in Corporate America** Edward Iwata and Barbara Hansen, "Pay, Performance Don't Always Add Up," *USA Today*, April 30, 2004.

192 Klaassen, like Anschutz U.S. Chamber of Commerce, IRS Form 990, 2004.

192 **it had restated its income by some $173 million** Change to Win, *Preaching Principle, Enabling Excess: How Tom Donohue Compromised the Credibility of the U.S. Chamber of Commerce* (Change to Win, October 2009), analysis of SEC filings and analyst reports.

192 **Union pension fund shareholders sued** *In Re Sunrise Senior Living, Inc.,* U.S. District Court for the District of Columbia, Civil Action No. CV-07-00143-RBW, May 4, 2009, unopposed memorandum for preliminary approval of shareholder derivative settlement and incorporated memorandum.

192 **advisory firms called for Donohue's ouster** Mark Drajem, "Donohue Should Be Off Sunrise Board, Risk Metrics Says," *Bloomberg News,* November 16, 2009.

192 **the board of Union Pacific** Union Pacific proxy statements, Securities and Exchange Commission.

192 **$3.9 million in compensation from the Chamber** U.S. Chamber IRS Form 990, 2009, accessed via guidestar.org.

192 **"That I serve on corporate boards gives me** Donohue quoted in Jeffrey Birnbaum, "Probe Amplifies Conflict-of-Interest Questions for Chamber of Commerce Chief," *Washington Post,* February 6, 2007.

193 **alleged accounting fraud against two executives** *U.S. Securities and Exchange Commission v. Sunrise Senior Living, Inc., Larry E. Hulse, and Kenneth Abod,* U.S. District Court for the District of Columbia, Case No. 1:10-cv-01247, judgments issued July 27, 2010.

193 **went to court to block** *Business Roundtable and Chamber of Commerce v. U.S. Securities and Exchange Commission,* U.S. Court of Appeals for the District of Columbia Circuit, Case No. 10-1305, petition for review, September 29, 2010.

193 **"sword of Damocles"** Bart Chilton, speech to Americans for Financial Reform, May 12, 2012.

193 **the SEC does not have to conduct a cost-benefit analysis** James Overdahl (former SEC chief economist), "Best of NERA 2011: Examining Economic Issues in Financial Regulation Under Dodd-Frank," Securities Industry Historical Society podcast, July 26, 2011, transcript available at http://bit.ly/13xcVQy.

194 **In that mutual funds case** Geoffrey H. Bobroff and Thomas H. Mack, "Assessing the Significance of Mutual Fund Board Independent Chairs: A Study for Fidelity Investments," March 10, 2004.

194 **Scalia argued that companies would incur** *Chamber of Commerce of the U.S. v. SEC,* U.S. District Court for the District of Columbia, 1:04-CV-1522, complaint, September 2, 2004.

194 **A federal judge was persuaded** James C. Cox and Benjamin B. C. Baucon, "The Emperor Has No Clothes: Confronting the D.C. Circuit's Usurpation of SEC Rulemaking Authority," working paper, March 2012, accessed via http://ssrn.com/abstract=2016433.

194 **"a significant victory."** Thomas Donohue to the U.S. Chamber board of directors, "President's Update," June 2005.

194 **Seven years later, fighting shareholders** Elaine Buckberg, Ph.D., and Jonathan Macey, "Report on Effects of Proposed SEC Rule 14a-11 on Efficiency, Competitiveness and Capital Formation: In Support of Comments by Business Roundtable," NERA Economic Consulting, August 17, 2009.

194 **"had failed to respond to substantial problems** *Business Roundtable and U.S.*

Chamber of Commerce v. Securities and Exchange Commission, U.S. Court of Appeals for the D.C. Circuit, No. 10-1305, decided July 22, 2011.

195   **twenty-one thousand staff hours** Mary Schapiro to Representative Scott Garrett (R-NJ), August 5, 2011, available at http://www.law.du.edu/documents /corporate-governance/sec-and-governance/SEC-letter%208-5-11.pdf.

195   **"We get to the point where we're so concerned** Bart Chilton, interview by author.

195   **"No matter how many times** Dennis Kelleher, interview by author.

197   **Scalia attacked Dodd-Frank's limits** *International Swaps and Derivatives Association et al. v. U.S. Commodity Futures Trading Commission,* Civil Action No. 11-cv-2146-RLW, September 28, 2012, memorandum opinion of U.S. District judge Robert L. Wilkins.

197   **The Business Roundtable and GE Capital** Lobbying Disclosure Act database, U.S. Senate: Michael Bopp (Gibson, Dunn), accessed at http://soprweb.senate .gov/index.cfm?event=selectfields.

197   **"If people can put Main Street instead of Wall Street** Matthew Magidson (Lowenstein Sandler), quoted in Eleni Himaras, "End Users to Blitz D.C. for Exemption," *Derivatives Week,* April 1, 2010.

198   **profited heavily from the corporate swap** *Hearing on OTC Derivatives Reform and Addressing Systemic Risk, Before the Senate Committee on Agriculture, Nutrition, and Forestry,* 111th Cong. (December 2, 2009), testimony of Blythe Masters, JPMorgan Chase & Co.

198   **the two firms would hold half the value** Office of the Comptroller of the Currency, OCC's *Quarterly Report on Bank Trading and Derivatives Activities First Quarter 2013,* http://1.usa.gov/1p707cY.

198   **played an instrumental role in positioning JPMorgan** Gillian Tett, *Fool's Gold: The Inside Story of J.P. Morgan and How Wall St. Greed Corrupted Its Bold Dream and Created a Financial Catastrophe* (New York: Simon and Schuster, 2009), pp. 46–47.

198   **"preventing them from managing risk** Masters testimony, December 2, 2009.

199   **estimated that a 3 percent cash cushion** "An Analysis of the Coalition for Derivatives End-Users' Survey on Over-the-Counter Derivatives," Keybridge Research, February 11, 2011, http://bit.ly/13lsqdT.

199   **"It was a hypothetical study,"** Quoted in Andrew Ross Sorkin, "Vanishing Act: 'Advisers' Distance Themselves from a Report," *New York Times,* February 11, 2011.

199   **Companies have to pay** *Hearing Entitled "Challenges Facing the U.S. Capital Markets to Effectively Implement Title VII of the Dodd-Frank Act," Before the Subcommittee on Capital Markets and Government Sponsored Enterprises, Committee on Financial Services, U.S. House of Representatives,* 112th Cong. (December 12, 2012), testimony of Dr. John Parsons. His testimony was subsequently published as John E. Parsons, *Hit or Miss: Regulating Derivative Markets to Reduce Hedging Costs at Non-Financial Companies* (Cambridge, MA: MIT Center for Energy and Environmental Policy Research, 2013).

200   **another fly-in of executives to lobby Congress** It took place on October 6, 2011, as described in "A Fly-In to Keep Capital from Moving Out," *Free Enterprise,* October 5, 2011.

200   **"Our members are united in one respect** *Hearing Entitled "Challenges Facing*

the U.S. Capital Markets to Effectively Implement Title VII of the Dodd-Frank Act," Before the Subcommittee on Capital Markets and Government Sponsored Enterprises, Committee on Financial Services, U.S. House of Representatives, 112th Cong. (December 12, 2012), testimony of Coalition for Derivatives End-Users.

200 **"We don't speculate."** John Parsons and Antonio Mello, "Chesapeake's Two Natures," *Betting the Business* blog, June 12, 2012; John Parsons, interview by author. Chesapeake discloses the U.S. Chamber as one of the industry groups to which it gives $50,000 or more; how much is unknown.

200 **"We offer customized hedges** *Hearing on Reform of Over-the-Counter Derivative Market: Limiting Risk and Ensuring Fairness, 111-85, Before the House Committee on Financial Services,* 111th Cong. (October 7, 2009).

201 **first nonbank to register** "Swap Dealers (SD) / Major Swap Participants (MSP) Registry," National Futures Association, downloaded at http://bit.ly/1rWx33r.

201 **"They've been captured by this fringe group** Parsons interview.

201 **The bill also removed** The Business Risk Mitigation and Price Stabilization Act of 2012, H.R. 2682, passed the House of Representatives 370 to 24, on March 26, 2012. The 2013 version of the same bill passed 411 to 12. It did not leave committee in the Senate.

202 **The same unfounded talking points** See, for example, Senators Debbie Stabenow and Tim Johnson and Representatives Frank Lucas and Spencer Bachus to Timothy Geithner, Ben Bernanke, Gary Gensler, and Mary Schapiro, April 6, 2011, available at http://1.usa.gov/1wghgSX.

202 **an estimated $2 trillion in cash** Joseph Stiglitz, quoted in "Vanishing Act."

202 **that baseline went up to $8 billion** See U.S. Commodity Futures Trading Commission, "Q&A, Final Rulemaking Regarding Further Defining 'Swap Dealer,' 'Major Swap Participant' and 'Eligible Contract Participant,'" http://1.usa.gov/1xFHIDa.

203 **Scalia's lawsuit on behalf of the derivatives industry** *International Swaps and Derivatives Association et al. v. U.S. Commodity Futures Trading Commission,* U.S. District Court for the District of Columbia, Civil Action No. 11-cv-2146-RLW.

203 **"First, if you don't like a bill, amendment** Bart Chilton, speech to Americans for Financial Reform, May 12, 2012.

204 **"crushing competitive losses"** *American Petroleum Institute et al. v. U.S. Securities and Exchange Commission,* U.S. District Court for the District of Columbia, 1:12-cv-1668-JDB, complaint, October 10, 2012.

204 **a Scalia lawsuit sought to block the CFTC** *Investment Company Institute and U.S. Chamber of Commerce v. U.S. Commodity Futures Trading Commission,* U.S. Court of Appeals for the D.C. Circuit, No. 12-5413, decided June 25, 2013.

204 **missed most of its deadlines** Davis Polk, *Dodd-Frank Progress Report,* June 2013.

204 **"Consumers can enter the market** Elizabeth Warren, "Unsafe at Any Rate," *Democracy: A Journal of Ideas,* no. 5 (Summer 2007).

205 **"A cop on the beat looking out** Elizabeth Warren, remarks to U.S. Chamber of Commerce Fifth Annual Capital Markets Summit, March 30, 2011.

207 **earned the eternal gratitude of the securities** Office of Representative Vito Fossella, press release, February 20, 2007.

208 **"would reduce liquidity"** News release from Representative Vito Fossella, "Rep. Fossella Urges Congress to Reject New Taxes on Futures Transactions on CFTC-Funded Exchanges," March 9, 2007, accessible via States News Service.

208 **"modernize a system to allow the markets** Representative Vito Fossella, interview by C-SPAN, April 1, 2008.

208 **A Washington State Pepsi bottler** *Noel Canning v. National Labor Relations Board,* U.S. Court of Appeals for the D.C. Circuit, No. 12-1115, January 25, 2013.

209 **"There will be lots of lawsuits** Pincus quoted in Robert Barnes and Steven Mufson, "Court Says Obama Exceeded Authority in Making Appointments," *Washington Post,* January 25, 2013.

209 **proposed alternatives to the CFPB** David Hirschmann, "Consumer Financial Protection Bureau Needs More Accountability," *Politico,* December 7, 2011; Peter Schroeder, "U.S. Chamber Seeking to Replace Provisions of Dodd-Frank Reforms," *Hill,* April 4, 2013.

CHAPTER 9: WHY AMERICAN JOBS COME LAST

211 **Shrinking paychecks, lower job security** Weekly and hourly earnings data from the U.S. Department of Labor, Bureau of Labor Statistics, "Current Population Survey," December 2013.

211 **6.9 million of us work part-time** Labor force statistics from U.S. Bureau of Labor Statistics, "Current Population Survey, Employment Level—Part-Time for Economic Reasons, All Industries," November 2014.

211 **cut 3 million U.S. jobs, while adding** David Wessel, "Big U.S. Firms Shift Hiring Abroad," *Wall Street Journal,* April 19, 2011.

211 **attributes the loss of 2.7 million U.S. jobs** Robert E. Scott, "The China Toll," Economic Policy Institute, August 23, 2012.

212 **125,000 people go to work** Darryl Green, ManpowerGroup president of Asia Pacific and Middle East, interview by author.

212 **The hourly minimum wage for Shenzhen workers** "Shenzhen Raises Minimum Wage Levels," *China Briefing,* March 11, 2013.

213 **"It's a matter of *when* China becomes** Jeff Joerres, interview by author.

213 **"I would say in five years from now, we** Darryl Green interview.

213 **AmCham has had a foothold in China** James Reed, *The Missionary Mind and American East Asia Policy, 1911–1915* (Cambridge, MA: Harvard University Press, 1983), p. 46.

213 **More than half the businesses surveyed** American Chamber of Commerce in Shanghai, *China Business Report,* 2013–2014.

213 **Daimler AG and Control Components** *United States v. Daimler AG,* U.S. District Court for the District of Columbia, No. 10-CR-063; *United States v. Control Components,* U.S. District Court for the Central District of California, No. 09-cr-00162.

214 **"government appreciation dinner,"** Eleventh Annual Shanghai Government Appreciation Dinner, December 8, 2011, RMB1000 per ticket. Event information at http://bit.ly/1DM3psH.

214   **"their eyes and ears on the ground."** Commerce Secretary Gary Locke, speech to American Chamber of Commerce in Seoul, South Korea, April 28, 2011.

215   **"views on feasibility and desirability** U.S. Embassy, Lagos, to State Department, "Chamber of Commerce of U.S.," November 17, 1976, cable no. 1976LAGOS12994–b, WikiLeaks.org.

215   **"about any particularly fruitful relationships** Secretary of state to all diplomatic posts, "Post Relationships with American Chambers of Commerce," April 19, 1976, cable no. 1976STATE094266_b, WikiLeaks.org.

215   **"political sensitivity to organizations** U.S. Embassy, Cairo, to secretary of state, "Post Relationships with American Chambers of Commerce," April 23, 1976, cable no. 1976CAIRO05560_b, WikiLeaks.org.

215   **"In previous times one sent gunboats.** U.S. Embassy, Bonn, to various Western European embassies, missions, and consuls, "DGB President Attacks American Chamber of Commerce on Mitbestimmung," October 15, 1974, cable no. 1974BONN16237_b, WikiLeaks.org.

216   **In Nicaragua, the AmCham president** U.S. Embassy, Managua, to secretary of state, "Nicaraguan Opposition Unity Efforts," August 25, 2009, cable no. 09MANAGUA837, WikiLeaks.org; and U.S. Embassy, Managua, to various agencies, "Ortega's Judicial Coup," October 23, 2009, cable no. 09MANA-GUA1045, WikiLeaks.org.

216   **In Egypt, the chair of the American Chamber** See, for example, U.S. Embassy, Cairo, to secretary of state, "Unesco Director General—Next Steps," December 30, 2008, cable no. 08CAIRO2584, WikiLeaks.org, in which Taher Helmy advised U.S. ambassador Margaret Scobey to support the nomination of Egyptian painter Farouk Hosni as head of UNESCO, despite Hosni's highly inconvenient promise to personally burn every Israeli book in Egypt's libraries.

216   **Taher Helmy helped write the law privatizing** James V. Grimaldi and Robert O'Harrow Jr., "In Egypt, Corruption Cases Had an American Root," *Washington Post,* October 19, 2011.

216   **USAID proceeded to also give $4.2 million** "American Chamber of Commerce: Business Information Highway Project—Final Evaluation," Development Associates, Inc., June 21, 2005.

216   **State Department routinely deferring** U.S. Embassy, Beijing, to various, "Indigenous Innovation," December 18, 2009, cable no. 09BEIJING3395, WikiLeaks.org.

216   **a special fast-track visa** U.S. Consul, Guangzhou, to secretary of state, "Visa Referral Program: Guangzhou Amcham Nearly Flawless," April 1, 2009, cable no. 09GUANGZHOU193, WikiLeaks.org.

217   **And when China sought to pave the way** U.S. Embassy, Beijing, "China's Draft Charity Law," June 8, 2007, cable no. 07BEIJING3884, WikiLeaks.org.

217   **U.S. Chamber's report rallying** James McGregor, "China's Drive for 'Indigenous Innovation': A Web of Industrial Policies," U.S. Chamber of Commerce and APCO Worldwide, 2010; Representative Ed Royce, "Royce Statement on China's Trade and Investment Policies," March 9, 2011, accessed via http://1.usa.gov/1szB6Dj.

218   **employees are entitled to open-ended contracts** Monique Garcia, "China's Labor Law Evolution: Towards a New Frontier," *ILSA Journal of Interna-*

tional and Comparative Law (Fall 2009); and Linda Liang, "Latest Development and Characteristics of Chinese Trade Unions," *China Bulletin,* June 2011, http://bit.ly/10Cgnb7.

218 **"acknowledges and supports worker rights in China** American Chamber of Commerce in South China, "White Paper on the Business Environment in China, 2008."

218 **"If an employer and any employee have** Liu Cheng, "The Draft Labor Contract Law of PRC and Its Background," lecture at Harvard Law School, March 19, 2007.

219 **In Beijing, KFC announced in 2006** U.S. Embassy, Beijing, to secretary of state, "Colonel Sanders Changes His Ways, but Labor Laws Remain Vague," August 22, 2006, cable no. 06BEIJING17324, WikiLeaks.org.

219 **"They very openly threatened, as we in the West** Ellen David Friedman, interview by author.

219 **An apology never** Friedman interview.

219 **"really hopes that the laws cannot be enforced** Liu Cheng, Harvard Law School, March 19, 2007.

220 **"The form of dispatched labor** James Zimmerman, American Chamber of Commerce, People's Republic of China, Comments on Draft Labor Law Contract, April 19, 2006.

220 **"once the Draft comes into effect, unemployment** AmCham Shanghai, "Explanation on Various Problems Under the Labor Contract Law of the People's Republic of China," April 2006.

220 **"AmCham Shanghai has never, and is not,** AmCham Shanghai, responses to questions from ABCNews.com on the China draft Labor Contract Law, http://abcn.ws/13buzYL.

222 **They won a 10 percent salary increase** "China Hiring Plans Rise to Six-Year High," *Bloomberg News,* June 8, 2010.

222 **Even after the new law was in place** 2008 White Paper on American Business in China, AmCham China, http://bit.ly/1wgxLOP.

223 **"For Europeans, the Chinese law is not so** Andreas Lauffs, interview by author.

224 **a Coke plant in southwestern China dismissed** "Chinese Students Go Undercover to Investigate Coca Cola," *China Labor News Translations,* September 16, 2009.

226 **"We're going to support this program because** Thomas Donohue, on Fox Business Network, January 28, 2009.

226 **fast-track environmental review for stimulus-funded** American Recovery and Reinvestment Act (2009), Pub. L. 111-5, 123 Stat. 115, Title XVI, Section 1605.

226 **a "Buy American" rule** Thomas L. Gallagher, "Trade Groups Want Fast NEPA Reviews," *Traffic World,* February 5, 2009.

226 **Buy American was an economic death wish** Veronica Smith, " 'Buy American' stimulus alarms US businesses, trade partners," Agence France-Presse, January 29, 2009.

227 **China explicitly gave preferences** *China's Indigenous Innovation Trade and Investment Policies: How Great a Threat? Hearing Before the Subcommittee on Terrorism, Nonproliferation and Trade of the Committee on Foreign Af-*

fairs, U.S. House of Representatives, 112th Cong. (March 9, 2011), testimony of Karen Laney, U.S. International Trade Commission.

227 **already released catalogs of products that government** James McGregor, U.S. Chamber of Commerce, *China's Drive for "Indigenous Innovation": A Web of Industrial Policies* (Washington, DC: U.S. Chamber of Commerce, 2010).

228 **the likely result would be Chinese retaliation** U.S. Chamber of Commerce, AmCham China/Shanghai/South China/Southwest China, Business Round-table, and other trade associations, to Senators Harry Reid and Mitch McConnell, September 21, 2011.

228 **the Chamber backed the bill but again objected** Tom Ichniowski, "Next Move Is in the Senate After House Passes Jobs Bill," *Engineering News-Record,* December 28, 2009.

228 **"The question is, are we going to become more protectionist?"** Thomas Donohue, Fox Business Network, January 28, 2009.

228 **dues payments from international chamber members** Lee Fang, "Foreign-Funded 'U.S.' Chamber of Commerce Running Partisan Attack Ads," Center for American Progress, October 5, 2010.

229 **it kept all international funds strictly** "AmChams are independent organizations and they do not fund political programs in the United States," the Chamber told reporter Ben Smith. "We have a system in place for ensuring that they are not government-controlled entities. The Chamber is proud to have global companies among our membership. We're careful to ensure that we comply with all applicable laws. No foreign money is used to fund political activities." Ben Smith, "Chamber: 'We Have a System,'" *Politico,* October 5, 2010, http://politi.co/1rWPO6R.

230 **an offensive to eviscerate the Foreign Corrupt Practices Act** The Chamber's vision is laid out in a paper commissioned by the Institute for Legal Reform from two Jenner & Block attorneys. See Andrew Weissmann and Alexandria Smith, "Restoring Balance: Proposed Amendments to the Foreign Corrupt Practices Act," October 2010.

230 **covered up their activities with bogus bookkeeping** Mike Koehler, "The Story of the Foreign Corrupt Practices Act," *Ohio State Law Journal* 73, no. 5 (2012).

231 **"an insidious plague"** UN Convention Against Corruption, adopted 2003, quoted as published 2004.

231 **Mercedes SUVs are standard-issue government cars** *United States v. Daimler AG,* U.S. District Court for the District of Columbia, No. 10-cr-00063. In a deferred prosecution agreement, Daimler AG acknowledged it was responsible for the acts of its employees as laid out in the government's case against the company; filed March 24, 2010.

231 **In Mexico, Tyson Foods bribed** *United States v. Tyson Foods, Inc.,* U.S. District Court for the District of Columbia, 1:11-cr-00037-RWR. In a deferred prosecution agreement, Tyson accepted responsibility for the actions of its employees, who worked for a subsidiary called Tyson de Mexico; filed February 10, 2011.

231 **Kellogg Brown & Root and partners** *United States v. Kellogg Brown & Root LLC,* U.S. District Court for the Southern District of Texas, No. 4:09-cr-00071. On February 11, 2009, Kellogg Brown & Root pleaded guilty to five counts of violating portions of the Foreign Corrupt Practices Act.

231 **The Chamber's wish list for the FCPA** Two law professors writing for George

Soros's Open Society Foundations warned: "The Chamber proposes to change the Act in ways that would substantially undermine the possibility for successful enforcement of America's anti-bribery commitments. The Chamber's proposed amendments would also set back decades of progress in the global struggle against corruption." David Kennedy and Dan Danielsen, *Busting Bribery: Sustaining the Global Momentum of the Foreign Corrupt Practices Act* (New York: Open Society Foundations, September 2011).

231 **if low-corruption Singapore ended up with the level** Shan-Jin Wei, "How Taxing Is Corruption on International Investors?" *Review of Economics and Statistics* 82, no. 1 (February 2000).

232 **Those were fewer in recent years** The Chamber's consultants cited sources to back up their claim that the FCPA had negative economic impacts on U.S. businesses, but they predated the UN convention and therefore reflected a now-vanished world in which U.S. businesses alone bore the burden of criminal penalties for bribery and other forms of corruption. One, from 1996, began by declaring "a warning to the U.S. Government that the bribery of Russian Government officials by U.S. and foreign businesses and businessmen is seriously undermining the transformation to democracy in Russia." It recommended making it possible for U.S. companies to sue one another for anticompetitive bribery of foreign officials. Scott P. Boylan, "Organized Crime and Corruption in Russia: Implications for U.S. and International Law," *Fordham International Law Journal* 19, no. 5 (June 1996).

232 **merely asking for "clarification"** U.S. Chamber of Commerce, Institute for Legal Reform, and other signatories to Lanny Breuer and Robert Khuzami, "Guidance Concerning the Foreign Corrupt Practices Act," February 21, 2012, http://advamed.org/res.download/33.

233 **The Department of Justice subsequently** David Barstow, "Vast Mexico Bribery Case Hushed Up by Wal-Mart After Top-Level Struggle," *New York Times,* April 21, 2012.

233 **"Walmart has never lobbied on the FCPA."** Dan Froomkin, "Dems Ask U.S. Chamber If Firms That Bribed Are Behind Its Push to Weaken Anti-Bribery Law," *Huffington Post,* May 22, 2012.

233 **Another six had undergone** Representatives Elijah Cummings and Henry Waxman to Thomas Donohue, May 22, 2012, accessed via http://1.usa.gov/1Ao9TrZ.

233 **One prime example: Johnson & Johnson, which in 2011** *United States v. DePuy,* U.S. District Court for the District of Columbia, No. 1:11-cr-00099 -JDB, April 8, 2011. Johnson & Johnson acknowledged responsibility and entered into a deferred prosecution agreement with the U.S. government.

234 **The SEC alleged the company** Schnitzer Steel, SEC Form 10-Q, period ending November 30, 2007; *Securities and Exchange Commission v. Si Chan Wooh,* U.S. District Court for the District of Oregon, No. CV 07-957.

234 **Under a settlement with the SEC** *In the Matter of Schnitzer Steel Industries, Inc.,* SEC Administrative Proceeding, File No. 3-12546, order instituting cease-and-desist proceedings; *United States v. SSI International Far East,* No. CR 06-398, plea agreement. Schnitzer entered into a deferred prosecution agreement with the Department of Justice, in which it stated: "Schnitzer Steel does not endorse, ratify or condone criminal conduct and, as set forth below, has taken steps to prevent such conduct from occurring in the future."

CHAPTER 10: WITH ENEMIES LIKE THESE

235   "We want capitalism unless our friends are involved Justin Amash, speech to the Charleston Meeting, November 11, 2013, http://www.youtube.com /watch?v=o6-HQORz-yg.

236   "unless my side has something that's completely "Karl Rove Accuses Justin Amash of Being Too Liberal," MOFO Politics, video, https://www.youtube .com/watch?v=WoFfx7ddbT8.

236   "It is not in the best interest of the employers Anna Palmer, "Trade Groups to Congress: No Shutdown," *Politico,* September 27, 2013.

237   told pollsters for MoveOn.org "Michigan 3rd Congressional District Survey Results," Public Policy Polling for MoveOn.org, survey of 665 district voters on October 15 and 16, 2013, http://s3.moveon.org/shutdownpolling /mi3results.pdf.

237   about half of all voters in Republican primaries Pew Research Center, "Few See Adequate Limits on NSA Surveillance Program," July 26, 2013, http:// pewrsr.ch/1o8DioD.

238   For every obstructionist vote on government spending U.S. Chamber of Commerce, *How They Voted* 2012. One perverse effect of the Chamber's *How They Voted* scorecard is that it doesn't penalize rebel members for obstructionism. For example, when the Chamber supported immigration reform, opposition killed its chances to even come to the floor for a vote in the House. No vote, no record to attack.

238   a generous $5,200 campaign donation Federal Election Commission, Contributions to Political Committees, Steve Van Andel, Federal Election Commission: two contributions of $2,600 each, June 30, 2013, http://www.fec.gov /finance/disclosure/norindsea.shtml.

239   "Tea Party—I'm not really sure Thomas Donohue, remarks at *Christian Science Monitor* breakfast, October 21, 2013.

240   "The people who come to me Amash at Charleston meeting, November 11, 2013.

240   the Swedish construction giant Skanska quit American High Performance Buildings Coalition, http://www.betterbuildingstandards.com/, accessed July 18, 2013. The Internet domain was registered to American Chemistry Council on July 2, 2012.

241   the target of $3 million in attack "education" Russ Choma, "Candidates in Little New Hampshire Get Big Out-of-State Money," OpenSecrets.org, September 10, 2014.

241   "a few single-minded businesses are creating Mike McNally, "Commentary: Don't Let Green Standards Wither," *Washington Post,* June 30, 2013.

241   "the U.S. Chamber reflects the grassroots views U.S. Chamber of Commerce, *The Policymaking Process: Roles and Responsibilities of Committees, Committee Chairpersons, Staff, and the Board of Directors* (Washington, DC: U.S. Chamber of Commerce, n.d.), p. 2, http://uscham.com/10hTKYJ.

242   "If corporations want to play in the political "SEC Should Make Companies Disclose Political Spending," *Bloomberg View,* May 8, 2013.

243   "The city is a place where people live," "Your City Is Your Business: A Complete Report of the Businessmen's Conference on Urban Problems," September 11 and 12, 1947, p. 9.

243   "Poverty in America is a problem that must not be U.S. Chamber of Commerce, Task Force on Economic Growth and Opportunity, *The Concept of Poverty* (Washington, DC: U.S. Chamber of Commerce, 1965), p. 28.

243   a National Symposium on Guaranteed Income " 'Guaranteed Income' Not Convincing," *Los Angeles Times,* January 2, 1967.

243   "80% of the world's purchasing power See, for example, John Murphy (vice-president for international affairs, U.S. Chamber), "The State of World Trade 2013: The Outlook for American Jobs, Economic Growth, and Global Leadership," remarks to the Go Global Conference, Rockford, Illinois, May 1, 2013.

243   global ambitions have split local affiliates In 2006 the U.S. Chamber announced that 200,000 small-business members of local chambers had automatically become members of the national organization via the Chamber's Federation Partnership. Press release, November 3, 2006.

243   "They're sort of the backbone Lawrence Kraus, interview by author.

244   "Frankly, it was very easy for us Tony Sheridan, interview by author.

245   the Seattle Chamber, which broke away Joel Connelly, "Severing Ties with the U.S. Chamber of Commerce," *Seattle Post-Intelligencer,* September 28, 2012.

245   the board of the Aspen Chamber Resort Association Andre Salvail, "Aspen Chamber to Cut Ties with National Organization," *Aspen Times,* April 24, 2012.

245   "The Greater Kansas City Chamber isn't affiliated Jim Heeter, quoted in McClatchy-Tribune Regional News Service, October 22, 2010.

246   "We had national experts come in and study Natalie Gochnour, interview by author.

246   "During this fund-raising season N.A. to Metro legislators, June 19, 2012, PoliticalVine.com, http://bit.ly/13vKvpz.

246   "Republicans have gained power by being anti-government Kyle Wingfield, "The L-O-S-T in T-SPLOST refers to public trust," comment by "Darwin," *Atlanta Journal-Constitution,* August 1, 2012, http://bit.ly/16umssx.

247   His Alaskan seafood company U.S. Environmental Protection Agency, news release, May 11, 2006.

247   Gardiner had to fight to renew NorQuest Seafoods, Inc., Project No. 620-009, U.S. Department of Energy, 2006, order issuing subsequent license; application filed October 3, 2003.

249   "American companies have to compete Terry Gardiner, interview by author.

249   In fact, his group grew out of battles "Small Businesses Form Pro-video Gambling Group," Associated Press, October 1, 1999.

250   Most saw a role for government Small Business Majority, "Small Business Views on Taxes and the Federal Government," October 25, 2012, available at http://bit.ly/1C1oQkV.

251   "inconsistent with long-standing democratic principles "Business Statement in Support of Government by the People," Business for Democracy and American Small Business Council, http://bit.ly/1xrLZOx.

251   "You're not going to be able to compete Frank Knapp, interview by author.

251   help get Congress to legalize crowdfunding Davis Polk, *JOBS Act Becomes Law: Reduced Compensation Disclosure for Many IPO Companies and Exchange Act Relief for Private Companies with Significant Equity Compensation,* April 5, 2012, http://bit.ly/13mg4lQ.

Index

ABOUT THE AUTHOR

ALYSSA KATZ, author of *Our Lot: How Real Estate Came to Own Us* (Bloomsbury, 2009), is a member of the editorial board of the New York *Daily News*. Previously, she edited The New York World, an investigative news project based at Columbia Journalism School, and *City Limits* magazine. She lives in Brooklyn, New York.

alyssakatz.com
@alykatzz

ABOUT THE TYPE

This book was set in Sabon, a typeface designed by the well-known German typographer Jan Tschichold (1902–74). Sabon's design is based upon the original letter forms of sixteenth-century French type designer Claude Garamond and was created specifically to be used for three sources: foundry type for hand composition, Linotype, and Monotype. Tschichold named his typeface for the famous Frankfurt typefounder Jacques Sabon (c. 1520–80).